WITHDRAWN

SCORING
POINTS

The Author goes on to say

The Author add

The book goes on to mention

In addition to this

SCORING POINTS

How Tesco continues to win customer loyalty

Clive Humby, Terry Hunt and Tim Phillips

KOGAN
PAGE

London & Philadelphia

Publisher's note

Every possible effort has been made to ensure that the information contained in this book is accurate at the time of going to press, and the publishers and authors cannot accept responsibility for any errors or omissions, however caused. No responsibility for loss or damage occasioned to any person acting, or refraining from action, as a result of the material in this publication can be accepted by the editor, the publisher or any of the authors.

First published in Great Britain and the United States in 2003 by Kogan Page Limited
Second edition 2007

120 Pentonville Road
London N1 9JN
United Kingdom
www.kogan-page.co.uk

525 South 4th Street, #241
Philadelphia PA 19147
USA

ISBN-10   0 7494 4752 4
ISBN-13   978 0 7494 4752 6

British Library Cataloguing-in-Publication Data

A CIP record for this book is available from the British Library.

Library of Congress Cataloging-in-Publication Data

Hunt, Terry, 1955-
    Scoring points : how Tesco continues to win customer loyalty / Terry Hunt, Clive Humby and Tim Phillips. -- 2nd ed.
        p. cm.
    Rev. ed. of: Scoring points / Clive Humby and Terry Hunt, with Tim Phillips. 2004.
    Includes index.
    ISBN 0-7494-4752-4
    1. Customer loyalty programs--Case studies. 2. Tesco (Firm--History--20th century. I. Humby, Clive. II. Phillips, Tim, 1967- III. Humby, Clive. Scoring points.   IV. Title.
    HF5415.525.H85 2006
    658.8'12--dc22

                                                                        2006018807

Typeset by Saxon Graphics Ltd, Derby
Printed and bound by Cambrian Printers Ltd, Aberystwyth, Wales

Contents

Foreword

I always smile when people refer to Clubcard as an outstanding loyalty scheme. In reality, a 'scheme' by itself cannot create loyalty any more than a promotion or TV commercial can. It is the whole customer experience that counts.

Clubcard isn't something that we added to our business to create loyal customers; instead it is one expression of what we do as a business. The philosophy of 'Every little helps' has made us successful, and continues to do so. It's how we earn customer loyalty.

How does Clubcard help us deliver 'Every little helps'? It lets us say 'Thank you', personally, for shopping with us. The quality of the insight it provides helps us make the shopping trip relevant. You could argue that even calling it a loyalty scheme is over-complicating things. We prefer to think of it as a simple 'Thank you'.

Clubcard's enduring strengths seem to be self-evident, and some people would consider them to be little more than common sense. It's simple: the more you spend, the bigger the 'Thank you'. It's fair: we don't give out platinum or gold cards to give special privilege to some of our customers. As our advertising says, we put eggs not customers, in boxes. Instead, we put all our effort into making the rewards personal. Every Clubcard statement offering rewards reflects what each individual, as a customer, wants to buy from us.

If this is common sense, it doesn't make it easy to do. Over 10 years, as this book describes, we have continuously worked to adapt and refine

Clubcard's strengths. Sometimes we got it wrong: we tried to be too clever, we over-complicated things, or we lost sight of our principles for short-term gain. We often think of successful businesses as moving smoothly forward, never making mistakes. When you're a retailer, you know that isn't true. Sooner or later you get it wrong. How do you know? Because customers tell you.

And that's a simple and obvious benefit of Clubcard that it's easy to miss. It is not now, nor has it ever been, a way to manipulate customers, to force them to buy things they don't want or need or can't afford. Instead the shopping patterns it reveals are a way for customers to tell us when we get it right or wrong, as long as we have the skill and desire to listen.

Today, Clubcard is stronger, and more deeply embedded in our business, than it has ever been. This book shows that it has taken 10 years of continuous enhancements, improvements, revisions and rethinks to get there, but as our customers tell us, every little helps.

Simon Uwins
Marketing Director, Tesco Stores

Introduction

It has been three years since we published the first edition of *Scoring Points*, and a lot has changed. The story of how Tesco Clubcard came into existence, how Tesco discovered the power of building strong relationships with individual customers, and how the company successfully used the data that the programme generated to drive business growth is increasingly being recognised as the most successful example of loyalty-based marketing anywhere in the world. The facts of how Clubcard was created have not changed. We've updated the statistics, but we have not attempted to rewrite the history of the programme's first 10 years.

However, supermarket retailing being what it is, the sector has seen many changes since the first edition. This has led to radical developments for Tesco Clubcard, concentrated in three areas.

First, Tesco has continued to win market share in the UK, and expand the scope of its business – both in the range of products and services it offers, and the store formats that it uses. Selling groceries on the internet or expanding its non-food range were new challenges for Tesco and its loyalty programme in the late 1990s. Coping with the dynamics of smaller format stores and making a loyalty-based customer programme relevant to customers shopping more spontaneously at lower basket value is now a new challenge for Clubcard. This is happening against the backdrop of a media backlash against Tesco. Some commentators are asking, 'Is Tesco too dominant?' In this context, it has never been more important for Tesco to engage even more effectively with customers and the brands who supply them, using Clubcard to deliver continuous improvement in the relationship with both.

The second big change – which is closely related to the first – has been Tesco's desire to refresh the Clubcard programme, to make sure that it enhances Tesco's brand promise that 'Every Little Helps'. That means testing whether Tesco's 'Every Little Helps' promise is delivered effectively to customers through Clubcard. We tell the story of this major internal project, which over a period of 18 months led Tesco to question every part of its loyalty marketing strategy and the role of the Clubcard programme.

The third development had already begun when the first edition of *Scoring Points* was published, but has accelerated since. Tesco has continued its international expansion, and has started to introduce loyalty marketing initiatives into new markets outside the UK, especially in South Korea. Dunnhumby, the data analysis company whose ability to translate Clubcard data into customer insight proved so valuable to Clubcard that Tesco bought a majority share of the company, has entered into a joint venture with US supermarket giant Kroger. The question: can the customer data techniques that have worked so well with Clubcard translate into the very different US retail model? The prize for Kroger is the ability to compete more effectively with cut-throat domestic competition, especially the behemoth of global retailing, Wal-Mart. We were granted exclusive access to this pioneering work.

At the time the first edition was published, some analysts still questioned whether Tesco was committed to loyalty marketing in the long term, and whether investing in Clubcard could continue to create competitive advantage for the company and its business partners. In the last three years, we have seen that the answer to both questions is a resounding 'yes'.

TWELVE YEARS ON

The 13th of February isn't an anniversary that Tesco's management publicly celebrates, but if they did, you wouldn't blame them. On that day in 1995, the company changed the way it did business so fundamentally that its effect is still seen in every part of the company. The events of 13 February 1995 changed the way Tesco makes decisions, develops products, manages its stores and, most important, the way it serves its customers. On that day, Tesco launched Clubcard, its customer loyalty programme.

Before Clubcard, Tesco was stuck as the UK's second-ranking supermarket. Today, not only is it the UK's largest grocer, it is the world's most successful internet supermarket, one of Europe's fastest-growing financial services companies and arguably one of the world's most successful exponents of what the jargon terms Customer Relationship Management, or CRM. Its 242,980 staff makes it the UK's largest private employer, and one of its fastest-growing businesses overseas.

Since the late 1970s, Tesco has transformed its perception amongst customers from a 'pile it high, sell it cheap' market trader stuck in the past, to a progressive retailer that delivers on its promise that 'Every Little Helps' – and Clubcard has been the catalyst.

Of course, Tesco was not alone in its massive transformation. The last 10 years of the 20th century were as dramatic a period of change in high-street retailing as any period in the 90 years before it. Nowhere was this as apparent as among the UK's giant grocers, who made takeovers (or were taken over), opened new formats of stores, created new categories of product and new ways to sell them, forged and broke alliances with other retailers, and left few stones unturned in their desire for a greater share of the UK's annual £100 billion grocery market. Yet from all this turmoil, Tesco has emerged the strongest. By 2005, it had been the biggest of the 'Big Four' – Sainsbury's, Asda and Safeway (now part of the Morrisons group) are the other three – for 10 years, and it had increased the margin of its lead in each of those years.

No one would claim that Clubcard is exclusively responsible for the success of Tesco. But talk to any of the senior executive team who have steered the company so skilfully over the last decade and it is clear that the business benefits of Clubcard are now written through the Tesco business like lettering through a stick of rock.

Tesco Personal Finance (TPF), the Tesco branded bank launched in 1997 and jointly owned with the Royal Bank of Scotland, has 5 million customers for its 11 products, and in 2004 made profits of £200 million. It has lent £1 billion in personal loans, 500,000 customers insure their cars using it, and more than 250,000 of their pets are insured by their supermarket's bank. Yet TPF owes its beginnings to a humble plastic card with a number to identify the customer. It was the Tesco Clubcard team under Tim Mason, now the group's board marketing director and chairman of Tesco.com, who first identified the opportunity for Tesco to sell financial services successfully to millions of card-carrying members who trusted their preferred supermarket to offer them more than fresh food and chilled meals. And it was Clubcard that provided the insight and the data to identify in which households those customers lived.

Tesco.com is the largest grocery e-tailer in the world, and since the late 1990s it has made an operating profit. It has delivered to more than 1 million homes, rents out 200,000 DVDs a month and in 2004 made sales of £700 million. Yet the chief executive of Tesco, Sir Terry Leahy, attributes much of the credit for this internet success story to Clubcard. 'We could not have created the dot-com business without the data from the loyalty card,' he says.

By the end of 2002 Tesco had massively increased its sales in the 'non-food' sector, the curiously unspecific description for the category spanning home electricals to clothing, books to furnishings. It came from nowhere in the mid-1990s and now has almost 7 per cent of the UK market, with non food contributing £6 billion of sales in the UK, and growth double that of the grocery business. Half of Tesco grocery shoppers have purchased non-food items like Tesco's £3 own-brand jeans. Tesco Clubcard fuelled that growth by identifying possible customers and communicating with them using a new medium – the Clubcard quarterly mailing.

Pop into the reception of Tesco's anonymous Cheshunt headquarters and you'll see clocks on the wall showing the time in Warsaw, Hong Kong, Seoul, Bangkok and Taiwan, because today, Tesco has stores in those fast-developing markets. There are also Tesco supermarkets in the Republic of Ireland, the Czech Republic, Slovakia, Hungary, and in 2006 Tesco announced that it was planning to open Tesco Express stores in the world's most competitive grocery market, the United States. One-third of Tesco staff are now outside the UK, as well as more than half of its floorspace. As a method of cementing customer loyalty, Clubcard is used in Tesco stores in the Republic of Ireland, Thailand and South Korea, with plans for the others to launch Clubcard too.

Tesco may well have got to this enviable position without Clubcard – but it could not have done so as quickly or as cheaply as it has done without the customer data and insight that Clubcard provides. This information has guided almost all of the key business decisions the management team have made in recent times, reducing the risk of taking bold new initiatives. As Mason, Clubcard's 'champion' at Tesco from its earliest concept stage admits, 'without Clubcard, the Tesco brand would be a significantly different brand… today we can say, "there's 10,000 people over here, how are we going to do a better job for them?"… and with the data, what we have to do becomes as plain as the nose on your face. It immediately changes the behaviour of the business.'

The recent history of Tesco is the story of a retailer's successful evolution: its diversification into new businesses and in particular its leap-frogging of long-standing market leader Sainsbury's to become the number one UK retailer. But the purpose of this book isn't to plot the rise in market leadership of one retail brand at the expense of the others: those changes in fortune have happened in retailing every decade in living memory. Tesco's rise to leadership is remarkable because of the culture shift that occurred within the company that made this change happen. Through Clubcard, Tesco has defied many of the principles of conventional food retailing that dominated the last 50 years of the 20th century. As self-service high street supermarkets were superseded by superstores and megastores, consumers became anonymous in exchange for improved choice and value. This, retailers argued, was unavoidable – until Clubcard.

With Clubcard Tesco had the chance to be personal again by introducing a medium through which it can treat customers as individuals. This is not in spite of its size as a business, but because of its size as a business. There is a term used in manufacturing: mass customization – meaning the ability to produce millions of products, but each one slightly different, according to what customers have requested. Think of it as the opposite of the Ford model T, where you could have any colour, as long as it was black. Thanks to Clubcard, Tesco can mass-customize to suit the needs of all types of customers, of all tastes and incomes and ages. Not on the basis of what they think the broad mass of customers want but in the knowledge of what individual customers actively choose and what they prefer.

Just as important, Clubcard has given Tesco a way regularly to show its appreciation to customers. Or as the theme of the launch advertising put it – Clubcard is the world's biggest 'Thank You' card. While every business talks about being customer-centred, Tesco has made that commitment tangible. Through Clubcard it has an explicit 'customer contract' that offers consumers a dividend-paying stake in the company in exchange for their business.

Tesco designed Clubcard not just to show customer loyalty to Tesco, but more important, to recognize Tesco's loyalty to its customers.

This is also the story of how a company famed for being careful – even mean – with its resources outflanked its competitors by investing in technology in a focused, practical but far-sighted way. It's also clear that, as Clubcard demonstrates, Tesco continues to apply new technology to improving the customer experience.

Like any business, Clubcard's story hasn't been free of mishap, but mistakes were identified and fixed using the same analysis and willingness to change that created Clubcard. One of the accepted principles of the programme is that there no such thing as complete success or total failure. Everything that happens to Clubcard is seen as an opportunity to learn, to refine, to improve and move on. There is constant monitoring and measurement of how well the card has been working and how it hasn't.

Clubcard is a reflection of the attributes of the business and its management: a strong team ethic, a commitment to serving customers, and most of all, top-to-bottom retailers' pragmatism. Tesco made customer loyalty marketing work, when every other major British supermarket loyalty programme in the late 1990s failed, faltered or never got started.

Every year since 1995, headlines have proclaimed the death of loyalty schemes, usually enthusiastically supported by other retailers whose loyalty schemes are distant memories. 'Loyalty cards have lost their lustre,' said Safeway in May 2000, when it abandoned its ABC card. 'Trying to analyse all the data is madness,' said Waitrose, after it abandoned its attempt. Yet Clubcard was never questioned as a strategic priority by the management. Instead Tesco has responded to the critics by measurably building sales through Clubcard, using the relevant knowledge it creates to improve the way it runs its business.

Clubcard teaches us how retail loyalty marketing works. It demonstrates how Tesco successfully overturned many of the preconceptions of supermarketing. It shows how it is possible for a mass retailer to know customers personally, and establish a long-term relationship with many of them, encouraging mutual loyalty. It is a case study of how to create a process of continuous improvement, not just in the promotional programme but also in the entire business. It shows how a bold leap of marketing imagination can help secure a massive achievement – propelling Tesco to the number one position in the UK's grocery business.

There is one more remarkable fact about Clubcard. Four times a year Tesco sends customers 'money' – vouchers that they can spend freely in the store towards the cost of their shopping. Each year, those rewards total more than £300 million – yet Tesco makes a profit out of doing it. Clubcard pays for itself. Since 1995, Tesco has covered the cost of running its loyalty programme with a sales uplift directly attributable to the promotions that have been created by Clubcard.

In short, Tesco hasn't found that its loyalty programme is a costly overhead. Because Tesco made Clubcard work, it can find out what its customers need and generate enough sales by satisfying those needs to cover the costs of finding out. Tesco runs Clubcard, and has been doing so since 1995, for no net cost.

1

Questions of loyalty

- ▶ In the beginning
- ▶ What is loyalty?
- ▶ The secrets of success
- ▶ Is customer loyalty genuine?

IN THE BEGINNING

Tesco Clubcard was by no means the first supermarket loyalty scheme. For that, we have to look back more than a century to the British Co-operative movement and the Dividend or 'divi' it paid its members.

The Rochdale Equitable Pioneers' Society was founded in 1844 by 28 weavers. It was not the first co-operative, but it is the origin of today's Co-op supermarket chain. Run by working people for working people, the Society had eight principles, the most important of which decreed that any surplus should be distributed back to the members, in proportion to their contribution.

So this was a retailer that considered its customers as members, where their regular custom, their loyalty, was rewarded in cash, and where the more they shopped, the more they got back. Fundamentally, this is exactly what Clubcard, and every other modern loyalty scheme, provides.

It is hard to imagine now, but from the time of World War I right up until the 1970s, Co-ops managed by this principle formed the largest grocery chain in the UK. The long-term success of the 'divi' makes Clubcard's decade-long story so far seem like a flash in the pan. As Andrew Seth and Geoffrey Randall point out in their book, *The Grocers*:

> Membership blossomed... bolstered by the unchanging appeal of the dividend, and by democratic ideals and a reputation for honest dealing. Two million members grew to... a staggering 11 million – more than today subscribe to the famous Tesco loyalty card – at its apogee by the Second World War. By 1950, market share was at least 25 per cent, and on some measures the Co-op had achieved one-third of the entire market, greater than all the multiples combined.

Yet although Tesco is a public company rather than a mutual organization, with a loyalty to its shareholders as well as to its customers, some of the principles that created the first mass-loyalty programme 150 years ago have been applied to its Clubcard customer membership programme. As Lord MacLaurin, the chairman of Tesco when the scheme was launched, explained in his autobiography:

> It was a direct result of comments from our customer panels that Tesco launched its Clubcard scheme... 'OK,' they said, 'so we're loyal to Tesco, why not show us a bit of loyalty in return?... And they were right, which was why, after examining the idea, Tesco launched its Clubcard.

The principle is also enshrined in the Tesco corporate mission statement. In the reception of the company headquarters in Cheshunt, on a plaque on the wall, it literally stares you in the face. The company's core purpose is to 'Create value for customers to earn their lifetime loyalty'. Not, in the first instance, value for shareholders. The list of company values starts with the goal to 'understand customers better than anyone'. (It also contains the promise to 'share knowledge so that it can be used'.)

If the Co-op dividend was the historical precedent for Clubcard, there were other schemes that demonstrated the efficacy of loyalty marketing for mass brands. Prior to Clubcard's introduction, Air Miles had been launched in 1988, and was a runaway success: a success fuelled by being adopted as the reward currency for the British Airways Executive Club. Air Miles had for its inspiration the predominantly US-based, single-airline brand frequent-flyer schemes.

When Tesco was looking to test Clubcard in a few stores in 1993, it also had many retailer precedents throughout the world to look at. In the United States there were many local loyalty schemes that had grown up with the regional supermarket chains and retail outlets. In Europe, several Scandinavian grocery chains were particularly advanced. Some offered preferential pricing to customers who joined their membership scheme. Some offered rewards only to their most valuable customers, or most regular customers.

So Clubcard did not invent the concept of retail loyalty marketing. What Tesco did do was take the thinking to a new level of business sophistication and effectiveness. Yet that effectiveness has often been questioned, so it is worth looking at loyalty more closely.

WHAT IS LOYALTY?

'Loyalty', in day-to-day life, implies an unselfish belief in institutions, or unswerving fidelity in marriage, or emotional commitment to friends. Loyalty also suggests monogamy: one choice above all others.

Retail loyalty isn't like that. There isn't a customer alive who will consider using one shop for every need. When retailers look at winning and keeping the loyalty of their customers they are looking to achieve a little extra goodwill, a slight margin of preference, an incremental shift in buying behaviour. This can add up to a massive contribution to the financial success of the business.

Types of loyalty

When the Nectar Loyalty programme was launched in the UK by Air Miles inventor Keith Mills in September 2002, backed by Sainsbury's, BP, Debenhams and Barclaycard, among others, the third in the UK's 'big three' supermarkets was unconvinced. Asda, a long-time opponent of loyalty programmes, responded by commissioning a public opinion survey from NOP. It stated that 93 per cent of shoppers would prefer lower prices to loyalty cards. 'On Monday, Asda will do what it's done virtually every week since it abandoned its own loyalty card pilot in 1999 – chip away at prices,' the company said.

'Customers aren't fooled by marketing gimmicks,' said Asda's deputy chief operating officer Richard Baker, 'Shoppers' real loyalty only comes from offering the lowest prices on the right range of products.'

Leaving aside the question as to whether 'everyday low prices' and loyalty rewards are mutually exclusive (Asda and Nectar's founder insists they are; Tesco's management begs to differ, and has an internal process by which it monitors its prices to match or better Asda prices), it is important to define what we mean by a loyalty programme – and what it can deliver to both parties.

There is an argument that Asda's discounting strategy is a loyalty programme of sorts: a clear public commitment to discounting that supports the claim that there is no point going anywhere else to shop. It is a technique most obviously used by US-based Wal-Mart, the world's largest supermarket – also the parent company of Asda.

We will concentrate on the results of explicit rather than implicit loyalty programmes: programmes that seek to create an active relationship with customers in which value is given in more ways than just price discounting, and that build a relationship between retailer and customer that extends beyond the immediate shopping experience. In 2000, a report from management consultancy McKinsey came down heavily in favour of loyalty cards as a technique to do this:

> McKinsey research found that about half of the ten largest US retailers in each of seven sectors have launched such programs, and the rate is similar among top UK retailers... Moreover, loyalty programs are popular with customers: in the United States, 53 per cent of grocery customers are enrolled in them, to say nothing of 21 per cent of the customers of casual-apparel retailers. Of those who join grocery programs, McKinsey research indicates that 48 per cent spend more than they would otherwise, though the figure is only 18 per cent in casual-apparel programs. Yet even 18 per cent represents a sizable number. If anything, we expect interest in loyalty programs to intensify. Faced with slowing revenue growth in many categories and the emergence of competing internet start-ups, retailers are eager to deepen their relationships with existing customers and to increase their share of wallet.

Management consultant KPMG calls simple Wal-Mart style discounting 'purge' loyalty. It has defined three other ways in which loyalty retail strategy can work:

1. 'Pure' loyalty means strengthening the existing bond between the customer and the retailer, so the retailer can find out what the customer wants, and give that customer more of it. If customers

would prefer a larger range of goods, or to have their shopping bags packed for them, or freshly-baked bread alongside the sliced loaves, 'pure' loyalty schemes aim to establish a two-way dialogue so that the retailer can act to improve the basic offer.

2. 'Pull' loyalty means attracting customers by augmenting a retail offer, so customers will find that buying one product means they get an offer on another, linked product. This might mean being able to receive discounts at another retailer – or it might mean being incentivized to try new products from the same retailer. At a simple level, 'buy one, get one free' is 'pull' loyalty. Effectively, it is an inducement to create more sales by encouraging customers to buy something new.

3. 'Push' loyalty means creating a scheme to encourage us to use a way of shopping that we would not have done before – pushing customers through new channels, or trying to create new types of behaviour. That might mean offering a combined credit card and loyalty card, or making prices cheaper on a website. Users get a discount, and so more of their spend is directed through that channel. It is a technique used by low-cost airlines to encourage customers to book online, or it can be used by a retailer expanding into non-core businesses to draw customers with it.

As we shall see, Clubcard's activity combines all three techniques – and when it has chosen to cut prices (KPMG's 'purge' strategy), those price cuts have also been guided by customer data. But whatever the combination of techniques used, there is still argument over whether these techniques genuinely create different customer behaviour.

How schemes create value

Defenders of loyalty schemes argue that they create a positive result in six ways:

1. More purchases more often. When they sign up to become members of your loyalty programme customers have made a conscious choice to commit to your brand in exchange for some sort of reward. You offer them an incentive to come back to your shop or airline or internet site, and they have an additional valued reason to choose you over your competition. Put simply: you sell more.

2. Loyalty programmes give the ability to mass customize marketing communication: to identify and talk to individual customers on a

massive scale. Over the past decade or more there has been much talk of one-to-one marketing. For retailers, particularly super-markets running a loyalty programme, it becomes a reality. The richness of customer transactional data created and collected as a by-product of running the scheme lets the marketers devise commu-nications and offers that are individually targeted or at least designed for a clearly defined customer segment. Loyalty schemes provide a two-way flow of information to and from the majority of a store's customers, something that self-service mass retailers could not normally achieve. If you know the names and addresses of customers, you can perform the most basic one-to-one marketing function: thank them if they spend more, and find out why if they spend less.

3. The asset value of the data. The transactional information produced by a loyalty scheme is enormously valuable if it is analysed and used well. As we've already said, these data are exact: they are not based on a small-scale study, a focus group or instinct – they're actually what is happening. And, as we discuss in this book, a torrential flow of live transactional data offers the possibility to transform how retailers manage their business. In itself the data can become a high-value asset, as Tesco has proved.

4. Loyalty programmes let companies track trends. Large organiza-tions are particularly vulnerable to changes in taste or behaviour: it's difficult to change overnight. So it's important to have early warning of significant changes in how customers are shopping, what they are choosing, what they are not doing. Loyalty data provide that information.

5. Loyalty programmes minimize waste. Conventional sales promo-tions are pretty indiscriminate, offering discounts or dreams to every customer, whether the offer is relevant or not. Most direct mail is inadequately targeted, so only the minority are expected to respond. In-store price promotions are available to everyone whether they are regular buyers of the brand or have never tried it before, so brands often expensively subsidize established behaviour. With the insight gained through a long-term loyalty programme marketers can target offers better than before (either by direct media or at the till) and reduce wasted spend. The result: companies waste less in communicating with people who don't want to know. Customers get less junk communications.

6. Loyalty programmes help promote trust. Who do customers trust? Their bank? The government? Their grocer? Results – for example

the success of Tesco Personal Finance (TPF) and Sainsbury's Bank – suggest the unlikely fact that grocers may be winning the trust war. And when a supermarket makes the effort to connect with customers in a more personal way, gets to know more about what each customer wants or dislikes, and cares about providing it for them, then that generally gives them more right to provide other services, and earn more of their loyalty and respect.

How schemes destroy value

Those who object to loyalty schemes argue that:

1. Loyalty schemes are just a bribe. Customers don't really care who they shop with. If they carry more than one card how can they be loyal?
2. Customers just want lower prices. In NOP's September 2002 survey, 55 per cent of supermarket shoppers believed that their supermarket raised prices to pay for its loyalty scheme.
3. It's a 'zero sum game' for the retailer. If everyone produces a loyalty scheme, how can there be any overall effect on loyalty? Profit margins are squeezed to run the scheme and to offer the rewards and discounts.
4. Handling the data is like drinking from a fire hose. Millions of shopping baskets a day, tens of millions of items scanned – the volume of data must be too big to make sense of it. So ultimately, they learn little of value about their customers that they could not already see.
5. They encourage a 'Big Brother' culture. We value our privacy. Loyalty cards erode that. How can you love a retailer who is spying on you? The relationship isn't trust, it is bullying on behalf of corporate giants who won't give discounts unless you give up your right to privacy.
6. Where are the incremental sales to pay for it all? A year after launch, how does the company know if the loyalty 'bump', the incremental sales effect of issuing the cards, is still there? Even if there is an effect on sales, the ongoing cost of a scheme may be better spent elsewhere.

Both fans and detractors are correct. A loyalty programme won't work if it is uncompelling, poorly conceived or inadequately managed. Asking, 'do loyalty programmes work' is like asking, 'does advertising work', or 'does direct mail work?' A programme will fail if customers do not value it or feel their interests are not being respected.

There have been more loyalty programmes that have failed than succeeded. This does not mean the objections are more important than the benefits of a loyalty programme. It merely means that many marketers have failed to think through their strategy well enough.

THE SECRETS OF SUCCESS

Love the programme

There is not one single design for a loyalty programme that will achieve all the benefits and avoid all the disadvantages. A programme cannot be lifted off the shelf and dropped into a business and be expected to transform sales performance instantly, and a lazily conceived loyalty strategy can harm customer loyalty. If it is to be a long-term success it has to be regarded as a strategic tool of the business, reflecting the brand's core strengths. Each programme has to be tailored to the brand, and the nature of the relationship that brand has with its customers. A brand is a collection of defined perceptions in the mind of the consumer, so the loyalty programme has to reinforce and live up to those perceptions.

Most important, the programme has to be loved by the business. Just as marketers and managers have to love the brand, they have to equally commit to the loyalty programme that represents that brand to its members. Loyalty programmes stand or fall on how they are represented by the employees that personify it.

This book details instances of companies half-heartedly getting involved in loyalty marketing, not appreciating the level of commitment it requires, expecting too much too soon and quickly becoming disillusioned. It is a marketing technique that effectively invites customers to become members of the brand, for example to become members of Boots or BA. And that's not the sort of relationship that can be kept at arm's length from the rest of the marketing that the company does, or from the rest of the company's operations.

It is, of course, possible to test loyalty marketing discreetly to part of the customer base before publicly committing to a business-wide programme, as Tesco did. But if it is to work, a programme's rollout must establish loyalty marketing at the heart of the business. The staff at every level from the main board to the frontline staff must understand why the scheme is important to customers and to the business' future and nurture and encourage it at every opportunity. A loyalty programme is a major commitment to customers. Marketers who have sat on the sidelines and waited to see if loyalty marketing fails for them have usually found their expectations realized.

Loyal to what?

Take the experience of Vodafone in the mid-1990s. It signed up as a partner of Air Miles and offered them to non-business contract customers. A large minority embraced the scheme because they were collectors of Air Miles and welcomed another source. That minority was loyal to Air Miles. The majority were not enthusiastic and saw no relevant connection between the Air Miles currency and their subscription to Vodafone. Not surprisingly their commitment to Vodafone wasn't noticeably influenced either way. Eventually the Vodafone programme was phased out. This was an example of the fundamentals of loyalty marketing being misunderstood, and the 'loyal to what?' question remaining unanswered.

In contrast, successful loyalty programmes around the world have been based on a clear view of what loyalty means and how it can be directed to increase customer goodwill. Customers are loyal to the brand. For Tesco, Clubcard is one of the key means by which it fulfils its business mission: 'Create value for customers to earn their lifetime loyalty... understand customers better than anyone.' It is the medium through which it can regularly demonstrate in tangible ways the brand promise: 'Every little helps'. The same consistency is found in other programmes that work. At Boots, the Advantage card invites us to 'Look after yourself.' At Hilton Hotels, the longest-running hotel loyalty scheme offers Hilton HHonors cardholders a 'Rewarding Experience'. These and other successes aim to focus and deepen an existing customer relationship by offering relevant rewards that reinforce the brand values.

So loyalty marketing is a strategy, not a tactic. The reward is no more a bribe than a birthday present from your partner or a dividend to a shareholder is a bribe.

Loyalty and CRM

Customer relationship management (CRM) is a very big subject, too big for this book to cover fully. CRM encompasses far more than the challenges of marketing. It is useful to see CRM strategy operating in two halves: 'structural CRM', the means by which a company joins up its operations to deliver better service to customers and better value to the business; and 'active CRM', the means by which it exploits that structural investment to drive sales, reduce costs and improve the customer experience. Loyalty marketing is very much an active CRM strategy.

A CRM strategy is driven by knowledge. That knowledge comes from data. For a mass retailer like Tesco, a loyalty programme should be the cornerstone of a CRM strategy. Clubcard provides a free mass-participation voluntary scheme that encourages users to identify themselves when they shop. Good-quality customer data – rich, relevant and recent – are essential for a CRM strategy.

One of the failures of CRM as a business discipline is an over-concentration on the means and a lack of focus on the end: too much attention to the IT and not enough on the customer. For companies like Tesco a loyalty programme is a customer-first approach to creating efficiency through CRM. This contrasts with the absolutist approach that is often part of CRM planning: an uncompromising view that insists that the IT platform has to be in place, the database 100 per cent populated, and the staff completely retrained before anything goes live. Forrester Research estimates that the CRM boom came to a sudden halt in 2002: the market for CRM systems actually shrank by 5 per cent, even though most companies still recognize they have the potential to make great improvements to customer service. One of the key factors the researchers identified was that the unrealistic expectations on the part of companies that were putting in the programmes had resulted in disillusionment.

Tesco Clubcard was developed by retailers. Retailers, especially supermarkets, are pragmatic by nature. Their businesses develop by a series of steps, doing more of the things that work for customers, and stopping doing the things that don't. For Tesco Clubcard, the definition of CRM is best summarized as: to improve our performance at every point of contact with our customers, to make them happier and the company richer. It's no more complicated than that.

IS CUSTOMER LOYALTY GENUINE?

Loyalty as a bribe

Are loyalty programmes really the opposite: *disloyalty* programmes? As Asda's former chairman Archie Norman was fond of claiming, loyalty schemes are a 'bribe'. This isn't real loyalty, he maintained, it's the opposite. They encourage customers to be mercenary by making them play one retailer off against another. In the 1990s, the UK's press carried a series of articles on how much that 'loyalty' was worth, drawing tables to compare the rewards, rather like a comparison of mobile phone tariffs. 'Don't be too dazzled by the discounts, magazines and exclusive shopping evenings offered by retailers,' said *House Beautiful* magazine in August 1996, surveying seven loyalty cards. 'Follow our guide to check out exactly what's in it for you before you sign on the dotted line.' Can this be called 'loyalty'?

Critics like the management of grocers Waitrose stress that it is the total customer experience that creates loyalty, not promotions. Loyalty is an emotional response based on empathy, not a logical response based on bribery. In that case, better to invest in bag packers at the checkout, crèches and nappy-changing facilities, or even better packaging design to create loyalty.

It's true that all these improvements can enhance customer loyalty. But this does not mean that a card-based scheme isn't creating it too.

Loyalty schemes supplement service

No one would contend that a card-based loyalty scheme is a credible alternative to being the right price, offering excellent service, innovative products and customer care – because any business that neglects factors like these is extremely unlikely to have long-term success in achieving customer loyalty. Innovative customer-care programmes offering services that customers want will develop loyalty. The important point is that these initiatives and a card-based loyalty scheme are not mutually exclusive.

A dynamic loyalty scheme like Boots Advantage generates the customer insight to help the store managers offer more relevant products and services. Retailers cannot afford to do everything that they want to do for customers. The information gained from their scheme helps them reduce the risks and to prioritize.

All major service and product innovation is inherently risky. For example, in October 2000 Iceland announced that all its fresh produce would be organic, in response to a perceived customer desire for it. 'Customers have told us they want organic food at no extra cost,' said managing director Russell Ford. By August 2001, Ford had left, and his successor was new chief executive Bill Grimsey, who had a different idea of what customers would want: and it wasn't organics:

> You have to understand what they need and telling them that they've got to have 100 per cent organics is clearly flawed. If the buying team is just sourcing those products, then they're not doing new product development in frozen ready meals. Which is when you start to run into difficulties.

A poor decision, based on poor information, had not only failed to deliver, but had disastrously distracted the management's attention away from its customers – for almost a year.

Risks like this can only be substantially reduced if there is a large amount of clear, reliable data that show how relevant a new idea is, and which customers like the idea – in this case, the core customers for Iceland were budget-conscious shoppers, and for them, shopping for organic produce was not as relevant or attractive as the company had thought it would be. But a lack of customer insight led Iceland into a damaging policy shift, and hampered them from identifying and resolving the mistake quickly.

By asking customers to join a brand, a loyalty scheme gives customers the chance to influence the direction of their chosen brand. Transactional data (even with questionnaire responses and the results of customer forums) do not completely replace the management's 'gut feel' – but they are a valuable support for experience and instinct. A loyalty programme gives a brand a way to talk to individual customers on an adult-to-adult basis, rather than in the patriarchal style of 'we know what you want' that has often been the case in the past.

So loyalty programmes create relevance for the customer – which may create an emotional bond, but will certainly create a measurable response. They are the starting point for deepening the customer relationship, which flourishes in many ways, through many types of innovation – provided the managers of the programme can turn the data into insight and the insight into business decisions. Ultimately though, it is also essential to turn the business decisions into profit.

2

Making loyalty pay

- ▶ The economics of loyalty marketing
- ▶ Playing a zero sum game
- ▶ The foundations of a loyalty scheme
- ▶ Four loyalty 'currencies'
- ▶ Does a loyalty programme pay?

THE ECONOMICS OF LOYALTY MARKETING

The investment in cash

Loyalty schemes certainly don't come cheap. McKinsey, in its report into loyalty in 2000, found that:

> 16 major European retailers had a total of some $1.2 billion tied up in annual discounts to customers, with several supermarket chains devoting some $150 million. Costs are about the same in the United States. Given large sales volumes, even programmes with modest rebates (up to 1 per cent) can cost a great deal of money.

For Tesco, that is an investment of £300 million a year in rewards, at a time when falling grocery prices have squeezed margins on its core business. The cost of the rebate is only one overhead of a loyalty programme. McKinsey again:

> the costs of marketing and managing a programme – investment in systems, fulfilment support, and so forth – which normally run well into millions… Many retailers seriously underestimate the full cost of setting up and sustaining loyalty programmes, so even those that increase sales might actually be draining money.

For a large retailer, McKinsey estimates set-up costs as US $30 million in the first year, and annual maintenance costs are between US $5 million and US $10 million. 'Very few retailers fully account for these incremental costs,' the report concludes, 'especially for marketing support required to sustain awareness of the programmes as well as their momentum and impact.'

So to justify this magnitude of set-up and running costs a loyalty scheme has got to deliver an acceptable return on investment. For the Clubcard launch, Tesco needed a 'bump' in sales of around 2 per cent to offset the cost. By the time that Sainsbury's launched its Reward card in even more demanding market conditions, its internal projections showed the like-for-like sales bump had to be nearer 4 per cent to cover costs and deliver incremental profit.

A loyalty programme also requires a huge investment of time, IT resources and talent. Tesco employs, directly or indirectly, nearly 100 people whose main job is to manage various parts of the Clubcard process. Add Clubcard's share of the customer care call centre staff in Dundee (500 of them), and then the training and processing time invested in thousands of stores and checkouts, and you appreciate the human resource implications of running a programme like Clubcard. It also employs many thousands of other staff who are marketers for its loyalty scheme: its customer-facing staff.

The investment in people

From the trials of Clubcard onwards, the staff have been an important ingredient in encouraging customers first to take up, and then to use, Clubcard. They are briefed thoroughly and early – not just about what will be different for their job, but about what Clubcard does for the business as a whole. If a loyalty scheme is to be integrated with the business, it has to be part of the working lives of the people who run the business in the stores, too.

It's not just a commitment of numbers. Loyalty marketing done well changes company culture and structure, because it encourages customers to contact the company as an implicit clause in the loyalty 'contract' that it creates. When Tesco invited affiliation from millions of customers, it uncorked the pent-up goodwill and frustrations that they had previously kept to themselves – so much so that Tesco had to create a dedicated call centre team to cope. It's not only the expectations of customers that change, there is also the need to change the mindset of everyone in the organization: it is no longer enough to say that dealing with customers is someone else's job. In a loyalty-driven company direct customer service happens at every point in the company.

The marketing department is suddenly challenged by the availability of a flood of new customer information. New knowledge means new skills, new ways of planning and working. Marketing departments of supermarkets traditionally allocate the responsibilities of their organization by product or brand: a loyalty programme invites them to think in terms of segments of customers instead. Market research becomes 'customer insight'. Success is measured in 'share of customer', not just 'share of market'.

This isn't always comfortable. The cost of this insight may be extremely high to managers and staff whose stores are under-performing, or whose product categories are revealed as less important than previously thought, or whose marketing initiatives are not working for key customers. There is a revolutionary effect on organizations when they are confronted with rich customer information. While it can transform business performance, in the short term the truth may hurt.

The Clubcard Customer Charter

Clubcard has also demonstrated that customers will expect more from a brand that runs a loyalty programme. When a scheme launches, it either implicitly or explicitly makes a series of promises. Tesco did this very explicitly on the first birthday of its programme with the 'Clubcard Customer Charter', shown in Figure 2.1.

Whether implicitly or explicitly, membership of a loyalty programme engages customers as stakeholders in the brand. It raises the bar of expectation. It implies that the company is trying harder to get its offer

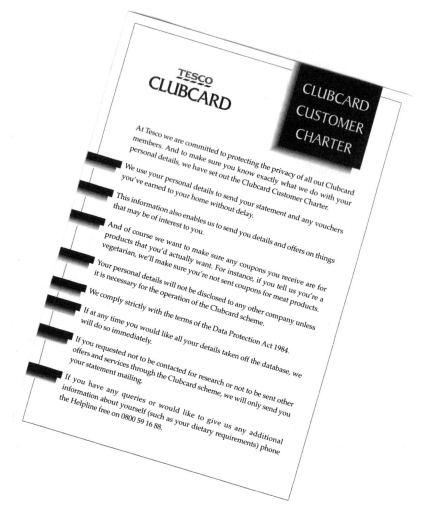

At Tesco we are committed to protecting the privacy of all our Clubcard members. And to make sure you know exactly what we do with your personal details, we have set out the Clubcard Customer Charter.

We use your personal details to send your statement and any vouchers you've earned to your home without delay.

This information also enables us to send you details and offers on things that may be of interest to you.

And of course we want to make sure any coupons you receive are for products that you'd actually want. For instance, if you tell us you're a vegetarian, we'll make sure you're not sent coupons for meat products.

Your personal details will not be disclosed to any other company unless it is necessary for the operation of the Clubcard scheme.

We comply strictly with the terms of the Data Protection Act 1984.

If at any time you would like all your details taken off the database, we will do so immediately.

If you requested not to be contacted for research or not to be sent other offers and services through the Clubcard scheme, we will only send you your statement mailing.

If you have any queries or would like to give us any additional information about yourself (such as your dietary requirements) phone the Helpline free on 0800 59 16 88.

Figure 2.1 The Clubcard Customer Charter

right for us, its customers. It opens up a two-way dialogue, which means that the company has to take note of what its customers are saying, and respond.

When Tesco sends a mailing every three months to its members, the mailing carries Clubcard vouchers, often to the value of £20 or more, as well as discount coupons for favourite products and brands. As an example of the dialogue this medium generates, the call centre receives hundreds of calls when each quarterly mailing is about to be sent out from customers who want to know when the mailing will reach them. It is one of the few direct mail programmes in the world that receives a response from the public – before it goes out.

The cost of stopping

This all adds up to an important and challenging fact: once you turn on a loyalty scheme, it is very hard, and costly, to turn off. According to McKinsey:

> Loyalty programmes take on a life of their own once they start, so mistakes can be very hard to correct. Even programmes with low benefits become entrenched in the minds of customers, who must be informed when they change or come to an end. Customers react pessimistically to any perceived 'take away' once a programme is in place, even if they are not actively involved in it... a negative experience with a programme heightens the scepticism of consumers when they are offered a follow-up programme and can undermine their trust in a retailer more broadly.

Be careful what you wish for, McKinsey concludes. Initial success heightens costs and risks: 'Curiously, the successful launch of a programme worsens the problems of ending it.'

Once a substantial number of customers embrace a loyalty programme, they are likely to be very reluctant to have it taken away. Customers quite reasonably consider that the benefits they received from the loyalty scheme are theirs by right, and react negatively to any perceived reduction in the value they receive from the company.

When Nectar launched in the UK, it combined two existing loyalty schemes: Sainsbury's Rewards and Barclaycard Profiles. While millions of Nectar users embraced the new scheme enthusiastically, some of the more active collectors of the schemes it replaced felt they were receiving less value back from the brands. 'Nectar, which is the largest loyalty scheme of its kind in the UK, was launched last month amid a blaze of publicity,' said the *Guardian* in November 2002. 'But some of these promises have now been exposed as empty, while evidence has emerged that a significant number of Barclaycard customers are worse off under the new scheme.' Barclaycard holder Barbara English had 12,927 Profiles points – meaning she had spent £129,270 on her card. Another 73 points would get a flight to Australia and back to see her son for her 70th birthday. Under the new scheme though, she was less than half way to the same flight. 'This has caught us on the hop,' said a Nectar spokesman, admitting that the company was aware of the problem that affected only a few customers who were collecting points for long-haul flights. A small number, but those customers are extremely loyal, long-term customers – who felt angry enough to complain to a national newspaper when slighted. Proof that customers do not take the commitments of loyalty programmes lightly.

PLAYING A ZERO SUM GAME

Split loyalties

Clever commentators and academics have argued that loyalty programmes are ultimately self-defeating when competition confronts the first mover. Two years after Clubcard and Sainsbury's Reward card launched, the Consumers' Association found that 4 out of 10 adults owned both cards. In 2004, 50 million loyalty cards were issued in the UK – about 2.5 cards to every household. From a customer perspective, can you be 'loyal' to both Sainsbury's and Tesco if you carry a card from both? In a 2002 MORI survey of UK adults, more than half used loyalty cards – but two out of three loyalty card users said that their cards did not determine where they shopped.

From the retailer's perspective, it is logical to ask whether the attempt to make loyalty a business strategy becomes futile if all your competitors adopt the same techniques. If only one supermarket runs a loyalty programme, then that may achieve its goals. But if three of them end up running loyalty programmes with similar rewards, they will surely all fail. As a result the entire industry has a new cost, but has lost the initial benefit because overall the 'loyalty' effect has been cancelled out.

These arguments have weight. When the UK's Competition Commission investigated supermarkets in 1999, it found that 92 per cent of the population lives within 15 minutes' drive of three major supermarkets. It also found that the average consumer held two loyalty cards. That's not surprising. The Competition Commission was measuring the number of supermarkets within this radius because it wanted to establish that the industry offered shoppers enough choice. After all, in the UK, the six largest supermarket chains are where we spend £7 out of every £10 that we spend on groceries.

So with this much competition in each locality, and more than one loyalty scheme in each customer's purse, it looks like we are back to square one, except with the addition of a new overhead that – as we have seen – has a cost measured in eight-figure numbers, and a commitment that cannot be reduced or eliminated without damage to the brand.

Loyalty not monogamy

The doubters would be correct if it were not for the fact that when we talk of loyalty in a commercial context we aren't talking about monogamy. We may want a bit more commitment from customers, but our expectations of commercial loyalty are not the same as our hopes of loyalty in a marriage – especially when our business model is that of a 'share of customer' supplier.

To understand 'share of customer', think of your own buying habits. At any time, you are likely to purchase your electricity from one company, your phone service from another, and you might return time after time to one motor trader to purchase your cars. On the other hand, almost all retail customers are 'repertoire' shoppers, using a number of suppliers to serve their household's grocery needs.

In the real world, a food retailer's loyalty scheme will never be about consolidating all of a member's food buying into its brand, or even aspiring to that goal. Even if no other competitor introduced a loyalty programme, that level of customer devotion is clearly unachievable. Even the most loyal Tesco, Sainsbury's or Asda household has a number of food retailers that it uses every week. The superstore may be the destination for a weekly shop, but the shop on the corner comes in handy for a pint of milk or a loaf of bread. There might be a competitor's supermarket closer to work. During the day, the shop at the local garage is the most convenient place to pick up a few groceries. The local butcher may be a family friend.

All that a loyalty programme attempts to win is a slightly larger share of the customer's spend than would otherwise be the case if the additional value of the scheme were not offered. It is no accident that Tesco has 'Every little helps' as its brand promise to customers. This slogan is based on the fact that regular yet modest improvements in Tesco's offer and service are appreciated by customers and accumulate their goodwill, and that equally constant but small shifts in customer behaviour are enormously valuable to Tesco's business. So thanks to the targeting power of Clubcard, Tesco has been able to encourage 'loyal' customers who will be most receptive and likely to change their shopping behaviour, for example to visit the pharmacy, or to shop for the first time at its off-licence, or to consider its clothing range, or simply to buy three bottles of Coke in one go rather than two.

These small changes of behaviour, achieved across the entire customer base of millions of households, add up to a considerable boost in sales and profitability for Tesco. Customers may not even perceive that their spending at Tesco has increased. But in general they definitely feel that they are rewarded for being a customer, and recognized and appreciated as a good customer. A loyalty programme does not change their life, it does not keep them awake at night in anticipation, but it does give them a reason to prefer the brand that is running the programme. By making more effort to win a customer's business the scheme helps the store remain one of several to which they are 'loyal'.

A commercial conversation

This is why Tesco Clubcard is as much about Tesco showing loyalty to the customer as it is about the customer showing loyalty to Tesco. It's a 'Thank you' to a loyal friend, not a 'Well done' to a constant customer. From day one, Tesco deliberately downplayed the idea of a 'loyalty card' when it talked about Clubcard to its customers. Instead, it presented it as a way for Tesco to say 'Thank you'. It is based in the realistic expectation of how we all behave as shoppers.

A loyalty programme like Clubcard opens a two-way exchange of value, a sort of commercial conversation. The outcome of that conversation, how useful it is to both sides, depends on the quality of the benefits being offered to both parties. For the customer, quality is about how relevant it is to them, and how valuable and tempting the 'Thank you' is. For the retailers, it is about how clearly they can hear what the customers are saying to them through their actions. That's not just about listening to the customers who call the helpline, or those who complain or compliment. Every time we skip an aisle that we normally use, or switch to a cheaper product, or decide to buy or not our fresh fruit in the store, we are communicating too. And the message we are giving can be heard through the mechanism of the loyalty programme.

It simply doesn't matter if we also hold and use a number of competitive loyalty cards. Millions of customers carry a Nectar card, a Boots Advantage card, a Clubcard and others. As long as that two-way conversation continues, then each of those brands has the opportunity to try and convince us to be a bit more 'loyal'. If the conversation dries up, then it's a sign that the relationship is faltering, that as a customer we are less engaged with the brand. Maybe we're not hearing propositions that are as relevant to us as before. Maybe the brand isn't listening closely enough to what we have told them through our actions. Either way it's not a disaster, because thanks to the relationship established by the loyalty medium the company has the ability to re-engage us in a mutually beneficial conversation.

By creating a loyalty programme the company turns into a media owner. A loyalty scheme isn't an end in itself, it is the means to an end, or indeed several ends. One of those ends is to create a way in which the brand can communicate that it didn't have before, and hopefully improve the quality of its 'conversation' with customers. And because this medium is founded on personal information that reveals our tastes and preferences it has the potential to be very powerful indeed.

Since the principal aim of all loyalty programmes is to reward customers for shopping more frequently and more broadly, it is arguably more accurate to say that retailers who use them are competing with those competitor brands that don't offer rewards for loyalty, not with each other. If a customer holds several loyalty cards, he or she clearly values brands that offer rewards for loyal custom. That customer is very likely to concentrate his or her spending in those companies that recognize and reward loyalty at the expense of those that do not. While Tesco, Boots, Sainsbury's, Asda, Safeway and some other large retailers like Morrison's and the Co-op have competed fiercely with each other using a variety of loyalty marketing techniques, the overall impact of their loyalty strategies has been to divert spending away from smaller retailers. There are arguments that this is a bad thing for communities. It's certainly not good news for smaller supermarkets. But it is undoubtedly a sign of success for retail loyalty programmes, and for customers who earn even greater rewards in exchange for their loyal custom.

THE FOUNDATIONS OF A LOYALTY SCHEME

All programmes begin with a basic who, what, why, how, which and when. Think of your customers: who do you really want to engage with, all of them or just the most valuable? Think of your business: what sort of engagement is credible given the current ways in which customers transact with you? How will you reward customers to best influence their behaviour? What's your 'currency'? Which loyalty model looks most appropriate, universal or hierarchical? One size fits all or tiered?

And when do you engage with members: when it suits them, when it suits you, or a bit of both?

Let's consider some of the basic mechanics of a scheme.

Opt-in or automatic?

Should the scheme automatically include everyone who is a customer, leaving them to decide whether they want to make use of it? This approach is used by some credit card issuers, for example. The advantage: you don't have to recruit, and everyone feels involved. There are disadvantages too: unless you are already collecting data on those customers, you have changed the relationship with them – and legally, will need their permission under the terms of the Data Protection Act to use that data for a new purpose. Also, if everyone automatically gets recruited, it is harder to encourage someone to be an active participant in the brand. In many ways it is much better to be a 'chosen' than a 'given'. There's plenty of proof that an opt-in has vastly more effect than an automatic offer of benefit to customers. When BT introduced its Friends and Family programme it turned a passive discount scheme that most customers took for granted into an active preferential pricing scheme that customers loved. It had a similar cost to the business, but massively greater return on investment.

The ultimate example of the power of the opt-in is with a programme that charges for membership – effectively challenging customers to be active in their loyalty behaviour.

Anonymous or personalized?

Both approaches are legitimate, but for different applications. When your coffee shop gives you a card, and stamps it each time you visit, you offer nothing in return, except your business. It does not try to capture your name and address, because there is little advantage in generating customer data about you. It judges that the programme is working if sales increase. If it did try to collect data, the cost of running the scheme would probably outweigh the value to the business. Similarly, a supermarket may offer discounts to try and build loyalty – but with the difference that if it doesn't capture customer data about which shoppers are taking advantage of the discounts, it may not be pleasing enough customers, or generating business value from its anonymous scheme.

Flat-rate or top-down?

Should a loyalty programme give disproportionate rewards to very high-value customers, and little or no reward to low-value customers, or reward everyone using the same flat-rate approach? Clubcard offers the same points reward for almost all its customers in every aspect of the business. It would be inappropriate for a 'democratic' brand like Tesco to offer a Gold Clubcard, for example. Conversely, a highly aspirational brand like BA is happily hierarchical in its approach to loyalty. BA Executive Club members who fly the most become Silver and then Gold members, and are given access to faster check-ins, lounges and upgrades. This approach certainly offers flyers an incentive to consolidate their spend, and a strong sense of being valued. But with a tiered approach the business has to cope with relegating customers when they spend less as well as promoting them when they spend more.

Are you happy to tell your customers they are less important than they were last year? If your brand values concentrate on serving all customers, big and small, high or low spending, it is difficult to see how a loyalty scheme can afford to erode that perception by adding a layer of elitism and still succeed.

Rewards-on-demand or cumulative value?

Should a loyalty programme pay out when the business wants, or when the customers decide they have saved enough? An example is Air Miles, which lets members keep collecting until they have all the miles they need to fly to the destination they have chosen. In this instance the advantage for the customer is a sense of control, and for the participating retailers there's the chance to offer aspirational, high-value rewards. But the disadvantage to the points issuer is that these points can build up: by 2002, world airlines had a liability for 8,500 billion frequent flyer miles, worth around US $500 billion. Indeed, calculations in the *Economist* in January 2005 suggested that the total stock of unredeemed miles was worth more than all the dollar bills in circulation. The record for the biggest individual account is 25 million miles (enough to fly from London to Sydney and back 250 times), reputedly belonging to a publishing executive who charged his firm's postage bill to his own credit card. Such cumulative reward schemes make it harder for the points issuer to measure the effect of the programme in the short term.

At the other end of the scale, a supermarket scheme that allows customers to take their rewards at the checkout as and when they please is likely to lose out on the impact of a cumulative reward presented periodically. We will discuss this further in the chapter describing the extraordinary success of the Clubcard quarterly mailing.

FOUR LOYALTY 'CURRENCIES'

The next thing to decide is which rewards customers most value. What is your gold standard currency that most of your customers will enthusiastically collect and use? There are effectively four types of loyalty currencies: points-led, discount-led, information-led and privilege-led. You can offer all four in different combinations to create a rounded benefits package to members: most of the major loyalty programmes do.

Points-led

This is a generic description for schemes that encourage members to collect and spend their units of value, either at a fixed or variable issuing rate, or at a fixed or variable redemption rate. So whether they're marketed as points, miles, stars, units or cents, the basic concept is the same. Customers view these points very much as an operating currency, with a clear link between the number of points collected and a particular value at redemption. Essentially, as in the perceived value of frequent flyer miles, they have a notional face value. Increase the number earned and you're giving more value away. Reduce the face value of your points, and customers will soon work out that you are taking cash from them. When considering a points scheme it's critical to understand what the perceived value of your currency will be. Economic history tells us that consumers flock to a strong, stable currency. Loyalty currencies are no different. Air Miles continue to succeed. 'Beenz', the loyalty scheme that rewarded users for registering with websites on the internet, did not.

Discount-led

Tiered or preferential pricing is based on the simple proposition that retailers make it worth your while to be loyal because the more you shop, the less you pay. There are several retail loyalty schemes in the United States that automatically offer members lower prices at the checkout. Each item stocked literally has two prices: one for customers and a lower one for members. Others prefer to concentrate rewards by encouraging customers to buy products that they would not normally purchase. It is worth noting that while preferential pricing or discounts can be valued highly by customers and guarantee wide participation, it can lead to 'spend substitution', where your most loyal customers cease to be your most profitable because the business has significantly reduced the price of items that customers would happily pay full price for, and only given small benefits to the less frequent shoppers whom you really want to attract. Nonetheless a more targeted offer of preferential pricing, directing customers to higher margin or less mainstream products, can be a powerful incentive.

Information-led

Loyal customers may value help and advice as much as cash. Take the special interest clubs that Tesco has added to its Clubcard programme, which we will discuss in Chapter 11. The Baby Club provides information at a time when potential parents really need it. The value of that information builds on the fact that Tesco is a trusted brand, offering straightforward advice on a range of relevant subjects. Tesco has found that when it provides information that is objective and useful, it deepens the trust among those customers who have opted-in to that part of the programme. The World of Wine Club provides easily digested specialist advice on wine enjoyment, and has been successful in engaging more experienced premium-wine purchasers who might otherwise not have considered Tesco as their wine merchant.

Privilege-led

American Express claims that 'membership has its privileges'. The underlying principle is that customers prize access to services or facilities that have a rarity value, or that might be difficult to attain without the negotiating muscle of the programme or club they belong to. By definition there is only limited capacity in airport lounges, so there is inherent value for many in being invited by an airline into their 'inner circle' to enjoy free access to pre-flight drinks and pretzels and a comfortable armchair. Being offered free theatre ticket bookings or ski insurance for being a fully paid up Gold Charge cardholder is a similar proposition. These benefits are non-cash, and ongoing, depending on the customer maintaining his or her side of the deal, that is, spending at the required level. A less elitist example of the privilege proposition is often designed into store cards, offered as a 'special' way to pay, perhaps with side benefits for heavy store-card users, such as a preview invitation to the store's sales.

This model is increasingly under strain. Retail research consultancy Mintel has found that few consumers today still use their store cards as heavily as they once did. Although 14 million UK shoppers have at least one store card, three-quarters of accounts are dormant and the average card is used only three times a year, compared to 26 times for the average credit card. Mintel attributes this to the high interest rates that store cards charge. Customers may enjoy the privilege, but they don't enjoy paying for it.

DOES A LOYALTY PROGRAMME PAY?

A mass-membership programme is a long-term, expensive undertaking. But when it works, it repays the investment many times over and in many ways – as Tesco has proved.

Clubcard has transformed customer behaviour and attitudes. It has provided unprecedented levels of hard information that no other source could provide. And this is systematically transformed into rich, actionable customer insight. Clubcard has helped Tesco create new businesses. It has created incremental sales and profits.

Clubcard demonstrates that the investments needed to set up and maintain a loyalty programme are not all additional spend. Much of it is replacement spend, diverted from traditional forms of communication and promotion – for example, door-to-door distribution or TV advertising. The Clubcard mailing communicates economically and effectively with millions of customers at a time. This means that Tesco is less reliant on bought-in media to reach those same customers (and many others that Tesco may not want to reach). This reduces wasted expenditure through sending the wrong offers to the wrong customer segments. To illustrate the point, Tesco's marketing director Tim Mason recalls an immediate side-benefit of Clubcard:

When a competitor opened up against one of our stores, we were able to see those customers that stopped shopping and we were able to do something about that. We knew the names and the addresses of the couple of thousand people whose behaviour changed. If you were being aggressive about defending your store, previously you would have taken out advertisements in the local paper which said that you could get £2 off every £20 that you spend and £5 off every £50 that you spend, come on down! All those newspapers went through the doors of people who hadn't changed their behaviour at all and the costs were so exorbitant that actually you couldn't really afford to defend yourself very effectively. This completely changed the whole way in which we were able to defend ourselves from people opening new space against us.

Even more significant: in 1993, before Clubcard launched, Tesco was one of the biggest buyers of TV advertising. The next year, after Clubcard successfully exceeded all its membership targets, that TV advertising budget was slashed, as individually targeted, Clubcard communications replaced some of the TV campaigns. Christmas 1995 was a success for Tesco, but the TV advertising agency could not take the credit that year. For the first time, in the run-up to Christmas, Tesco tried a new strategy for its TV advertising. It didn't run any.

benifits of the scheme.

3

Clubcard on trial

- ▶ The trials
- ▶ Tesco and loyalty in history
- ▶ Project Omega
- ▶ The DNA of loyalty
- ▶ Rediscovering the customer

THE TRIALS

In November 1993, the press began to report strange goings-on in the UK's supermarkets. 'Tesco has started a customer loyalty programme,' reported *Campaign* magazine, the weekly journal for advertising and marketing:

> The company… has introduced electronic 'swipecards' in three outlets. Although Tesco is playing down the launch of a branded 'ClubCard' as 'a test', it has already had a 50 per cent take-up from customers in all stores applying to join the scheme. Sources say that Tesco is now planning a national rollout from next year.

Whoever the 'sources' were, they certainly weren't the official ones at Tesco. A cautious press office was giving away few details, and officially there were no plans for a national rollout of a loyalty programme. But the journalists were sitting on a scoop: the tests in the Dartford, Sidcup and Wisbech stores had already produced some remarkable results that suggested that Tesco was on to a winner – and the marketing team at Tesco had already started in 11 more stores to host the Clubcard trial in January 1994.

This was no sudden decision from Tesco. The origins of the Clubcard trial dated back to at least three years before: and appropriately, the story leads us back to the original purveyors of retail loyalty rewards, the Co-op. The Tesco marketing director in the early 1990s was Terry Leahy (now the chief executive), who had once spent a year working for the Co-op. In 1990, having risen from the shop floor to the board at Tesco, he had his interest grabbed by the news that the Co-op in Bury was experimenting with a loyalty scheme based on a plastic card with a magnetic stripe on the back. The Co-op was still awarding its customers the Co-op dividend – but now, in return, it would be able to collect information on that store's customers' shopping habits. Leahy, who had hankered after a loyalty programme for Tesco customers for several years, without successfully convincing his fellow board members, was intrigued, even if the Co-op's initiative fizzled out, not to be revived until a decade later. 'If they can do it in one shop in Bury,' he said to his marketing team, 'why can't we?'

With basic retail loyalty schemes commonplace in the United States, Tesco marketing staff had crossed the Atlantic several times already to see whether the idea would translate – each time reporting back that the start-up costs were too high, and the chances of ever making an acceptable return on the investment were doubtful. But by 1993, three things had changed that opinion and opened up the debate once again.

The first was that it was now technologically possible to process the volume of transactional data that a loyalty scheme would generate. Not all the data, and not in the detail that Tesco can now analyse. But the early 1990's vogue in the IT industry for 'data warehouses' – large databases of operational information that could be linked to the retailer's networked point of sale systems at the checkouts, and that could be used for business planning and marketing competitiveness – had created both the software and the expertise that meant for the first time there was a realistic prospect of collecting and managing masses of accurate customer-based transactional data and using it to provide insight and advantage.

The second was that Terry Leahy and Tesco were not alone in being intrigued by the possibilities. Market leaders Sainsbury's and an energetic management team at Safeway were also looking across the water. Sainsbury's had started a two-store trial of a loyalty promotion, and if the long-term market leaders of British supermarketing were beginning to see this as one way forward, Tesco didn't want to be left behind. Safeway, in that period boasting a track record for innovation, was also testing customer response to a prototype loyalty card. Other retailers that might take business from Tesco – high street clothing and household goods chain British Home Stores and petrol retailer Shell – were interested in their own loyalty programmes.

The third factor was that in the early 1990s, Tesco was not in the market leading position it now enjoys. Pressured from above by a seemingly unassailable market leader in Sainsbury's, with a looming threat from below from price-cutters like Asda and Kwiksave, and facing the prospect of an invasion from German and US discounters like Costco, Tesco needed to fight back against the competition. It needed to protect its current market share by sustaining and developing the value of its customer base. By mid-1992, Leahy's repeated conversations with the board advocating a loyalty scheme began to get a more sympathetic hearing.

The pilot

At the beginning of 1993, a £1 million research and development budget was earmarked for the project. The implications of introducing a scaleable electronic loyalty programme were well recognized by the business. The group's Electronic Point of Sale (EPOS) till system would need to be modified with card readers. A robust data collection and management system would need to be built. Data storage analysis and security were vital. Staff would have to be trained and the impact on in-store customer service would have to be planned for and monitored. Tesco would also need to create a compelling message so that customers would join, and design a marketing communications campaign that would launch and sustain the programme.

The senior marketing team – from Leahy, at its head, through Tim Mason, his marketing operations director (and later successor on the board as marketing director), to Carolyn Bradley with the Tesco brand specialists – were enthused about the potential of some sort of loyalty programme. Mason selected a young New Zealander, a recently appointed manager in strategic promotions called Grant Harrison, to head up the day-to-day development of what was then beginning to be known as Clubcard. Harrison was selected for his self-confidence and pushiness as much as his knowledge – he would have to convince not only the marketing team, but persuade store managers to take the trial seriously. It did not hurt, however, that Harrison's recently completed MBA thesis was on the little-known subject of loyalty marketing.

Harrison had researched retail loyalty marketing around the world. He knew what had succeeded and what had failed, and his earliest conclusion was that Clubcard would fail unless it was designed to appeal to customers' 'hearts as well as heads'. He argued that Tesco couldn't just use loyalty as a one-dimensional sales promotion aimed at encouraging customers to spend more. That would just be a repeat of the blunt and decreasingly effective scheme that Green Shield Stamps had become for Tesco by the late 1970s. Harrison said later:

> In my mind it was about two things, behavioural change and attitudinal change. Combined together those two things add up to genuine customer commitment. And that's the most valuable goal for a loyalty programme. Right from that point, as soon as we had agreed that, we knew our scheme was going to be different. Even before Clubcard was tested live in the first few stores, that was our premise. If you just set out to improve and measure behaviour, we didn't believe the programme would take root and develop over time. It had to be behaviour plus commitment.

From the outset, the Clubcard team shared his ambition for the project, believing that loyalty could deliver more than a boost to like-for-like sales, the traditional measure of effectiveness for a retail promotion. Clubcard had to be about both emotional and rational behaviour. It had to boost customer goodwill to Tesco.

One of Harrison's first acts in charge of the project was to appoint in May 1993 Evans Hunt Scott, now EHS Brann, a 40-strong direct marketing agency to help him turn Tesco's loyalty plans into a reality. Since 1991 EHS had been helping Tesco promote a business incentive programme, but this was their first opportunity to contribute significantly to one of Tesco's major initiatives. Partly thanks to its long-term relationship with Tesco Clubcard the agency has grown tenfold, and left its 1993 headquarters above a carpet shop on London's Edgware Road, where it first served the Tesco account, to a smarter office in the City. But it's still working intimately with Tesco on Clubcard, 13 years later.

Harrison was going to need EHS: for the first six months of the Clubcard trial he was administering the day-to-day working of the programme alone, until he managed to obtain an assistant. Tesco wasn't exactly throwing resources at this unproven concept.

An urgent need

If a positive shift in shopping behaviour and emotional commitment was the goal for Clubcard, no one could deny that Tesco was in serious need of more of both from its customers. Results during the recession in the early 1990s were disappointing: while its market share was some way ahead of Asda and Safeway, it was permanently the number two supermarket, lagging behind Sainsbury's. As Seth and Randall describe it in their history of British supermarketing, *The Grocers*:

> [for Tesco] 1991 and 1992 were bleak trading years and early figures for 1993 again showed they were losing customers vis-à-vis their 1992 levels... there were talks of a crisis at Tesco... Did Tesco have a strategy to respond? There were widespread doubts... It had hit a brick wall, having got as close to Sainsbury's as the present approach could.

Clubcard became one of a series of initiatives created in 1993 to break this cycle of under-achievement. There were the 'Value' lines, low-price basic goods, which at the time were misinterpreted as a return to times when Tesco cared more about cost than quality, but were created as a response to Tesco customer requests, and have since been copied by the rest of the UK market. The 'one in front' policy to cut queues at checkouts (whenever there was more than one person in front of you, the store would open another checkout) was a radical service improvement launched by Tesco's then chief executive Ian MacLaurin (now Lord MacLaurin) so quickly that the store managers were as surprised to hear of it as customers were. 'One in front' was an effective marketing coup that won goodwill from shoppers and acknowledgement – and imitation – from competitors. There were other signs that Tesco was starting to shed its lack of confidence and take bold initiatives, rather than always following Sainsbury's lead. There were MacLaurin and Leahy's plans to reverse the trend of supermarkets to desert town centres, by opening the smaller high street 'Metro' stores, and there was the beginning of serious investment in Tesco's 'non-food' offering started in the early 1990s – both proved to be a long-term success.

But the most innovative of the initiatives for change, its biggest leap into the unknown, was the launch of Clubcard. Unlike new store formats, or in-store service improvements or new product lines, there was no precedent in the Tesco culture for a membership programme for customers, driven by data and requiring unheard of levels of customer interaction. As one of the pioneers of self-service stores, Tesco did not have a tradition of building relationships with customers as named individuals. That was the legacy of the old-fashioned corner grocery store, not a modern out-of-town retailer. Clubcard depended on a radical, uncomfortable transformation in Tesco's management thinking. If those managers had followed their instincts as conventional super-marketers it's unlikely that Clubcard would ever have been launched. Fortunately, by this time the management of Tesco were getting more confident in challenging convention.

TESCO AND LOYALTY IN HISTORY

Terry Leahy's colleagues had taken a while to consider loyalty marketing with anything other than scepticism, but that wasn't surprising. The last time the company had invested in a full-scale promotional scheme, it had nearly driven it out of business. Tesco in 1993 might not have been the fittest supermarket, but it was in a signifi-cantly better state than it had been two decades earlier when it was pumping out millions of Green Shield Stamps.

Piling it too high, selling it too cheap

Ask anyone aged over 50 in 2003 what the early Tesco stores had been like, and they would have told you: cheap. Built by 'Slasher Jack' Cohen (later Lord Cohen) from his market stalls in East and South London, the stores he started in Becontree and Edmonton in 1931 were tiny by today's stan-dards: 500 square feet, offering a cut-price range of goods at bargain-basement prices. A trip to the United States had convinced Cohen that the new breed of 'supermarkets' was the way forward (the King Kullen Market, titled 'The world's greatest price wrecker' – a name that must have been inspirational to Jack Cohen – had opened in Long Island in 1930, and hundreds of similar shops were changing the face of retailing across the United States). Jack Cohen's Tesco opened its first supermarket in 1956, and by 1961 the company had opened a 16,500 square foot store in Leicester – at the time, a spectacular size for a supermarket.

Over the next 25 years, Tesco grew big, but increasingly vulnerable. Tesco had an admirably straightforward sales philosophy, but inadequate management depth to apply it to an increasingly complex business. The methods employed by Cohen to run his empire were no different to the way he had run his market stalls. As his former managing director Lord MacLaurin recalls, the Tesco corporate gift was a tiepin with the initials 'YCDBSOYA' on it. Cohen told visitors it was Yiddish – but actually it stood for 'you can't do business sitting on your arse'.

One of the most powerful drivers of Tesco's growth in the 1960s was its commitment to an early customer loyalty currency, originated in the United States: Green Shield Stamps. From 1963, shoppers at Tesco were rewarded with a sheet of stamps of proportional value to the amount they spent, which they saved by licking and then sticking into books. Completed books could be exchanged for consumer goods like transistor radios or garden tools. 'No question it was a gimmick, but no question it was a powerful one' says MacLaurin in his autobiography. In reporting the effect of introducing Green Shield Stamps in the Leicester store in November 1963, the *Sunday Express* agreed:

> In Leicester yesterday, the giant Tesco store was besieged by thousands of housewives. Twelve women fainted. The staff was completely overwhelmed. Finally store manager John Eastoe cleared the shop and closed all the doors. Mr Eastoe said, 'I have never seen anything like it in my life…'

Green Shield Stamps were a powerful expression of the core promise that had built Tesco's empire: squeezing the last drop of value from the weekly shop. They also displayed Tesco's common touch, in contrast to the more genteel appeal of Sainsbury's stores.

Yet a decade and a half after their introduction this first Tesco loyalty strategy had run its course. The company was in a mess, losing customers and reputation, and the cost of using the Green Shield Stamps currency to buy repeat spend was out of control. By 1977 Tesco was spending £20 million a year on an outdated gimmick that was no longer valued by the majority of customers, who increasingly were finding Tesco's prices uncompetitive. As MacLaurin points out, there 'was a very real possibility that the company would go to the wall… as prices rose, it focused the public's mind on the diminishing value of the pound in their pockets… all the indications were that the stamps were becoming increasingly counter-productive.'

Tesco's board was emotionally committed to Green Shield Stamps, and they were sucked into their own inflationary spiral. They offered ever greater numbers of stamps through double and treble promotions for the same level of customer spend. This runaway stamp inflation made the cost of the scheme more outrageous, but with diminishing effect. MacLaurin described the situation as 'the ludicrous game of having to collect a barrow load of [stamp] books to obtain a TV set'. Tesco had also fallen into a trap that other loyalty schemes before and since have experienced: it had no accurate way to measure the true sales effect (or lack of effect) of the scheme, and no adequate way to control the cost.

Tesco's Green Shield Stamps experience illustrates one of the major problems of a loyalty programme. Imagine that you create a loyalty programme from scratch, and you see like-for-like sales go up by 4 per cent in the next month. Not only that, but they stay at that level. You can give the loyalty scheme credit for the first month's sales increase. If sales stay at the higher level a year later, you may link that to the positive impact of the loyalty scheme, but it could be a combination of other recent initiatives or economic factors that are making the difference, and disguising a decline in the contribution of the programme. Without the ability to directly measure its effect, loyalty marketing is an act of faith rather than a management science.

There's another fundamental challenge: how do you stop the scheme when it ceases to be economical? Logic may say that's it's time to withdraw a loyalty scheme, but will this create a downturn in sales? When Lord MacLaurin argued that it was time for Tesco to cease issuing Green Shield Stamps, he also insisted that the saving would have to be reinvested in new revenue-building strategies like store modernization and, even more important, price cuts.

Killing off Green Shield Stamps

The Tesco board was split over whether to keep or drop Green Shield Stamps. MacLaurin led the opposition; Cohen wanted to keep his creation intact, no matter what it cost and how little evidence of a return on investment there was. The Tesco board, dominated by Cohen and an 'old guard' of management, some of them his family, had enjoyed success by rubber-stamping his decisions, and were not accustomed to innovation or rational decision-making. In MacLaurin's words, it was 'like a meeting of the Chicago mafia'. Disagreements became rows, rows became fights (at one point using a pair of ceremonial swords that had been displayed on the wall). The Cheshunt head office, which Tesco still occupies, was known throughout the company as 'the snake pit'. Politicking was rife and no decisions were made without first enduring gossip and rumour. The company's reputation for low prices was all it had, but other supermarkets were now cheaper. It had never had a reputation for quality, and that reputation showed no sign of improving.

Nonetheless MacLaurin won the day. After four rounds of voting in a fractious board meeting on 8 May 1977, Cohen finally conceded defeat: Green Shield Stamps were history. The Tesco revolution started. One month later, Green Shield Stamps disappeared from the shops, and everyone knew change was in the air. It was the end of an era in the company's history – and was marked by the demise of its first customer loyalty strategy.

Now established as the leader of innovation at Tesco, MacLaurin set about modernizing the company. He recruited a new breed of managers to help him force through the 1977 revolution. The core of that revolution, which defined Tesco's future as a brand, as a store and as an organization – and paved the way for Clubcard – was called 'Operation Checkout'.

Operation Checkout

The 'Checkout' campaign was designed to destroy the tired old image of Tesco, literally overnight. Test marketing in two Tesco stores had shown the potential for success in a fresh new way: price cuts and new store design, with larger formats and standard layouts. Pricing would be unified, and a new, cleaner, refined image would be created. The desire was to change, but also to return to the fundamentals of the Tesco brand: championing the customer, offering best value, and its populist image.

On 9 May, MacLaurin briefed 250 top managers. The next day, he and David Malpas, his deputy, set off on a nationwide tour to address the other 34,750 staff to tell them what was going on. Four weeks later, over the weekend of Queen Elizabeth II's Silver Jubilee, to the astonishment of customers and competitors, all Tesco shops shut. Their windows were whitewashed to heighten the secrecy, and behind those blank windows every Tesco store in the UK was refitted, every product repriced and every aisle redressed, all in one weekend.

It was the single most audacious gamble in the history of Tesco, and probably of British retailing. The loss of sales and profits from the self-enforced closures was unprecedented. On the evening of Wednesday 8 June, while waiting for the shops to reopen the next day, Malpas and MacLaurin drank a toast laced with gallows humour: 'Here's to Checkout, or we won't be here this time next week'.

On Thursday morning the shops opened to instant success. In scenes that mirrored the first crazy days of Green Shield Stamps, and which were to be echoed by the customer excitement over the launch of Clubcard, the numbers of customers arriving at the store forced Tesco in Pontypridd to prematurely close the shop for the day. Shoppers bought all the stock in Preston, emptying the shelves, and determined grocery buyers queued for 25 metres outside the shop in High Wycombe.

The fallout from Checkout

Tesco's Checkout revolution started a momentum that carried Tesco through the hypermarket era of the 1980s. It created a company that was no longer frightened to innovate, and one that was now hot on the heels of Sainsbury's, even if through that decade it was never quite able to catch up. The new Tesco had successfully freed itself from outmoded management practices and a self-destructive culture. As the old guard bowed out in the 1970s and 1980s, to be replaced by figures like David Malpas and Ian MacLaurin, a spirit of consensus replaced the sword fighting – so much so that the board today rarely, if ever, needs to take a vote.

Tesco's senior management team had also learnt that radical change was possible – if managers and staff are informed and brought enthusiastically behind a great idea. The 10,000-mile tour of the stores that MacLaurin and Malpas completed meant that everyone was aware of the scale and importance of Checkout. And they were made to feel that they were key to the success of that change.

The speed and secrecy of such a major undertaking as Operation Checkout were critically important. To go from the successful but traumatic board vote to national store relaunch in two months was a daunting challenge for such a large retail group – but they had little choice if they wanted to reverse Tesco's decline. As a rebranding exercise, it had less to do with repainting storefronts and everything to do with revitalizing the structure of the organization and its core offering. The risks were high. The change would have had much less impact if the plans had leaked out and the competition had been able to create a spoiler campaign. The theatrical flourish of whitewashing the windows and closing all the stores for a working day created maximum impact on the customers, and created the sort of excitement around the Tesco brand that it had not achieved for years.

Operation Checkout taught Tesco the importance of 'first mover' advantage. MacLaurin's radical and risky strategy let Tesco management rediscover the value of being an innovator. Tesco left the opposition to either copy the strategy, or stay on the sidelines. Mason points out how that has carried through to the Tesco we see today:

> One of the things that Tesco holds dear is doing things first. When you do things first, the customer views it as you doing something for them. But when you do them second, the customer is quite ready to take the discount, if it is a discount, but if it is Sainsbury's who are second, they will recognize that Sainsbury's motivation is not to try and do a better job for the customer, but to try and neutralize the advantage that Tesco has gained.

The success of Checkout in 1977 was aped by Sainsbury's with its 'Discount 78' – as the name implies, a year later. The impact was considerably less, though in fairness, they were still ahead of Tesco in market share. An important precedent was set.

Another enduring lesson for Tesco came from the stage-management of the launch. The campaign had been masterminded by Tesco's advertising agency of that era, McCann-Ericsson, whose strategic impact went much further than creating advertising copy. In effect, the agency acted as impresario of the event to gain maximum news coverage. This was a strategy that Tesco later calculated gave the company £5 million of free publicity (worth approximately £22 million in 2003).

Tesco had never been a stranger to publicity stunts. Cohen marked the opening of Tesco stores in the 1960s with the appearance of a knight called 'Sir Save-a-Lot', mounted on a white horse, and at its Leicester superstore opening in 1965, the ribbon was cut by comedy actor Sid James, the personification of the 'common touch'. With Checkout, Tesco magnified its traditional local press stories to become a huge prime-time national television and front-page newspaper story, at a time when business news stayed on the sober business pages. England may no longer have been a 'nation of shopkeepers', but Tesco calculated that its citizens had developed a taste for supermarket stories as a business soap opera. Tesco was determined to land the leading role.

This taste for the limelight contributed much to the extraordinary publicity surrounding Clubcard when it was launched onto an unsuspecting public.

PROJECT OMEGA

Fast-forward 16 years to 18 October 1993. Some impromptu customer service desks appeared in the foyers of Tesco stores at Sidcup, Wisbech and Dartford Tunnel, piled high with application forms and Tesco branded ballpoint pens, with a modest display of recruitment posters (two per store) and a little custom-built post box. Shoppers were encouraged to sign up for their 'Tesco Clubcards' and save on their shopping. These were the humble beginnings of a customer programme that was to become as radical and far-reaching in its effect as Checkout. In fact the project team developing Clubcard was able to reap the benefit of Checkout's hard-learnt lessons. Shoppers were invited to give their names and addresses and tick a box indicating the size and ages of their family. They were rewarded with a plastic card, six vouchers for a free cup of tea or coffee, a letter from the store manager and the promise of good news to come.

This was the trial that Leahy had been agitating for since the early 1990s. Grandly codenamed 'Omega' (plucked at random from the furniture warehouse next door to Tesco's Cheshunt headquarters), the trial had a simple purpose: to demonstrate whether or not a card-based loyalty programme was worthy of the board's attention. Many thought it at best a distraction, which was why the trial was modest, even by the standards of marketing pilot programmes. This was also why, even in November 1994, a Tesco spokesperson was still talking about 'The potential to operate the scheme on a nationwide basis', when the launch was less than three months in the future. Clubcard's success was certainly not guaranteed, or even confidently expected. For almost the whole of 1994, the debate internally was: could this thing work for long enough or on a broad enough scale to justify serious investment?

To find an answer, the tiny Clubcard team at Tesco had to work out exactly what they were offering, and whether or not that was compelling enough to get the majority of store customers to sign up and become committed card-carrying members. Harrison had some answers – his research had shown him that customer data was the big prize, and he was certain that sending rewards to customers at home was the best way to keep them interested. Jane Lacey, the planner for the trials, had come up with the vital ingredient: that Clubcard had to be recognized by customers as a reward for their existing loyalty rather than increased loyalty, a decision which has had a dramatic effect on the long-term success of the scheme.

Yet there were plenty of decisions still to be made. How big a dividend or cashback should Clubcard offer (the word 'discount' was banned internally, suspected of sending the wrong message)? What was the least they had to give away to get the most response? Should there be a 'minimum shop' – a basket value below which Clubcard loyalty points would not be awarded? What about pensioners or students, who only spent modestly? In the early days of the trial, different offers were tested in different stores, because the Clubcard team had no idea what would succeed.

Omega's fixed points

Some principles of Clubcard, however, based on research work or just plain common sense, had already been established. The most important – and with hindsight, obvious feature, was that Clubcard needed to capture the customer's name and address.

Tesco had the technology to track every item that was purchased from whichever store, at what price and when. The only piece of the jigsaw missing was 'Who bought it?'. The capability was there. In 1993 the newest Electronic Point of Sale (EPOS) tills had been upgraded so they could swipe credit and debit cards. There was no new checkout technology needed to extend that to read the magnetic stripe on a loyalty card, although Siemens Nixdorf programmers had to write new code for the EPOS tills. As Harrison points out, this was also a new concept for Tesco IT staff. 'We also set up a small internal IT team who worked hard to understand what on earth we were talking about,' he recalls.

Direct marketer Terry Hunt of Evans Hunt Scott described the challenge to the Clubcard team in their first meeting in June 1993:

> My mum shops at Tesco Pitsea twice a week. She spends around £20 each visit. That adds up to £2,000 every year. That is her biggest annual household outlay. Yet Tesco doesn't know who she is or where she lives or what she likes. In fact Tesco doesn't know anything about my mum at all. She's just an average to you. So what can you do if my mum decides to take her grocery 'account' elsewhere? Nothing.

More worrying, he pointed out, what can the manager of Tesco Pitsea do if a hundred customers like Hunt's mum decided to shift their 'accounts' down the road to one of the competitors?

The standard retail technique at the time would be send out untargeted promotions to everyone in the area, hoping that the customers who had deserted got them. 'If you don't know your customers as individuals it's like trying to play the piano in boxing gloves,' Hunt said. 'You make a lot of noise but it's not always very pretty.'

Without the name and address specifying who the member is and details of the household, Clubcard would be no more useful to Tesco than the store's daily till roll, and no more motivating to customers than a discount card.

With the member's name and address Tesco was able to accumulate the rewards earned by the customer and send them directly to his or her home in the form of money-off vouchers. The vouchers would be posted to the member every three months. A Tesco internal document, explaining the scheme to store staff, said:

> The scheme allows customers to accumulate points which are converted quarterly to a cash value in the form of vouchers, which may be used to purchase goods at the trialling stores. No special purchases are necessary, but with the points earned in the Tesco Clubcard scheme, shoppers can treat themselves to a little extravagance now and then – on Tesco.

Thank you

Sir Terry Leahy has always emphasized that Clubcard does not create loyalty by itself – it creates a medium that allows Tesco to say 'Thank you' to customers for their loyalty in proportion to how much of that loyalty Tesco has earned. The idea that Clubcard is a 'Thank you' from Tesco to its loyal customers was established by Lacey early in their project planning. From the outset the Clubcard team wanted to make sure that the relationship they were strengthening was the one between the customer and the Tesco brand. They were wary of setting up a new relationship that created loyalty between the customer and Clubcard. The approach has to allow Tesco to recognize what changes create that loyalty, and enhance it. Clubcard was always intended to be the servant to Tesco, not a brand in its own right.

If Clubcard was always meant to be a 'Thank you', the way that gratitude was to be expressed was left open in the trial. The Clubcard team needed to leave Tesco the freedom to take Clubcard in different directions according to customer response, or even abandon it altogether. Even the name, Clubcard, was chosen to be bland enough to allow the card to be used in a number of ways depending on results and subsequent board commitment. Although the programme was set up so that it could easily be scaled nationally, and was designed to one day be a company-wide scheme, one option was still to run it locally on a store-by-store basis rather than launch it as a universal nationwide scheme. Not every store would need to offer Clubcard. 'At the very least,' Harrison recalls, 'Clubcard could have just have been a short-term sales promotion'.

Trialling on the cheap

This was only one of many marketing programmes that Tesco was trialling that year. At best most supermarket promotional initiatives prove useful for a short time, or in a certain locality, or for a certain format of store. Finding one that can 'go national' is the exception. Around the same time as the Clubcard trials, Sainsbury's was experimenting with the prototype of its Reward card, primarily as a local marketing tool.

Harrison and his team didn't have a blank cheque. One of the attributes that Tesco had retained from the Cohen years was its thrift. Cohen called his autobiography *Pile It High, Sell 'em Cheap* for a good reason: he, and therefore Tesco, never spent more money than was strictly necessary. In the 1990s, Tesco marketing teams could try out radical ideas, but never with radical budgets.

At the Cheshunt headquarters, marketing staff who were delegated to sort the Clubcard applications manually had no money for office partitions to keep the noise down. So they built their own from cardboard boxes (of which there must have been a ready supply).

Thrift was most important in the economics of the programme – and that meant deciding how big the cashback percentage would be. A 1 per cent cashback would be cheaper, but might not be significant enough to change customer behaviour. If it became 2 per cent, would it be too expensive to pay for those changes?

Tesco wanted a scheme that appealed to the majority of customers, not just the highest spenders. This was partly because Tesco wanted to be a democratic, inclusive brand (former Clubcard Director Crawford Davidson refers to Tesco having a 'strong democratic streak' in the brand). It was also basic economics. If a membership programme, with all the IT and customer service investment that required, was to be worthwhile it had to demonstrate an impact on the total Tesco business.

For many retail loyalty programmes that Tesco had researched, especially in the United States, asking how many percentage points of reward would create more sales was as deep as they thought. They created a discount or dividend structure, rewarded shoppers for spending money, and trusted that the excitement and goodwill they created would drive additional sales over an extended period. Tesco's team thought this deferred discount was not smart enough. For its trials, the Clubcard team decided to go one step further.

That extra step was to use Clubcard to generate knowledge about its customers, and to use that knowledge to serve those customers better. The Clubcard team realized that with Clubcard, for the first time, Tesco would be able to look into the shopping trolleys of its customers in detail, and that knowing what they bought, linked to knowing where they lived, would be a powerful insight. A one-dimensional reward scheme that does not analyse these customer data might create a change in sales performance, but it leaves little room to improve what the company offers its customers.

Retailers that are not able to record and use their transactional data to track trends, behaviour changes and sales, and apply that to known groups of customers, are not much better informed than before – and are probably making the same mistakes week after week, unaware that they are doing so.

The thinking behind building a customer relationship was supported by Hunt's thinking at EHS, where his focus on brand created a three-strand model for a brand-building loyalty programme.

THE DNA OF LOYALTY

The model assumes that there are three intertwined 'strands' that create a loyalty programme.

1. Brand values

This is the key ingredient of a loyalty programme's genetic code. The programme is the active expression of the brand's personality and its values. Whatever the characteristics of the brand are, the qualities that customers recognize and admire, the loyalty programme is that brand in action. It is the brand putting its effort and money where its mouth is.

2. Business dynamics

A loyalty programme cannot exist in isolation from the day-to-day business dynamics of the company. Whatever opportunities or constraints exist for the business as a whole, they have to be reflected in the construction of the programme.

For example, the concept of loyalty and its measurement will vary radically by product sector. Take the impact of customer defection. A statistic showing that 98 per cent of customers who purchase a brand of coffee are likely to buy the same brand the next time they need coffee sounds good. But when you look beyond the average to the heavy users who are buying coffee every two weeks, the defections in that group will increase dramatically after only a few months. Compare this to a washing machine manufacturer's experience. It may find that only 50 per cent of customers are likely to buy their next washing machine from it, but that retention rate may be the best in the industry and the value to the business of retaining those 50 per cent is enormous. A pay-as-you-go phone company that retains 97 per cent of its subscribers month by month but loses 30 per cent of them over the course of the whole year could be facing financial meltdown, but a new consumer product that retains 40 per cent of its first-time buyers for a second purchase could represent a stunning success. No loyalty programme can succeed if it ignores these principles.

Also, if the customers of the business tend to visit on a very infrequent basis, but spend a lot of money when they are shopping, there is no point devising a points scheme that most benefits frequent low-spending customers. Or say yours is a particularly low-margin business and you can't afford to sacrifice margin on every purchase, you'd do better to base your scheme on added-value service for best customers, or by providing instant-win prize draws at the point of purchase, where the cost of the reward is capped by the finite prize pool. If your business has not got a standardized till system at every outlet, there's no point devising a scheme based on the latest smart card technology, unless of course the business is ready to make that commitment to infrastructure to meet its broader commercial objectives.

3. Customer behaviour

It is axiomatic for Clubcard, and any other loyalty programme that aims to succeed, that the focus of the programme should be to encourage profitable customer behaviour – 'Reward the behaviour you seek', as it is known at Tesco. Call these goals the Key Performance Indicators (KPIs) of the programme. Establish priorities for the changes you want to see in customer behaviour. An example may be the need to increase the frequency of customer visits, or to consolidate spending in the main departments. Judge the programme on simple measures like that at the outset and there is a clear-cut way to measure the performance of the scheme. It is probable that if it doesn't achieve its most basic goals, then it will not succeed when it is trying to achieve more subtle, targeted changes in customer behaviour. Large or small, a scheme needs to work from a basic principle: work out what you want your customers to do, and create a reward system that encourages them to do it. It also means trying to dissuade senior management from seeking to achieve every desired behaviour change at once.

The DNA of a loyalty scheme isn't fixed. All three strands can change and evolve. But a scheme that does not create specific goals that are relevant to all three strands has less chance of succeeding, and little chance of surviving beyond the first few years.

REDISCOVERING THE CUSTOMER

Early results

While there were many new challenges for the Tesco marketers to face during the trials of Clubcard, one thing helped maintain their enthusiasm for the project. It was working.

By the middle of 1994, it was clear to the project team that customers loved Clubcard. In the three stores participating in the first phase of the test, out of every £10 spent by customers, £6 was spent by Clubcard holders, and that was by the end of the first week of its introduction. Over the following two months the proportion of sales attributable to Clubcard members rose to 80 per cent in some cases. That take-up exceeded all targets. Most important for the cost of the scheme, customers responded just as well to 1 per cent of their spend as their reward as they did to 2 per cent, which made the cost of the 'Thank you' much more manageable for Tesco.

For Terry Leahy, this was a huge relief. If he was to make the Clubcard attractive to the board, he had to be able to minimize the risk in the business case. There was no point generating higher sales through loyalty marketing if it resulted in an unsustainable dilution of margin. 'Even with a 1 per cent discount, we would be giving a third of our retained profit away,' he explains.

The marketing department may have been sold on the potential of Clubcard, but to convince the board that this was more than a revamped Green Shield Stamps, Terry Leahy and Tim Mason needed evidence that Clubcard delivered a lot more value to Tesco than an occasional sales blip.

Recruiting a specialist

That proof would come from customer insight based on the transactional data from the Clubcard trials. Tesco needed a specialist partner that could make its dream of data-driven marketing a reality. The Clubcard team knew that they would need to look outside the company's IT department to get the dedicated data analysis expertise they needed. So the search started for an outside company that knew how to take the massive volumes of transactional data and turn them into customer information.

In the early 1990s these weren't common skills. Site research was a well-established discipline at major retailers like Tesco, which realized the economic advantage of putting the right store in the right place. In-house teams used census and research data about communities, their affluence, their travel habits and spending patterns to position new stores, or adjust the ranges in existing stores. Geodemographic data like this can give a fair representation of what type of households make up any given community – it is the type of data that decides how much your home contents insurance premium will be, or what clinical facilities are needed in the local doctor's surgery. But it only works on an aggregated basis; it is not designed to offer insights at an individual household level.

With Clubcard, Tesco wanted to respond to information on an individual customer's needs and preferences. This would be information based on what customers do, not what they say they do, or what a research project guesses they will do.

Fundamentally, retail systems are not set up to provide customer information at this level – instead, their job is to give a snapshot of the sales activity and stock status. There is a similar contrast between a transactional view and a customer view in high street banking – in most cases, still not resolved. While a bank might know that during a week it issued £500 million in loans and took £500 million on deposit, its systems find it harder to identify an individual customer with savings of £5,000 and no borrowing, or a customer with £5,000 in borrowings and no savings, and so it tends to communicate with both customers in the same undifferentiated way. In 1993, the principal task for the Tesco IT department was to maintain the vital flow of transactional data 24 hours a day, 52 weeks a year. They were certainly not accustomed to thinking about household shopping habits or the peculiar new demands of the marketing department.

To achieve this insight, Tesco turned to another small agency: dunnhumby, marketing data specialists. Already working with EHS, but with only five clients, it had a reputation as a clever innovator in the use of geodemographic data for companies like Mercury, the telecommunications provider, and BMW. The brief from Mason to dunnhumby's 'chief data doctor' (now chairman) Clive Humby was simple: 'Convince the board that Clubcard adds value to the business.'

The question was simple to ask, not so easy to answer.

The problem with data

Any store manager in the trial sites who was worried about giving up his or her store's innermost secrets for examination needn't have worried. The only information that Tesco could collect from the transactional logs in 1994 was the amount each customer had spent, and the date and location where they had spent it. Tesco could see where the regular shoppers were, and who the big spenders were. But whether the big spend was on five bottles of champagne or 100 loaves of sliced bread was still a mystery.

As the trials progressed through 1994 and were extended to 14 stores, the demand for more profound insight became more pressing. The good news was that the Clubcard results would be presented to the autumn chairman's conference, to a group of directors who needed to be convinced that their £1 million had been well spent – convinced enough to give the go-ahead for millions more to be committed to preparing for a national launch. Just to get Clubcard on the agenda was a victory for the team.

Luckily, dunnhumby's first look at the sample data revealed an overlooked but very useful basis for analysis. The Clubcard-linked transactions at the till could be broken down by spend by department.

Although Tesco was still some way away from being able to tell if its trial customers were buying Coke or Pepsi, the Clubcard data could reveal if they were buying soft drinks or nappies. The implications of cutting the data that way were very exciting to Humby and his team. Computer tapes holding Clubcard transactions were delivered to dunnhumby's West London offices, and for three months over the summer of 1994 a dedicated team looked into what discoveries would most impress the Tesco sceptics – and whether they had that information.

What did they find? A simple, yet at that time unknown statistic gained from the data was that a small proportion of its customers accounted for a massive part of its profitability – the 80–20 principle. These 'Premium Loyals' would have a massive influence, but before Clubcard, they were anonymous. Neither store managers nor the marketing experts at Cheshunt were aware of the economic significance of the most loyal customers to Tesco. Other insights showed the profile of different customers based on the combination of store departments they used, highlighting departments that were failing to attract customers who shopped heavily in other areas. (The small number of departments visited on average was quite a shock, and led to the drive to encourage customers to 'shop the shop'.)

By analysing the penetration of Clubcard membership by postcode, the Clubcard data gave a sharply defined picture, store by store, of how far valuable customers were willing to travel to shop. It showed in which neighbourhoods the competition was really biting. The analysis showed who was coming back several times a week, and who saved up their shopping for a weekend.

In 1994 even the most advanced retailers were unaccustomed to being confronted with their customers' behaviour in such fine detail. They were used to measuring footfall (how many people had come in and out), or the number of checkouts that were active during the day, or the number of baskets of shopping and their average size and value. These were the standard measures displayed on their 'control panel' that they used to drive their businesses. This was different. This was what was really happening, not an average.

The data were strong enough to form the basis for an experiment in direct mail. In September 1994, Grant Harrison briefed EHS to create the first large-scale Clubcard direct mail campaign for 100,000 members. They had already been sending out local mailings to contact customers of individual stores, but for the first time Tesco could target customers based on a basic analysis of shoppers' buying habits. The mailing was not too ambitious in its targeting and the offer test was simple – giving high spenders £3 off a £30 shop, while low spenders were incentivized to spend just a little more, with a £1 offer off a £10 shop. The results were, even compared to the expectations of EHS and the Tesco team, staggering. Redemption rates on the coupons exceeded 70 per cent in some cases. Spend was up among the recipients by 4 per cent.

The trials had also unleashed a stronger customer reaction than Tesco expected, as customers responded to being contacted by name by their supermarket for the first time. Mason remembers offering 300 customers of its Amersham store the chance to pop in for a free glass of Tropicana orange juice and a croissant one morning, to meet the store manager. Amersham, where some of Tesco's most-well-off customers shop, came out in force. 'The car park was crammed with BMWs and Mercedes,' Mason recalls. 'Why did they come? I am not sure I fully understand today.'

As the chairman's conference approached, another supporting argument began to emerge. The managers of the trial stores loved the card, particularly the new power it gave them to see exactly who had stopped shopping at Tesco in recent months, and then do something about it. This impressed Dave Clements, at that time one of the local marketing team:

> I knew this was only a trial, and it was going to be very expensive to rollout so we didn't know if we ever would, but I was very quickly aware about how powerful it could be. One of the stores had a re-fit, and so I thought that rather than buy space in the local press and say 'sorry for the disturbance', we could write to the Clubcard customers with a personal letter from the store manager saying, 'We would like to give you advance notice, we are sorry and here are some money off coupons.' Response rates were huge. We also identified who had stopped using one of our stores, and sent them a letter saying, 'we really value your custom, please come back.' Again, the results were fantastic.

We know more in three months...

While the number crunchers were excited by the potential of Clubcard data, the bean counters at Tesco would be a tougher audience. Even if the results of the trial were positive, they were asking, what if everyone does it?

It was already well known that Asda, Safeway and especially Sainsbury's were interested in the idea – and Sainsbury's had its own localized pilot project in development. 'The question going round was, will the competition go too?' recalls Carolyn Bradley, Harrison's boss at the time, and one of the sponsors of the scheme, 'If everyone does this, have we all just knocked a [percentage] point off our margins and that is that? The big reservation was, are we just instigating a downgrading of the entire industry's margins?' If Tesco wanted to sacrifice margin for short-term growth, there were proven ways to do it. In 1977 Tesco had redirected the costs of the cancelled Green Shield Stamps scheme into price cuts, and had almost doubled market share as a result.

The ghosts of Operation Checkout haunted the Clubcard proposal in another way. The members of the board who would have to approve Clubcard were, in many cases, coming to the end of their Tesco careers. Sir Ian MacLaurin was chairman. His managing director, David Malpas, was the other architect of Checkout. 'When the decision on Clubcard came to be made,' Mason remembers, 'you were asking the people coming to the end of their careers, and who had built their careers around dismantling a loyalty scheme, as one of their final acts in the business to introduce a new one.' Tough sell.

It was also tough to be arguing for a loyalty scheme when it meant recognizing that for all the success of Operation Checkout, it had ultimately failed in its biggest ambition – to make Tesco the largest supermarket chain in the UK. Research showed customer perception of quality put Tesco and Sainsbury's on a par. Tesco had made massive strides forward under MacLaurin's leadership, innovating faster and recruiting higher-quality managers, but the fact remained that in 1994 it was still number two. The argument for Clubcard was very simple. By replicating the sales growth that Clubcard had created in its trial, Tesco could become the UK's number one for the first time.

On the morning of 22 November 1994, Tim Mason, Grant Harrison and a nervous Clive Humby presented the results of the Clubcard trials to the Tesco board meeting. In half an hour they laid out the data findings, the response rates, the customer research results and the like-for-like sales boost. The board listened in silence. At the end of the presentation, more silence.

Sir Ian MacLaurin spoke from the chair: 'What scares me about this,' he said, 'is that you know more about my customers in three months than I know in 30 years.'

4

Because we can

- ► The national launch
- ► The need for speed
- ► 'Electronic Green Shield Stamps' catch on
- ► What made the launch a success?

THE NATIONAL LAUNCH

Tesco has never been a company to spend money on fancy offices. The company headquarters building in Cheshunt, an unfashionable satellite town northeast of London, is an ugly, concrete box nestling incongruously among streets of modest semi-detached houses. So the spirits of the Clubcard team lifted when they discovered at the beginning of December 1994 that they would be moving off site. Until, that is, they discovered where they would be going.

The board meeting at the chairman's conference was a success. Project Omega was going national. A few voices had counselled caution, suggesting a larger but still limited trial. But under Sir Ian MacLaurin, Tesco senior management had the ability to make bold decisions when there was evidence that they would work. In this instance the decision was to roll out Clubcard as soon as possible. David Malpas had caught the mood of the meeting on 22 November. He argued that if Tesco was a customer-centred business, and it wanted to fulfil that promise, it could not afford to ignore an opportunity that was possible for the first time. 'We ought to do this,' he said, 'because we can.'

Entering 'The bunker'

To the small marketing team who had struggled for 12 months to manage the Clubcard trials in 14 of Tesco's 600-plus stores, who were just at the beginning of building a customer database and who had only produced the first of their new targeted mailing programme, 'as soon as possible' looked like May 1995 at the earliest. To the board, it meant January – less than two months away. January was physically impossible, the team said, there's too much to do, too many risks. Tesco's board of seasoned retail negotiators were accustomed to compromise, their way. The result was a launch in the second week of February. 'OK,' said MacLaurin to Mason. 'You have 12 weeks.'

Bolstered by a couple of extra members of staff, the Clubcard team took possession of their new office, or as Carolyn Bradley (who stayed at headquarters) named it, 'The bunker'. The reason was secrecy. Sainsbury's was also trialling its card – although, as it turned out, was less satisfied with the results – and retail gossip implied that Safeway's trial scheme had worked well, and it was ready to go nationwide any time. The race for first-mover advantage was on. A news blackout was ordered. Clements, Harrison and the others were officially working on a new home-shopping initiative (another of the decisions from the Chairman's conference was to create the Tesco home-shopping service, which was to become the second major innovation of a busy 1995), and with this as their cover, they were sent to an abandoned Tesco office nearby, as Dave Clements recalls:

> It was in Riverside House. It used to be a Tesco office, but they had moved everyone else out; either they were going to sell it or knock it down. We were in it for three months, from November through February; it was pretty grim but very exciting. There was the dedicated Clubcard team of Grant, myself, Jane Lacey, a couple of others and two or three IT people. We disappeared because we didn't want anyone to get wind of what we were doing, so we were pretty much the only people there, in a room that was 20 feet by 20 feet, with a phone, a fax and a coffee machine down the corridor.

THE NEED FOR SPEED

Cards, phones and forms

To make its 12-week deadline, the team worked over Christmas, keeping in touch by the new-fangled mobile phones they were issued with, and relying on help from suppliers who had cooperated with the trials.

Clements's task was to source the producers of enough plastic cards to satisfy the demands of all Tesco customers, estimated to be around 10 million. There was a question whether or not any manufacturer could cope with the production schedule, but a company called ID Data, still supplier of Clubcards, convinced Tesco it was up to the job.

At the time, this was the single largest card-issuing programme yet attempted in the UK. Tesco exhausted all the card manufacturing capacity in the UK; ID Data had to outsource much of the demand to factories in mainland Europe. Even so, Tesco ran out of Clubcards a week after the launch.

Extra telephone capacity was needed, because if millions of people were going to join the programme and use their cards, there would be a torrent of customer enquiries. There were 10 customer care operators at headquarters. They would be completely overwhelmed, even if the launch went perfectly. The team had to plan for problems too.

Card application forms had to be designed, printed and distributed to every store in the UK. They had to be as easy as possible for the customer, because anything that made applying for a Clubcard difficult would have a significant impact on the take-up of membership.

The testing of different formats by EHS had shown that an all-in-one sign up form, as opposed to a two-stage application for a personalized card, was more successful in generating majority take-up. In the launch version the card was adhered to the application form, both were printed with the member's unique number as a way to identify the form with the card user, and the application asked the minimum of questions to make the process of joining as painless as possible.

Advertising

The need for speed also affected Clubcard's launch TV campaign. The previous autumn, the same marketing team had been working with Tesco's advertising agency Lowe Howard Spink to announce the One in

Front campaign when they heard that Sainsbury's was ready to go with a similar project. The Tesco initiative, with completed TV advertisement, launched the next Monday, less than a week later.

Fortunately, Clubcard's face fitted perfectly the new brand positioning developed by Lowe Howard Spink for Tesco. Its 'Every little helps' advertising line, which customer panels were overwhelmingly positive about, was less than a year old. Customers told Tesco they found this straightforward, honest and believable. Where many loyalty programmes seemed like a moustache painted on the face of the brand, Clubcard fitted Tesco values as snugly as the 'divi' had fitted the Co-op.

There was the small matter that this preparation was all happening in December, traditionally the busiest month of the year for supermarkets. But the advertising brief was very simple: join Clubcard and you'll discover for yourself that every little helps. 'Could we have done better ads?' Bradley asks. 'Yes. But because it was so simple, it worked. The positioning was easy for customers to get and it was celebratory, and that is why it worked.' The announcement that Tesco splashed across the nation's TV screens, poster sites and newspapers was not witty or clever, but it was to the point: 'At Tesco we wanted to say a big thank you to all our customers. So we're giving everyone a thank you card... pick up a card and full details, with our thanks.'

Telling the staff

Advertising alone would not make the launch successful. There was another audience that Tesco needed to convince, without whose enthusiasm Clubcard would fail: the staff. Tesco needed to repeat the success of Operation Checkout when MacLaurin criss-crossed the country to make sure that every member of staff knew exactly what was needed, and felt valued and understood. Already, the trials had shown that staff – especially managers – responded well once they knew what the purpose of Clubcard was, and how well their customers received it. The job was to spread that understanding and commitment to all 130,000 staff.

To spread the news around the country Tesco produced a Clubcard video, presented by Mason. Senior managers were given aeroplane tickets for 8 February. Flying from Stansted airport, they made a whirlwind tour of four locations on that day to tell regional and store managers the news. Clements says:

I remember flying to Glasgow with Tim Mason and John Gildersleeve. Then we flew to Birmingham later on the same day to do the same launch. The message was that this was the icing on the cake, the culmination of what we had been doing for 10 years. All the managers had turned up, all their bosses were there – there was a sense that this was a huge thing.

Harrison recalls:

We put board members with Clubcard team members, and most importantly, store trial managers, and we presented simultaneously all over the country. Each store brought their store manager and customer services manager. Managers were given a few days' notice of the compulsory meeting and were to be the targets of the biggest internal marketing campaign they had ever seen. We knew from the trial that if the stores really got behind it and sold it to customers for all they were worth, it probably made a 10 per cent greater impact on the bottom line than just going through the motions.

The next day, all headquarters staff were taken to Tesco's 'Country Club', a slightly grand name for its works club just off the M25. Elliot Weider, a junior employee at the time, remembers the first time he heard of Clubcard, on 9 February:

I joined Tesco in a graduate training scheme, and I have been here ever since. It was new and wondrous to me at the time... I still remember going down to the Country Club. It generated a load of excitement; there was a real buzz because it was a first, that was exciting. I would say that was one of the reasons that Clubcard worked, that we really had the hearts and minds of our staff. They believed in it, thought it was a fantastic opportunity, and it was really sold to us.

Timing was critical. The first weeks after launch would be vital to maintain the momentum of the programme: if customers weren't made aware of the importance of the programme, recruitment would not gain the 'snowball effect' that Tesco predicted. Encouraging staff to sell the card to shoppers – and making sure they knew what the benefits were when they did – was effectively grassroots marketing using Tesco's own staff.

Checkout staff were coached in how to ask for the Clubcard and when to swipe it, asked to point out the portion of the till receipt which showed the Clubcard number and an updated points total in order to convince customers that 'points are definitely being added to their account, and the account is growing.' They were encouraged to feel that they and their store owned the scheme. 'It's your Clubcard too. Be part of it... over 70 per cent of sales in participating stores are made by Clubcard customers. And sales are significantly up. Make sure you encourage as many people as possible to register and use their card,' the EHS-produced literature exhorted the staff. 'If they don't, they will be missing out.'

Having already recruited 250,000 cardholders from the trials and seen the power of word-of-mouth recommendation, Tesco also knew that its customers would act as recruiters too. 'Everyone was saying to their friends, "Have you got one of these cards?"... we only really understood the full impact of that when we saw it happening,' Dave Clements remembers.

Telling the press

The last challenge was to get press coverage. On Friday 10 February, three days before the launch in every Tesco store in Britain and just two days after Tesco managers found out that the 'home shopping' project being planned in 'The bunker' was nothing of the sort, the press heard about the national launch of Clubcard for the first time. 'Tesco says "Thank You" to customers,' said the press releases. Significantly there was not one mention of the controversial L-word, loyalty. 'Reward' was in there, 'relationship', 'thanks', and of course, 'every little helps' – but not loyalty.

'The news hit shares yesterday as rumours swept the city,' reported the *Sun*, excitedly. 'Rivals' shares also slumped as dealers viewed the move as the latest round in the supermarket price war.' The press had, not for the last time, missed the point of Clubcard, seeing it as the start of a price war – but even though Tesco's motivation wasn't commonly understood, the effect for the customer was. At the end of a period of recession, the message that Tesco was giving something back to all its customers was a powerful one. On the day that Clubcard launched, the *Mirror* splashed the depressing results of a survey by the Joseph Rowntree Foundation on 'Divided Britain': 'During the 1980s the poorest 30 per cent gained no benefit from economic growth,' it lamented.

The secrecy around the national launch wrong-footed competitors, who had assumed that Tesco would move to a larger trial, or that it would take until the autumn to launch nationally. An off-the-cuff response from David Sainsbury, then chief executive of his family firm, that Clubcard was simply 'an electronic Green Shield Stamp' got plenty of coverage in the national press. It was a neat quote – but one that he would regret. It was also received with delight at Tesco headquarters, where the directors realized that Sainsbury's not only were behind in the race to launch their scheme, but also that they had no clear idea at the most senior level what a data-creating loyalty programme was for. 'I was in Tim's office at the time we heard about it,' Bradley remembers. 'Ian MacLaurin came down to see the TV advertising at the same time and I remember us being convinced that it would come back and bite Sainsbury's in the bum. And it did. Oh, we enjoyed that a lot.'

Clubcard had arrived, causing what can only be described as a media frenzy. From Radio 4's 'Today' programme, through the daytime shows, national news and the newspapers, the launch got the sort of coverage normally given to a celebrity wedding. At 10 am, MacLaurin said that the Clubcard 'is an extension of the process of listening... we reckon that most of our 8 million weekly customers will become Clubcard holders over the next few months.'

'In the old days a manager knew all his customers personally and did his own market research just by talking to them,' Mason added. 'We're now able to recreate that contact. That was something that Ian MacLaurin could appreciate, and really buy in to.'

The story had strong local impact too – regional managers were briefed, and encouraged to invite the press in for pictures of shoppers clamouring to sign up. The momentum exceeded even Leahy and Mason's expectations.

'ELECTRONIC GREEN SHIELD STAMPS' CATCH ON

Two weeks after the launch, 7 million cards had been delivered to stores yet supplies were nearly exhausted: 70,000 a day were being sent out to replenish stocks. With such a full-blooded invitation to the country to come and join Tesco it would be a poor show not to have enough cards to go round. Within days more than 70 per cent of all Tesco sales were being recorded and matched to Clubcard holders – 3.5 million transactions every week. The Clubcard hotline was taking between 1,000 and 2,000 calls a day. More budget was found, and the advertising was extended until 12 March.

The competition responds

Asda brought forward the launch of its fuel card, as did Safeway – hoping to score a hit against Clubcard as Clubcard points could not at that stage be earned by customers when buying petrol, already almost 12 per cent of Tesco sales. Of the major retailers, Sainsbury's, which had less than a year earlier been the clear leader in loyalty card trials, was the most wrong-footed, having no immediate response apart from disdain. The 'electronic Green Shield Stamp' had become more immediately popular than anyone, including the Clubcard team, had expected.

To offset the £10 million launch cost of Clubcard and the cost of issuing membership cards and reward vouchers, Tesco calculated that a 1.6 per cent uplift in sales was required. Early results showed a lift in sales nearer 4 per cent – an almost unheard of sales spike from a single marketing initiative – and settling well above 2 per cent. In some stores, the Clubcard effect was so dramatic that like-for-like sales soared into double-digit amounts. Two weeks after launch, the marketing of Clubcard had been a public relations triumph by any standards. Some critics argued that customers were only signing up for a discount – and when they discovered that the discount was only 1 per cent, they would soon desert Clubcard and possibly Tesco. However, it wasn't long before that scepticism looked unfounded. Customers' enthusiastic participation in the programme grew steadily over the first quarter.

There were unexpected results from the Tesco stores that had not been refurbished, where sales had been in gentle decline for many years. Sales started to grow again.

If some people around Tesco were surprised by the impact, Mason and his team's step into the unknown was exactly what they had expected. It showed that the trial results would not just be replicated nationally, but they could be improved on.

As the scale of the success of Clubcard became apparent, Bradley realized just how important it would be to Tesco – and how costly failure would be. 'Oh my god,' she remembers thinking, 'what have we created?'

WHAT MADE THE LAUNCH A SUCCESS?

With hindsight, the launch of Clubcard is a case study in how to roll out a large marketing initiative quickly, efficiently and with maximum impact. Why?

Momentum

The speed to market that the board demanded didn't suit the Clubcard team at first – but it was a brilliant example of a courageously self-imposed white-knuckle challenge. Tesco's determination to gain first-mover advantage paid off. Tesco set the agenda – the only option for the competition was to react.

Simplicity

The message was right – 'Save on your shopping today'. It was simple, direct and emphasized what customers got out of the deal in the most basic terms. And it fitted customers' expectations of their supermarket brand: 'Every little helps' and 'Thank you' were a natural fit.

Control

The Clubcard team did not have a committee to negotiate with. 'The board trusted us to do what we wanted to do, driven by customer response and our growing vision of what customer understanding could do for the business,' says Harrison. 'Very few people made the decisions very quickly without the pontificating and justification which often slows other companies.'

Involvement

The front-line staff were always informed and closely involved at every key stage. They acted as marketers for the scheme too. Because it was 'their Clubcard', they backed the advertising messages in their dealings with customers at the local level.

Preparation

The lessons of the trial were learnt well. One year of experimentation had produced 250,000 test cases of how to do the job right. The phone lines were in place to handle customer queries, the marketing material was tested, the IT infrastructure was in place, the processes and means to deal with customers in a new way were ready.

Ambition

To convince the business and shareholders, Clubcard had to prove itself big and quick. After the trials the team was confident that 70 per cent of all Tesco customers could be attracted in weeks, and that those customers would continue to use their cards in the future. Because the reward was set at a sustainable level, pegged at 1 per cent, and this had been proven to be sufficiently attractive to customers, the upside was huge and the risks controlled. The response figures convinced the City, persuaded the board to back Clubcard wholeheartedly in its first year and quickly built the conviction that Clubcard had a big, popular future.

Commitment

If there is one factor that more than any other contributed to Clubcard's immediate success, it was the enthusiasm for bold innovation shown by the Tesco board. As a seasoned management team they could have been forgiven for dismissing loyalty marketing as a failed idea. As retailers they had achieved enough in their careers not to take unnecessary risk; they could well have consigned Clubcard to months or years of trialling, and probably a quiet lingering death. Instead they had the vision and energy to see the prize and to grasp it. They didn't just take what was on offer either – they pushed for an accelerated launch. They gave the project to a young team with more energy than experience and trusted them. The decision that the board took on 22 November 1993 wasn't business as usual – it was the act of a company that intends to be the first in its industry.

If the Clubcard team felt a degree of quiet satisfaction in the days that followed the 13 February launch, then that period of calm wasn't destined to last long. Behind the scenes, the hard work was only just beginning: the first customer mailing was due, and that was a bigger job than the launch had been. 'We realized that our successful Sunday amateur football team had suddenly been promoted to the Premier League,' Harrison says. 'We had a hell of a lot to do to continue the success.'

5

Every little helped

- ▶ The Clubcard effect
- ▶ The loyalty contract
- ▶ The first quarterly mailing
- ▶ Waiting for the zero sum effect
- ▶ Maintaining momentum

THE CLUBCARD EFFECT

The Clubcard team at Tesco hoped that they might have a few months to establish Clubcard before Sainsbury's retaliated with a national launch of its Rewards loyalty programme. 'We kept thinking, they must launch soon,' Harrison remembers. As it turned out, his team had a year and a half. In that time, according to market researcher Taylor Nelson AGB, customers spent 28 per cent more at Tesco, and cut spending at Sainsbury's by 16 per cent. Dr Stephan Buck, a director of the company, told a retail conference in September 1996 that 'Sainsbury's has lost out, and it looks likely that Tesco will maintain its lead.'

Nobody at Tesco would claim that Clubcard was the exclusive reason for Tesco's success. Almost simultaneously with the introduction of the Clubcard loyalty programme, Tesco beat competition from the other supermarket chains, notably a strong bid from Sainsbury's, to purchase Scottish supermarket chain William Low, transforming Tesco into a truly national retailer. William Low operated 57 stores, and doubled Tesco market share in Scotland overnight. The stores were instantly rebranded and refurbished, and with 545 stores by the end of 1995, Tesco had more supermarkets in the UK than any other retailer.

Nonetheless, the effect of Clubcard was fundamental to Tesco's accelerating business success. In the 18 months that followed the launch the card changed and developed the way Tesco rewarded customers, the way it was marketed, and the way that Clubcard data was turned into knowledge. We will look at what Tesco did with its customer data later, but it was clear that the data would not be generated unless Tesco customers implicitly accepted the company's 'loyalty contract'.

THE LOYALTY CONTRACT

Through Clubcard, Tesco was making a new promise to its customers.

The principle behind the Clubcard loyalty contract, shown in Figure 5.1, is simple but profound. It says to each customer 'Join Tesco', become a member of our brand, a long-term stakeholder. Open a Clubcard account with Tesco, and the more you shop with us the more benefit you will accrue. The benefit will become more and more relevant to you because we progressively improve our understanding of your priorities and preferences. So the data gathered by Clubcard is part of the contract. It becomes knowledge used by Tesco to deliver more value. Customers had been demanding the contract for a long time, without knowing it – they asked for it every time they complained that Tesco was sending promotions that they couldn't use.

The concept of a loyalty contract also led to a critically important decision in Tesco's communication strategy. To maintain the commitment on both sides to the Clubcard agreement between the customer and the brand, the benefit had to be regularly communicated and updated. In short it led to the quarterly mailing programme, arguably the world's most successful sustained use of direct mail as a customer communications medium.

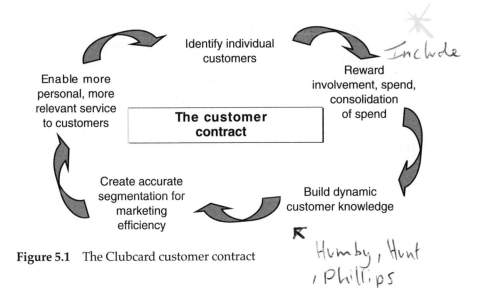

Include

Humby, Hunt , Phillips

Figure 5.1 The Clubcard customer contract

Creating the mailing

There are strong arguments against Tesco's decision to mail every member of its loyalty programme four times a year. Why make customers wait for their reward? Why not let them take it as and when they feel like it by claiming it at the checkout and getting an instant discount on their shopping? Why go to the massive extra cost of sending out millions of mail packs?

When Sainsbury's launched the Rewards programme, it rejected the concept of accumulated value, deciding to let customers take rewards on demand. Yet this also dissipated the effect of the Rewards investment, turning it into a small discount casually accepted – and often taken for granted – by most customers. Nectar, the replacement scheme for the Reward card, has adopted the Tesco mailing strategy.

Keith Mills, the creator of Air Miles who now runs Nectar, agrees that Tesco got it right, adding another disadvantage of rewards given only on demand: 'One of the problems with the Sainsbury's idea of giving rewards at the checkout was that there was no incentive for customers to tell you where they live. The value of the data they give you quickly goes out of date.'

The Clubcard team was very clear from the outset that the investment in a mass-mailing programme would pay much higher dividends to Tesco's business than the cheaper at-the-till alternative. They realized that if Clubcard were to become more than just a margin-sacrificing discount scheme, it had to provide the opportunity to be valued highly both by customers and in stores. It meant being top of the store manager's agenda a few times a year. It meant direct mailing the Clubcard cashback into the member's home, dramatizing the benefits of membership and at the same time encouraging more sales.

Surpassing Sainsbury's

By 1998, three years after Clubcard leapt to prominence in the consciousness of customers, UK retailers were spending £400 million each year on their loyalty schemes, according to Datamonitor. Most of those schemes launched in 1995 and 1996. Tesco could not stay ahead of the pack by standing still. If Sainsbury's was slow to acknowledge that Clubcard had changed the UK retail landscape for good, it was one of the few retailers who did not respond.

Tesco led the promotional hoop-la – the nation could not get enough of loyalty programmes. Clubcards even adorned a specially created tree at the 1995 Chelsea Flower Show, designed with the Institute of Horticulture to show off the 12 types of apple that Clubcard owners could buy at Tesco. 'Will own-label Clubcard Crunch follow?' asked *The Times*.

If senior Tesco management needed motivation to keep the Clubcard bandwagon rolling, and to encourage their staff to spend valuable hours attaching Clubcards to a tree, they got it early. Tesco's board enjoyed the publicity around the launch, but they enjoyed the lift in sales more. Combining the Clubcard effect with the purchase of the William Low chain of supermarkets in Scotland and its other promotions, Tesco had its most important victory: for the first time, its market share passed Sainsbury's – and stayed ahead, as Table 5.1 shows.

Table 5.1 Supermarket UK market share (%) (Source: Taylor Nelson Sofres)

1995	Jan	Feb	Mar	Apr	May
Sainsbury	19.4	19.0	19.1	18.7	18.8
Tesco	18.1	18.5	19.3	19.9	19.4

THE FIRST QUARTERLY MAILING

Quantifying the risk

Five million Tesco customers used their Clubcard to collect points in the first collection period, which ended on 14 May 1995. That meant that Tesco was committed to paying back £14 million in Clubcard vouchers that could be spent by customers on anything in the store. At the time, the scale of the reinvestment was unprecedented in Tesco – but is eclipsed by the latest reward value figure, for May 2006, of over £80 million paid out to members in one quarter. No one knew exactly how the first collection period might affect normal trading patterns, whether customers would buy something special, as Tesco would like, or just buy their usual items and use the vouchers to cut their normal shopping bill. No one knew whether the customers would use their vouchers on the first day, or save them up.

Quite apart from the financial risk, the logistical challenge to Tesco was formidable. Five million households, containing Tesco's most valuable and committed customers, would have to receive the Clubcard 'Thank you' they were promised, without a hitch, in the three-week period between 18 May and 5 June. Tim Mason admits that the first mailing gave him his first and only sleepless nights as a Tesco board member. No one at Tesco knew if such a large-scale mailing could even be done.

Grant Harrison and Dave Clements, released from 'The bunker', now took on the responsibility of controlling the operational demands of the statement mailing. As Clements recalls:

> We had just got to the second week of the launch, and all the membership displays were in the stores, the cards were in the stores, posters and the TV campaign were out. In many respects we had achieved the easy bit. Now we had to switch our focus immediately, because we had our first mass-statement mailing in 10 weeks. In the trials we had mailed the customer base, but that was only about 250,000 people. The scale of this was completely different. Now we would have to start predicting what impact it would have on the stores nationwide. When our customers had this extra cash in their hands we had to think about the impact right across the business.

The first national statement mailing would be around 20 times the size of any direct mail campaign that had been attempted at Tesco before.

It became clear that the statement mailing was a much more complex and risky challenge than the launch. Tesco had to deliver on the Clubcard contract. If customers weren't impressed by what they were sent they might not use their vouchers or product coupons. Then they might stop using their cards and the scheme would die. If they used their Clubcard vouchers but only to replace spending they would ordinarily have made in the course of normal shopping, the scheme would turn out to be unsustainable for the business, an expensive and elaborate promotional experiment that had no hope of covering its costs. And if the mailings were poorly managed, the statements inaccurate, the personalization awry, or delivered to the wrong addresses, then the press would quickly switch from admiration to mockery.

Then there was a reasonable fear over security. Sending out 5 million letters containing £14 million of Clubcard vouchers – essentially, sending piles of cash through the post – meant that the Clubcard team faced unprecedented responsibility to safeguard Tesco's financial interests. Security printing was introduced to make it difficult to colour photocopy the vouchers and thereby minimize fraud. Any customers receiving more than £100 in vouchers (not unheard of even in the earliest days of the programme and commonplace today) would get their statement sent to them by registered post.

Vouchers and coupons

Tesco did not want to end up in a mess like the world's airlines, with millions of unredeemed frequent flyer miles accumulating as a growing liability. So every Clubcard voucher carried an expiry date for a year ahead, long enough away for shoppers to feel they were not being coerced into spending them before they wanted (many customers saved up their vouchers to put towards their Christmas shopping, for example) but soon enough that Tesco wasn't building up financial exposure for the future.

The first quarterly mailing did not just include the Clubcard vouchers that represent the membership dividend, it also introduced the targeted product coupons that gave the customer money-off specific products or brands. Over the years the selection of these offers has become quite a science, with full use being made of the transactional data to maximize the relevance of the offer to the individual. In the first mailing, Tesco did not have the knowledge it needed to do this – either about the customer, or what the likely demand would be. Consequently customers received a limited range of coupons.

At the time of the first mailing there were no historical data to use for anything more complicated, so the team had to make their own projections based on experience and common sense. Too little product in the stores would mean frustrated shoppers and unused coupons. Too much would mean an over-stock problem, eating into profits. Store managers were warned: 'It is essential that no store runs out of products featured in the Clubcard coupons… It will reflect badly on your store and damage [customers'] view of the Clubcard scheme.' After much anguishing redemption rates for the product coupons in the first mailing were estimated at between 20 and 40 per cent, compared to a normal sales promotion redemption rate at Tesco of less than 5 per cent.

The first mailing was planned using the basic information that had been collected. The Clubcard team monitored how many shoppers used their cards in the first few weeks and predicted how many members would have spent enough in-store to earn Clubcard vouchers. (Shoppers who would not have spent enough to qualify were sent a simpler promotional mailing encouraging them to use their Clubcard more to get vouchers next time.)

The rewarded customers were sent two Clubcard vouchers with a range of face values depending on how many points they had accumulated. Shoppers had to spend at least £10 in one shop to qualify for any points at all – although after the first few months an exception was made for pensioners and students, who had a £5 entry level. Every £5 spent earned one point, which made each point worth 5 pence. So 50 points would convert to a £2.50 Clubcard voucher, 100 points equalled a £5 voucher, 150 points £7.50 and so on. The idea behind the £5 threshold was to encourage a higher level of spend – but by 1997, Tesco reverted to a simpler 'pound a point' strategy. In addition to the 'real money' of Clubcard vouchers, each Clubcard member received their six targeted product coupons offering discounts – 50p off a bottle of wine, 50p off a large box of washing powder, 50p off 12 cans of Coke. The idea at this early stage was to represent a broad variety of tastes and preferences, because Tesco could still only analyse the basket value of each Clubcard shopper, not the items that made up the basket. They knew how much the shoppers spent, but not what they bought.

The response from the first mailing showed how a lack of targeting was a disadvantage. Says Clements:

> We understood very quickly how important it would be. When we did our first mailing, and we put the coupon in for money off Coca Cola, we sent it to everyone, and then pensioners and [other] older people started calling, saying 'I never buy this, you have to give me offers for something I want'.

Tesco research showed that customers were also comparing their offers among themselves – and that any offer that might be seen to be an unfair reward for an occasional shopper would be destructive to the relationship Tesco was trying to build. 'Customers are too savvy to ever be manipulated, and any company trying to do so will be in for a headache,' is how Harrison analyses his experience of setting up the mailing.

A continuous customer survey

This unleashing of customer opinion, both positive and negative, is a valuable by-product of the Clubcard programme. First, Tesco management could now see that Clubcard created a new type of customer feedback – the equivalent of a continuous customer survey based on a panel of 5.5 million active customers. If something was wrong, customers would soon let Tesco know, mostly through their measurable actions in the stores, but also through spontaneous calls and letters to the contact centre. This was real time customer insight, on a scale and immediacy never experienced before.

The feedback from the first quarterly mailing also showed the need to divide customers into segments, with tailored communication and offers relevant to each clearly defined audience. The first segmentation was based on the life-stage information provided by customers on the application forms. Beyond that, segments were formed from the needs and preferences that customers told Tesco they had. So, based on calls and letters to the contact centre, the Clubcard team decided to invite customers to identify themselves as diabetic or vegetarian, which meant that in future they would get only offers that were appropriate for them. Tesco reasoned that offering a vegetarian cheaper beef mince was saying something to them, but it certainly wasn't 'Thank you'.

The limited capability for segmentation in the first statement mailing allowed Tesco just 12 different configurations of message and offers tailored to specific audiences. By August 1996, 18 months later, that increased to 1,800 different permutations. Today, every statement is effectively an individual one – with over 8 million significant variations of the mailing, governed completely by the differences in customer behaviour.

Although it was constrained by its lack of knowledge in the first mailing, Tesco's desire to segment the mailing from the start was a clear signal of its intention. The technology and the data weren't sophisticated – but instead, Mason recalls, there was the 'desire to be relevant'.

In the 10-week run-up to the first quarterly mailing Tesco's call centre logs revealed another concern among customers that needed a swift response. While there were less than 300 complaints about the scheme, the majority of them were about a common gripe: the £10 minimum spend that each customer was required to make before qualifying to earn Clubcard points. This threshold was deliberately set to restrict the benefits of Clubcard: it reduced the cost of the scheme by several million pounds, and focused the data collected to shopping baskets of a meaningful size. It rewarded behaviour that Tesco wanted.

It worked for Tesco, but it didn't work for customers. In particular, pensioners hated it. Many older people, certainly those who lived alone, found that their shopping trips did not qualify. They could not physically carry – even if they could afford – a larger quantity of items each trip. Yet they were far more likely to visit their Tesco store more frequently than young families or affluent single people. Despite their loyalty, the early version of the Clubcard scheme locked them out.

The Clubcard team calculated that to reduce the qualifying spend to £5 for everyone would cost Tesco an additional £2 million per year. At this early stage, Tesco had risked enough on Clubcard, and didn't want further investment in Clubcard on that scale. Nevertheless, reducing the £10 qualifying spend for pensioners was made a priority. So the quarterly mailing to customers over 60 years old included one more component: an invitation to register at their local store's customer service desk, qualifying them to earn Clubcard points on any purchase over £5.

The £18 million reward

After much planning and revising the first full-scale Clubcard statement mailing was sent out to 5 million homes in May 1995. One year previously, the company had barely used the medium at all. The campaign was phased to go out in three waves over a three-week period, so that Tesco could manage the dispatch and the customer response. The Clubcard team held its collective breath.

It wasn't long before it could let out a sigh of relief. It was clear within the first few days that it was a success. What had been observed on a small scale in the test year was magnified accurately across the country. When Tesco said 'Thank you' to customers, they responded by opening wallets wider. The incremental sales benefit from the mailing was a like-for-like sales boost of £17.8 million, 40 per cent of which was from customers redeeming their Clubcard vouchers, and then spending more on that visit than usual. 'Tempting? Why not use your Clubcard vouchers to treat yourself to something special?' said the point-of-sale posters in every store, and customers did. The vouchers were not simply being used for the basics: customers were using them to splash out on goods they might not have bought before. Sales went up in the health and beauty department, wines and spirits – the areas of the store that Tesco was encouraging shoppers to visit. The other 60 per cent of the sales uplift came from the money-off product coupons that were positioned in the mailing as an added bonus. The overall incremental sales uplift was enough to cover the costs of Clubcard, and more. It made a profit. And each of the quarterly statement mailings has achieved that ever since.

The mailing has become an advertising medium in its own right, one that offers targeting opportunities for brands that want access to the Tesco customer base. Clubcard can charge manufacturers and other suppliers for the opportunity to make offers in the statement mailing. This effect means that even today, coupons are half-funded by suppliers.

WAITING FOR THE ZERO SUM EFFECT

Sainsbury's loses momentum

The 'electronic Green Shield Stamps' comment with which David Sainsbury dismissed Clubcard rapidly became an own goal. Despite being ahead of Tesco in the early test period, Sainsbury's project had lost momentum. It was in no shape to launch a credible competitor to Clubcard.

The Sainsbury's local store-based scheme was called the 'Saver Card', which reached its greatest coverage across 200 of the chain's 355 stores in July 1995. It had some key differences to Clubcard. While Tesco told shoppers that it wanted to say 'Thank you', Sainsbury's told shoppers that its card was 'A new way to save'. Each customer's Saver Card could only be used at a single named Sainsbury's store; customers could not present their card at any Sainsbury's store and earn their points – although as many as 20 per cent of high-spending supermarket customers habitually shop in more than one store.

Sainsbury's also promoted a 'sliding scale' of loyalty rewards in order to give proportionately higher benefits to the highest spenders. 'It makes sense to go for the big bonuses with a Sainsbury's Saver Card' said the company's promotional literature. With Saver Card each point earned from a £10 spend was worth 0.5 pence, while the redemption value of points accumulated from £2,000 of shopping was 2.5 pence for each point. The scheme lacked the simplicity that Clubcard offered, and as the Tesco trials of Clubcard proved, a 2 per cent discount did not create significantly different customer behaviour compared to a 1 per cent dividend.

The biggest disadvantage of Saver Card to Sainsbury's was that it could not promote it widely. It could not generate national news coverage or advertise on national television. In fact, in several areas, it could not even use the local press, as not all stores in the region offered their customers the card. While Clubcard became eponymous, the category leader, Saver Card was stubbornly anonymous, barely mentioned by customers in research groups.

By not appreciating that a loyalty programme was more than an in-store promotional gimmick, Sainsbury's had left the field wide open and Tesco was allowed to prove one of its primary arguments for launching first: 'We will win customers from Sainsbury's'.

What would happen when Sainsbury's eventually launched its own version of Clubcard? Tesco had worked out that some defectors would return, but Tesco would still have a competitive advantage because it would have the names, addresses and transactional data of the customers it had persuaded to move from Sainsbury's to Tesco. Sainsbury's would only able to guess which customers it had lost. Tesco would know precisely which customers were most at risk by moni-toring those who stopped using their Clubcard. Tesco could then send them individually targeted Clubcard mailings. This was a large part of the advantage that Clubcard had secured by being first.

Sainsbury's eventually introduced its nationwide loyalty programme, Reward card, on 17 June. That is, 17 June 1996, a full 18 months after Clubcard. Even in January 1996, Sainsbury's was claiming that its customers only wanted 'pounds, not points'.

The Reward and ABC cards...

On the day that Sainsbury's finally replaced the Saver Card, a giant balloon shaped like a Reward card hovered over London. Some City analysts speculated whether Sainsbury's chances of market leadership had already floated away. Tony MacNeary, at the time a food retail analyst at NatWest Securities, said to *The Times* that: 'The question is, how much damage has Tesco already done and is Sainsbury's doing enough to get it back? What Sainsbury's has done with the Reward card is imaginative but only time will tell if it works.'

Evans Hunt Scott sent two staff to the launch at the Brompton Road store that day, disguised as press, to pick up competitive information: by that afternoon (after they were spotted and swiftly ejected) they were working on the Tesco response.

The damage to Sainsbury's wasn't just measured in lost leadership. By the launch of its programme, Tesco had grown a membership base of 8.5 million active Clubcard holders, customers who were consolidating more and more of their supermarket spend from competitors into Tesco. For the former market leader, Sainsbury's, 18 months of serious market share loss had already been suffered. The question ever since has been, can it recoup from such a prolonged period of marketing paralysis?

In the first year of Clubcard's life the most significant threat came not from Sainsbury's but from a then vibrant Safeway. The marketers of Safeway launched the ABC card, backed by £7 million in advertising, on 23 October 1995. It was the launch that Tesco feared most, but it was a launch of a programme that Safeway would later admit had lost £250 million, before it was scrapped in April 2000.

The company had three main goals when it launched ABC, according to the then marketing director Roger Partington. Like Mason at Tesco, he wanted to create a data-driven view of his customers. And he wanted to use that single-customer view to identify and provide what customers wanted with ever greater accuracy and relevance. Where ABC was a departure from the Clubcard model was that Safeway customers could redeem their points outside of the store, using the dividend from their supermarket shopping to buy from a mail order catalogue of toys and clothing, or taking family days out at theme parks.

Customers liked what they heard – the ABC card eventually signed up 9 million members. By waiting before it launched, Safeway was prepared to let Tesco grab the credit for being first, but while Tesco and dunnhumby were working out how to manage and analyse the torrent of transactional data, Safeway's management had made sure they had the right analysis tools already in place.

'Successful companies are those that know how to manage data,' said Partington at the launch, 'and that is why we have spent 12 months getting this right.' Very quickly, through smart data analysis, the Safeway marketers were able to identify and put a value to the segment of shoppers who would be most critical to Safeway's future profits in the years ahead – families with young children. This insight became the foundation for all its advertising and marketing for many years, as it portrayed its brand and its business as the best friend of young families.

Some things went very well for the ABC card. Among the target group of customers, average household spend with the brand increased by 22 per cent between 1996 and 2000. Unfortunately the company's strict interpretation of which customers it wanted to become most loyal tended to alienate the other customer segments. What was in it for affluent retirees, or metropolitan child-free yuppies?

Despite a £20 million promotion of ABC in 1998 to encourage regular card use, which it was claimed caused a sales bump of 6 per cent in the first six weeks of April and May, Safeway profits suffered because of the prevailing price wars. In November 1999, profits plunged by 20 per cent. Something had to give and in April 2000, the ABC card programme was withdrawn. Safeway promised to reinvest the ABC card's annual cost, which it claimed was £50 million, into price cuts, claiming that it would save each of its shoppers £70 a year. 'People have lost interest in [loyalty card] points, and don't think they give value,' said chief executive Carlos Criado-Perez. 'We haven't got enough customers and loyalty cards are not good for getting new customers. I don't think that companies are using data nearly enough,' added finance director Martin Laffin.

Tesco immediately offered to give 250 free Clubcard points to any Safeway shoppers who swapped their ABC card for a Clubcard. On the first day, 33,000 did. In the first week, 100,000. Safeway, concerned that Tesco was learning the names and addresses of its loyal shoppers, claimed the cards were its property, and demanded them back, threatening legal action. The threat allowed Tesco the chance to retaliate in the press: it moved the cards outside its headquarters to a 'safe house', and Mason gave a statement: 'We have an obligation to protect their identities and prevent coercion.'

When the brouhaha died down, Safeway chose to continue price cutting, and the ABC card was never revived. As Taylor, the head of loyalty marketing at Safeway at the time, who left before the scheme was abandoned, commented, 'Safeway didn't make a priority of the ABC card, and failed in using its technological expertise to gain a truly customer focused approach.' Ironically, it had a far greater ability to use data than Tesco had at the time – but Safeway had perhaps forgotten that the scheme could also drive more sales, as well as provide data. Tesco staff have a saying: 'It's not the skill, it's the will'.

... and the rest

There were other burnt fingers and bruised egos in the loyalty wars of the period. Esso had its soon-to-be-withdrawn Tiger Tokens campaign. Asda was trialling its own card in 14 stores, but without relish. The Asda management threw in the towel and abandoned its loyalty scheme trial in 1999, never having got anywhere near a national launch. 'It cost us £8 million per year just to run the loyalty card trial,' said company spokesman Nick Ararwel at the time, 'and would have cost £60 million to roll out nationally.' Few companies, it seemed, were able to see a return on investment: everyone, though, could count the cost.

The other significant retail programme launch in the first half of 1995 that came anywhere near the impact of Clubcard was the Bhs Choice Card. In May 1995 Taylor Nelson AGB measured the spontaneous awareness – that is those respondents who would name different loyalty programmes without prompting. Clubcard was three times more famous than Sainsbury's Saver Card scheme, and achieved two and a half times greater awareness than any other card, while 15 per cent of adults canvassed claimed to use Tesco Clubcard. Esso was next most popular with 9 per cent, and Bhs third with 6 per cent.

A very different model for retail loyalty marketing emerged around that period, the Catalina system. This was not a reward programme based on individual customer membership and insight gained from recorded transactional data. Instead it was a checkout-based system that rewarded customers based on an instant analysis of items within each shopping basket. Effectively, Catalina performed one half of the loyalty programme's function: it rewarded consumers. As their baskets were scanned, Catalina checked the product codes, and automatically printed related coupon offers, depending on what promotions were running that week. For example, customers who purchased cat food might get that week's offer on cat litter. The proposition to the customer was: here's a coupon for something you might want to buy, come back and spend it next time. For the brands it was: here's a way to target your competitors' customers and encourage them to brand-switch. And for the retailer the deal was: here's a cheap way to encourage repeat visits by outsourcing the cost of your promotions to your suppliers. Asda enthusiastically embraced the concept and launched it in all 207 of its stores on 13 January 1996, Somerfield introduced it alongside its Premium Points loyalty programme in June 1997, and Sainsbury's flirted with the idea while it anguished over whether or not to compete head on with Tesco and launch the Reward card.

By January 1996, Catalina vouchers were used by 35 per cent of UK households, and the company announced plans to become a fully fledged loyalty programme by issuing customers with unique ID numbers to create customer behaviour databases. Said managing director Blair Jenkins:

> We will now build up a history of the retailers' customers over some time by tracking the ID number against the purchases. This will enable the retailer to encourage the customer to trial certain products... in the past we have been capturing a little bit of data. We have always had the capability but we have never used it.

Every time a shopper was identified as part of the Catalina membership he or she would get a coupon offering the chance to win a prize if he or she called a free number and took part in a market research survey. Nothing very much came of the idea.

Nevertheless, and despite no longer being used in Asda stores, Catalina is still a force in retail loyalty marketing, though a very small one in Europe. In the United States, 170 grocery and drug retailers, a total of 5,500 stores, use the system and its database holds 100 million customer records.

MAINTAINING MOMENTUM

An evening with Clubcard

While competitor retailers struggled to emulate the Clubcard effect for their businesses, Tesco's loyalty marketing programme concentrated on maintaining the momentum it already had.

One of the most spectacular – if short-lived – triumphs the team achieved early on was the 'Clubcard evening'. These were invitation-only events held at stores and hosted by the store managers – where Clubcard cardholders were welcomed outside of normal trading hours to enjoy an evening devoted to a particular theme, and where the manager could introduce him- or herself to the top-spending customers. What seemed an unlikely experiment in deepening relationships with the most loyal customers turned into a marketing triumph, as response rates to the invitations touched 40 per cent. Said Harrison:

> We tried the first Clubcard evening back in the trial days at Lakeside
> Thurrock where the 100 best customers were invited to a wine and cheese
> evening with the store manager. The top shopper ran a chain of rest homes
> for the elderly, and was spending £147,000 a year! We had a response rate
> of 70 per cent. It was incredible that the customers turned up in numbers –
> it really cemented my view that the British just love their supermarkets.

By July 1995, Tesco was ready to launch a more ambitious events
programme – a mini tour of Tesco stores by hairdresser and TV star
Nicky Clarke. For 'An Exclusive Evening with Nicky Clarke', Clubcard
members were invited to meet the celebrity 'hairdresser to the stars...
Nicky's star-studded salon clientele includes The Duchess of York,
Yasmin Le Bon and Queen Noor of Jordan'. Clarke, whose new hair-care
range was available at Tesco, was going to spend three nights in Tesco
supermarkets in Watford, Sandhurst and New Malden. Only the 100
best customers of each store were invited to see him work his magic –
and enter a free draw to win a personal consultation at his salon.

From the data collected from each store over the previous six months,
Tesco knew exactly which 100 customers to invite. They also knew that
because these customers bought so much from Tesco (spending as much
as £7,000 a year), and were in the store so regularly, there would be a
high proportion of acceptances. They were right: acceptance levels
reached 80 per cent, and at 7.30 pm on 10, 11 and 12 July, three Tesco
supermarkets became unlikely hair salons for a couple of hours. Tesco
had begun its commitment to its 'Premium Loyals', the high-value
customers the company is most determined not to lose, and that rival
supermarkets most want to gain.

By the end of the first 18 months, 175,000 of these most valuable
customers had been invited to social events in Tesco stores, and over
50,000 of them accepted. With themed evenings offering everything
from beauty care to flower arranging, wine tastings and the chance to do
their Christmas shopping in peace, by the end of the programme 100
stores had held 'shopping evenings' for their best cardholders.

The Clubcard events were a success. Customers loved them and store
managers loved them too. It gave them the chance to break down the
barrier between themselves and their customers by talking and
listening to them, explaining how the store worked, engaging with
them as 'stakeholders' in their store. The problem with Clubcard
evenings was time. You can only hold 'out of hours' events if you have
any spare hours in the trading day. With the introduction of longer
opening hours leading to 24-hour opening in all the top-performing

stores, the opportunity to invite a select few customers into the store was squeezed out of the promotional calendar.

Include , shows failure.

Student Clubcard

Rather less successful was the attempt by Tesco to use Clubcard as a way to engage with the valuable customers of the future by introducing Student Clubcard. Launched in September 1995, in anticipation of the new academic year, Student Clubcard was the result of research among 600 students which had shown that they were aware of supermarket reward schemes but that they didn't think that loyalty cards offered any benefits to them.

In its early stages, Tesco learnt the lesson that students would be a different audience for them. Focus groups traditionally put consumers in a room, with beer, wine and sandwiches to put them at their ease, with a moderator to guide the discussion. Company staff watch through a one-way mirror. The first focus group didn't go to plan. The students swiftly drank so much wine that they made little sense to anyone still sober. At the end, not knowing that Tesco staff were still watching in amazement through the mirror, the students stuffed all the leftover food and drink into their pockets, including a couple of bottles of wine, and left.

Members were offered their own distinctively designed card, a lower qualifying spend (£5, as opposed to the £10 at the time that all others had to spend), and their own statement mailing focusing on products and news that was most relevant to them. Student Clubcard had the backing of the students' union, the NUS, at 75 campuses where the scheme was being trialled. In the stores Tesco staff were giving out money-off vouchers to try to tempt students to become part of the Clubcard family.

Perhaps influenced by its focus group, the Student Clubcard statement for Christmas 1995 announced that 'It's party time!', enclosing a £4 National Express voucher, 'so you won't have to walk home this Christmas', a competition – 101 things to do with a Student Clubcard – and an encouraging 'Good luck if you have any end of term exams – and don't spend too much time in the library'.

By August 1996, one in five UK students was a member: 4 per cent of Tesco turnover was from Student Clubcard holders, in some stores as much as 20 per cent. At the first anniversary of the card's launch, students at 30 'Freshers Fairs' found a new diversion – a Tesco stall squeezed between the Film Club and Rag Week, signing up new card-holders. The target for recruitment was a comparatively modest 250,000.

On the face of it Tesco had another Clubcard success on its hands, but closer examination of the transactional data told a different story. Students may have been a desirable target and recruitment a relative success, but they simply didn't engage with the idea of a loyalty programme. By definition, loyalty marketing requires some planned behaviour from customers, and students did not organize their lives that way, let alone their visits to the supermarket. They tended to move house at least once a year, and even when they didn't, it was virtually impossible to keep track of who lived in which household, and so very difficult to communicate with them effectively. Students existed as a well-defined group, but in the end they turned out to be an example of segmentation that was commercially impossible to profit from by using loyalty marketing techniques. Student Clubcard was a 'Thank you' too far.

A Christmas present

The run-up to Christmas is the annual sales bonanza for supermarkets. Shoppers buy much more food and drink than normal, not to mention all the seasonal purchases like Christmas decorations and gifts. They also visit the supermarket more frequently than they usually do. Many UK retailers make up to 40 per cent of their sales over the two-month pre-Christmas period. At a supermarket, the uplift in sales can be up to 10 per cent, but what would be the Clubcard effect?

The Clubcard team decided to find out by taking the 'Thank you' theme and expressing it in typical yuletide fashion – a gift. And what more appropriate gift from Tesco to millions of homes than a free turkey? Every shopper who earned more than 40 Clubcard points between 16 October and 12 November received a coupon qualifying them for a free turkey. Four out of five members who spent up to the required level in the run-up to Christmas used their coupon to claim their free bird – a total of 1 million free turkeys, at a cost of £3.55 each. It was arguably the most successful single promotion Tesco had created. The customers loved it. And so did Tesco.

The December statement mailing was now of a scale that put Clubcard firmly at the top of Tesco's marketing agenda. Eight and a half million members now qualified for a reward mailing and £17 million in Clubcard vouchers was to be sent to customers to spend in-store (with one shopper alone getting £253 in Clubcard vouchers), along with £22 million worth of product coupons for luxuries like Bell's whisky, Luxury Cookies in a Santa Tin, and Bristol Cream sherry. This brought the total of 'money through the post' in this one mailing to £40 million. The Christmas mailing of 1995 was a major marketing investment by Tesco and the stakes were high.

When grocers attack

So it was a shock to the Clubcard team when, on 9 December, Asda chairman Archie Norman, no friend of loyalty cards or Tesco, announced a promotion that could threaten to derail the Tesco 'Thank you' not just for Christmas, but for good. Asda, he announced, would be accepting Clubcard vouchers at 16 of its 200 stores in the weeks leading up to Christmas. By selecting only stores close to a Tesco, Asda maximized its chances of peeling away Tesco's loyal Clubcard customers at the most vital time of the year. Not only was the Christmas mailing the largest of the year, it had already been fully dispatched by 24 November, so Tesco had no opportunity to change anything in response to Asda's spoiler attack. It was perfectly judged to reinforce Norman's assertion that loyalty programmes were 'bogus'. If Tesco could bribe, went the reasoning, then Asda could too, by honouring Tesco 'money' in its own stores.

The news was covered with glee. 'Asda has successfully hijacked the marketing campaign of [its] rival,' said *Marketing* magazine. '[It is] telling shoppers, "Your Tesco Clubcard voucher is worth more at Asda."'

Tesco attempted to head off the promotion by complaining to the Advertising Standards Authority. But accepting a rival's money-off coupons was already an established industry tactic – not least by Tesco. Neither trademark law nor Clubcard's own terms and conditions could stop Asda. Early analysis was worrying. The transactional data suggested a 1 per cent drop in sales in the vulnerable stores – not life-threatening in itself, but significant, with potential to grow as more customers heard about the Asda offer in the run up to Christmas.

Was this the 'zero-sum-game'? A neutralizing of the Clubcard effect by competitors accepting the Tesco currency in their own stores? As it turned out, the impact Asda's move had on the overall performance of Clubcard was less than negligible. The total of voucher redemptions at Tesco through the Christmas period easily outstripped the total from the previous two mailings combined – and 30 per cent of the Clubcard vouchers that had been sent out over the year but had not been used by customers were spent during December, as customers put the value gained from their membership towards a merrier Christmas.

Every partner helps

After the first Christmas rush, January 1996 saw the first Clubcard partnership with another brand. Although designed as an offer to Tesco customers, the Clubcard managers had frequently been contacted in the early days by other brands, hoping to share promotional opportunities and take a ride on the Clubcard bandwagon. At a very early stage the Clubcard team were approached by Air Miles, the UK's other major loyalty brand of the 1990s. Nothing resulted from the talks at that time, although subsequently Air Miles formed a redemption partnership with Sainsbury's Reward programme. In early 2002 Air Miles switched allegiance to Tesco as partner in the Clubcard Deals scheme, as we shall see later.

Why did Tesco need to bring in other brands as either partners that issued Clubcard points or partners that redeemed Clubcard vouchers? Clubcard was always meant to be an expression of the Tesco brand. The reinvestment in customers represented by the Clubcard reward for loyalty was always meant to return to Tesco stores in the form of incremental sales, not be spent outside the brand with other companies. Nonetheless there was clear evidence that customers did value having more opportunities to earn points on their spending than those offered at Tesco alone. Some customers also said they valued the holiday and travel offers that they could get with the Safeway ABC card. As Terry Leahy explained many years later: 'Let me tell you a secret. The secret of successful retailing. It's this: never stop listening to consumers and giving them what they want. I am sorry if that is a bit of an anti-climax... but it is that simple.' What is true now was true then, so the Clubcard partner programme began.

For its first partner promotion, Tesco made a deal with Thomson Holidays and Lunn Poly. The offer to Tesco customers was simple: book a Thomson holiday through Lunn Poly travel agents, and earn a Clubcard point for every £5 spent – so buying a £1,000 family holiday would earn the equivalent of £10 to spend at Tesco. The opportunity to save £10 on groceries for the cost of a two-week family holiday seems small beer compared to the elaborate schemes that Tesco and now Nectar are operating in the UK in 2006. But for the first time it was a demonstration that Tesco could make a success of joint ventures with third parties: the scheme was a test, running from 15 January to 6 April, the time of year when rain-soaked Brits book their annual holiday abroad.

Much more significant was the partnership with fellow retail brand B&Q, launched on 2 April with a six-month tie-up. B&Q was the UK's biggest DIY retailer, and with 260 retail outlets (compared to Tesco's 548 stores), and 3 million customers a week, it was designed to increase the Clubcard spend, to increase B&Q's sales – which it did – and to bring new customers into the scheme, in which it was also successful. Designed for six months, the partnership lasted two years, being withdrawn when Kingfisher, B&Q's parent, decided that a close partnership with Tesco was against its strategic direction.

While these were experiments, the case for Clubcard partnerships was getting stronger. They helped to defend Clubcard against the broad range of benefits offered by Sainsbury's, and the incremental sales benefit of broadening the points-earning base were good. In 1996, an additional £1.5 million in points value was earned by 1.3 million Clubcard customers, representing a profit approaching £1 million for Tesco. Of that number, 126,000 customers signed up for Clubcard in non-Tesco outlets during the first eight months of 1996, introducing valuable new custom into the brand. 'If these customers shop with us once, the incremental profit is £500,000,' a Tesco memo revealed. 'If we can keep 5 per cent of them over the next year, the incremental sales will be £18.9 million.'

Points on petrol

Tesco's emergence as a major player in petrol retailing coincided with the development of Clubcard.

By the beginning of 1996, Tesco had 254 filling stations. For every £9 spent on groceries at Tesco, £1 was spent on petrol. Yet for the first year of Clubcard, customers' spend on petrol did not earn them any points. The original decision to exclude petrol from the programme was based on the difference in margins between store and forecourt, as well as the principle that Clubcard existed to promote grocery sales. It soon became necessary to review that decision.

Competition at the pumps continued to escalate. Tesco was confident that Clubcard could create the margin of preference that would secure the brand an even greater market share. So on 11 March 1996, Tesco launched 'Points on Petrol', and millions of Clubcard-carrying motorists could now boost their points earning power by filling up their tank.

The immediate effect on sales was yet more evidence of the power of Clubcard to shape customer behaviour. Analysis of Clubcard data revealed that the top 4 per cent of customers for petrol were responsible for 17 per cent of sales. Points on Petrol brought in almost a quarter of a million new Clubcard users, with a significant male bias. And the inclusion of petrol allowed Tesco to see precisely who was buying petrol but not visiting the store, and who was visiting the store but not buying petrol. Then it could incentivize each group to do the thing that they weren't doing already.

Shop the shop

The power of points was further demonstrated in early 1996, when Tesco marketers first used bonus points to encourage Clubcard members to 'shop the shop', that is, extend their purchase in more departments in the store than they normally would.

On 22 April, Tesco launched its first four-week programme of extra Clubcard points on 70 Tesco own-label products. The concept is simple. By using the Clubcard currency of points to attract customers to particular departments, or encouraging them to sample particular products, the overall basket size increases. More important, it has the potential to increase Tesco's overall share of purse as customers go on to consolidate more of their grocery budget to Tesco once the promotion has ended.

The use of points instead of money-off as an incentive had a side benefit for the overall Clubcard strategy, because it brought more of the marginal Clubcard users into the reward cycle. With more points on offer in-store, low spenders had more of a chance to earn enough to qualify for Clubcard vouchers, and in turn that encouraged them to keep using their cards. Tesco gained transactional data on customers who spent small, irregular amounts. The picture of customer activity that Clubcard produced became broader and clearer.

Offering extra Clubcard incentives in-store has become an established way to boost spend on particular lines or departments. It is a relatively inexpensive way to target product promotions at particular customer groups. It created incremental sales – by August 1996, the extra points promotions had generated a sales uplift of £16.4 million – and profits. Even with the extra £3.6 million worth of Clubcard vouchers the promotion generated in the first quarter, the net effect for Tesco was positive as suppliers largely funded the extra points.

By summer 1996 Clubcard was set for the next steps in its evolution. In their first 18 months, the Clubcard team at Tesco had learnt valuable lessons. The basic principles of how to run a mass-scale, value-creating loyalty programme had been tested and proven, and are still followed today. With 8.5 million customers actively using Clubcard by August 1996, Clubcard was an unequivocal success. Tesco had the most popular, and the most recognized, loyalty programme in the UK. Tesco could collect data from two-thirds of the 600 million shopping baskets processed at its tills every year. Tesco was now number one retailer in the UK.

Yet the number one position was not going to be easy to defend. In the next three years, price wars would lower the average cost of a basket of groceries by 7.5 per cent for every supermarket. To remain useful, Clubcard data had to be turned into customer knowledge that would create value for the Tesco business beyond the targeting of offers.

It was the potential to generate competitive advantage from data that had sold the board on the Clubcard project in November 1994. Clubcard's next phase would have to deliver on that promise: to transform that data into knowledge.

6

Data, lovely data

- ▶ Drinking from the fire hose
- ▶ Measuring customer loyalty
- ▶ The problems with data warehouses
- ▶ Making a warehouse work
- ▶ What Tesco learnt about data

DRINKING FROM THE FIRE HOSE

Clubcard could have been little more than a targeted discount, as many other retail loyalty schemes became. Most of those loyalty schemes are no longer with us. Says Air Miles founder Keith Mills:

> The mechanics of the reward had been done elsewhere in the world before Tesco. But the thing that set Tesco apart was the depth of its data analysis. The big step forward wasn't to launch a card with a magnetic stripe on it, it was understanding the value of the information it provided. There were a lot of high-profile schemes in the 1990s that were effectively deferred discount cards.

From the first days of the Clubcard trial, Grant Harrison had known the value of the data he was collecting. He also knew that unless the data were exploited to change the way Tesco did business, Clubcard would not have succeeded in fulfilling its concept. Harrison says:

> This means do the stores want to run differently, do the retail directors, do the buyers? We all know that you can find 'interesting stuff' in the data. The challenge is how you get the business to engage and be prepared to change processes or decisions based on a new more detailed source of customer understanding.

Too much data

Using data to help run the stores better was an admirable idea, with a big practical problem: in 1995, there was too much data, not too little. From the first days of Clubcard's launch, customer transactional data flooded in. The comparatively simple task of transmitting the customer data between Tesco's IT department, where they were held to run the points accounting database, to dunnhumby, where they were analysed for marketing and business information use, took 30 hours using the highest bandwidth connection then available. As owners of one of the most complex customer databases in the world, Tesco handled the output of more than 50 million shopping trips in the first three months, comprising more than 2 billion purchased items, from the shopping of more than 5 million Clubcard members.

The challenge of analysing every purchase of every cardholder was wholly beyond the technology available in February 1995. Whereas Tesco launched Clubcard nationally 'because we can', it didn't try to collect and analyse all the data for the opposite reason: 'because we can't.'

Tesco today has enough capacity to take the information from every shopping basket processed through its checkouts and use it to drive marketing and management decisions. But in 1995 the prospect of breaking down the logs from every till on a product-by-product basis, analysing every scrap of information from every transaction, was a fantasy. In fact, the experts' advice to Tesco was: don't even try.

Tesco was willing to let dunnhumby take the lead in developing the strategy for data analysis. The supermarket had never looked at mass volumes of individual customer data before. It didn't have the skills in-house, or anything like them, to do the job. As Tim Mason points out, the sort of people who could successfully analyse customer loyalty data to create useful insight weren't readily available in 1995:

> Because we entered this discipline early, we were able to incrementally develop our use and understanding of the information over time. But it took us two years to identify the sort of people who were good at analysing Clubcard data. You have to use intuition and creativity as well as statistical know-how, and you have to hope you have identified the right things to test.

In effect, Mason is talking about analysing data like a grocer analyses his or her business. Good grocers are born, then get better by experience. Grocers from Jack Cohen to Sir Terry Leahy have used 'instinct', they back hunches, they stay close to customers and respond swiftly to what's important to those customers. To extend this approach to the use of data was natural to Tesco. Trying to achieve perfection with transactional data is next to impossible: far better to have a good idea based on experience and instinct, then to go looking for the data to prove it, or at least strongly support it.

One in ten

The first insight from the dunnhumby team was not to struggle making sense of all data on all customers, but to use a matrix of data samples to achieve a statistically valid picture of customer behaviour. The analysts took 10 per cent of the data once a week, processed it and applied the findings back to the other 90 per cent of the file. As far as they were concerned the challenge wasn't to waste time and energy building a data warehouse, but to use intellectual agility to accelerate learning and put the insight to work as soon as possible.

Tesco management was happy with this approach. dunnhumby at the time was a 25-person company, and Tesco had agreed to underwrite the cost of the hardware required to deliver the analysis at the speed required. Investing in the computers to handle 10 per cent of the activity once a week suited Tesco's thrifty instinct. Simon Hay one of the original team on the Clubcard project, recalls being given 24 hours before the national launch was decided to come up with a budget for the computing resources needed to do the analysis. The team hurriedly did its sums and decided on what they thought was an astronomical sum as a negotiating position – though a sum many times less than rivals would fritter on their far more ambitious loyalty data projects in the next 18 months. The following day, 'We handed over a piece of paper with this figure on it,' Hay recalls, 'and Tesco immediately said, "fine". We were kicking ourselves, saying we should have asked for more.'

But from the constraint came an important commercial insight. The 10 per cent sample gave Tesco more raw data than they needed to create useful information. One of the quirks of statistics is that you don't need to analyse every record to be able to make reasonably secure assumptions. If there is a trend to observe, then analysing a small set of data enables you to identify a result with 90 per cent certainty. Analysing a larger set gives you 95 per cent certainty, and larger still, 99 per cent. Analyse all the data, and you can be 100 per cent certain, but it is certainty that has been bought at a disproportionate cost.

The Customer Insight Unit

Explain about the Insight unit.

Proof that Tesco recognized these analytical skills as critical for its business future came in 1997, when it established a team called the 'Customer Insight Unit'. The idea was to combine the skills of people from its site research team, who made proposals for new store development based on a cocktail of local information sources, with new skills from marketing and commercial. As Mason explains:

> These people were geographers, statisticians who had spent a lot of time applying those skills to understanding how customers would behave. They could crunch through the stuff that came from Clubcard, see the patterns in it and they could start to help the management of the business understand what was going on, but also point towards what should be done about it. They had to find the data, and present it in a way that makes the decision stark, and clear.

Professionalism, not perfectionism

Examples of data errors

No transactional data can ever be perfect. There will be errors or unknown factors that can upset the results of analysis. For example, cardholders move address and do not change the address for their Clubcard statement. Or there are multiple users of one card, displaying very different buying patterns. Or someone opens a new

Clubcard account on a frequent basis because they constantly lose their card. Results can often be distorted by unique occurrences or local effects – maybe a store runs out of stock of a key product, or a water main bursts on the ring road and visits to the store are disrupted for a period. And of course, in the broader view, if Clubcard usage only identifies 60–75 per cent of shoppers at any store, then 25–40 per cent of customer behaviour is not traceable and individual data aren't being collected.

In developing the Clubcard data strategy the data analysts were backing an educated hunch. Having worked with geodemographic data – that combination of where you live and who else lives there – for years, they were aware that the power and accuracy of that source of data were very limited, and over-use by marketers had reduced their efficacy. The major geodemographic databases had been compiled and marketed for years, and there were thousands of brands using them to target offers as accurately as possible – including Tesco, for example when choosing where to position a new store. The trouble with a geodemographic model of customer targeting is that it is based on the premise of 'you are where you live'. It's clearly not true: are you exactly the same as your next-door neighbour? Imagine two geographical districts in a big city, side-by-side. One has been designated by the geodemographical analysis as a poor district, the other as wealthy. There has to be a border, which could well be a line right down the middle of the street. So in terms of a simplistic geodemographic model, the odd number houses on one side of the street are deemed to be poor, while the even numbers are in the other area, and are described as rich. Yet simple common sense tells us that, in real life, the profile of the residents is more likely to be very similar from one side of the street to the other.

The Tesco model, by contrast, is based not on crude averages, but individual particularities: 'You are what you buy'. Rather than forcing a profile onto households using generalized data from their postcode, the customer behavioural approach starts from the distinctive actions of customers and creates genuine like-minded groups of customers sharing similar tastes and activity from real purchase choices they make.

When Safeway abandoned the ABC card, it complained that trying to generate useful insights from the data was 'like drinking from a fire hose'. It was the same for Tesco, but instead of drowning, the company simply decided to siphon off what it could deal with at any time, and get on with the real work of selling to customers.

MEASURING CUSTOMER LOYALTY

Successful retail loyalty programmes are created by matching good marketing skill and commercial pragmatism with a hard-headed attitude to data. This is especially clear in the way in which 'loyalty' is measured. The basic measurement is known in the jargon as 'RFV' – recency, frequency and value. Any shopper regularly using a loyalty card can be measured by monitoring how he or she behaves according to a mix of those criteria.

Recency

Recency is a simple measurement – recording when the customer last shopped. But its simplicity as a measurement belies its usefulness. When a group of customers' recency behaviour declines, that is the surest sign that they are deserting the retailer. The company might be able to recruit more to fill the void, and those customers might be of equal value, but to ignore significant evidence of defection is seriously dangerous for a retailer fighting to thrive in a fiercely competitive market. After all, those defecting customers do not simply disappear. They become customers of the rivals. It was an awareness of this problem that alerted Tesco to the need for a loyalty strategy in the first place. And if a retailer fails to respond to customers who are leaving the brand, eventually the company acquires a larger problem. As Frederick F Reichheld explains in *The Loyalty Effect*:

> Persistent defection means that former customers – people convinced the company offers inferior value – will eventually outnumber the company's loyal advocates and dominate the collective voice of the marketplace. When that moment arrives, no amount of advertising, public relations or ingenious marketing will prop up pricing, new-customer acquisitions, or the company's reputation.

But recency alone is a poor measure of an individual's loyalty. It needs to be combined with a measurement of the type of shopping the customer performs when he or she visits the supermarket.

Frequency

Frequency is, as it suggests, a simple measure of how often you shop. Frequency measures how much contact a retailer's customers have with their stores: it can give a rough guide to how robust the relationship is between the customer and the brand. It seems obvious that the customers who are most loyal visit most often – but that does not take account of the differing buying patterns of superficially similar shoppers. A family with two young children might shop out of town once a week as a unit. Or one parent might visit a local store three times a week. Or the family might try to buy everything, on the internet, once a fortnight.

Frequency therefore isn't a one-size-fits-all measure – that is why frequency is incomplete without a measure of what type of shopping is done on each visit. In short, the quantity of visits might be OK, but what about the quality?

Value

Hence, the tracking of value. As we have already described, loyalty is not about monogamy in a retail context. Customers may like a supermarket, but very few are exclusive in their affections. Value is an indication of the profitability of your customer base – a decline in it means a decline in basket size, which means that more of those purchases are being made elsewhere. It is more than a simple measure of the value of a shopping trip: it is a measure of how much 'value' the retailer is perceived to provide to that household. Reichheld argues:

> Creating value for customers builds loyalty, and loyalty in turn builds growth, profit and more value. While profit has always occupied centre stage in conventional thinking about business systems, profit is not primary. Profit is indispensable of course, but is nevertheless a consequence of value creation.

The main advantage of RFV is that it can be quantified accurately – and the information it provides can be an empirical basis for useful, productive action. For example, RFV analysis can highlight a group of vulnerable customers that need more attention to retain, or it can provide a comparative measure between stores, or it might help a retailer create simple customer segments that can be used to differentiate communications and offers.

These were certainly the ways that Tesco used RVF analysis to look at its customers, breaking them into simple segments, and making informed assumptions on what these groups of customers liked – and didn't like. But even on this simple basis the challenge to make the raw data manageable was enormous, and achieving that would make or break the future of Clubcard.

THE PROBLEMS WITH DATA WAREHOUSES

In 1996, 81 per cent of executives surveyed by consultant AT Kearney believed that technology helped their profits. Yet only 20 per cent were confident that they could measure the benefits. The story of many large IT systems built in the 1990s boom was that if it was big and costly enough, then the companies that installed the system believed that it must work, otherwise the investment would have been a mistake. Yet invariably months, and sometimes years, later many had to admit that those benefits had not been realized, especially when it came to analysing customer data in a meaningful, actionable way. In fact, the common experience of marketers in the mid-1990s was that the scale of their organization's IT ambitions was often the main impediment to getting them to use customer data usefully.

In March 1997, KPMG reported that '[t]he largest organizations are actually losing market position to smaller companies'. The reason KPMG hit upon was that the vast stores of customer data that big corporations had created were organized so badly that they could not be used to create any useful insight, and were indeed slowing down the companies' ability to react to their customers' needs and to swiftly changing market conditions.

The technique of taking large amounts of operational data and putting them into a large database, with the aim of analysing them every which way to yield useful information, is known as 'data warehousing'. At the time that Tesco Clubcard launched, it was the fashion in technology, and Tesco was not the only major company looking to collect and use vast amounts of customer transactional data. In the United States data warehousing was spectacularly popular. According to market research in 1996, 46 per cent of large companies were attempting to build a data warehouse, with a further 26 per cent planning to use one by the end of the year (Forrester Research).

Building a data warehouse sounds straightforward: surely a large database is only a small database with more information in it. The aspiring data-warehouse builders had plenty of small databases in HR, logistics and customer service. In theory the essential character of a database does not change, whether it is storing 30 names and addresses for a bridge club, or 30 million for HM Revenue & Customs: records are created, which can be sorted according to the fields in them (that is, the types of information – such as your name or your address). They can be interrogated – for example, to find anyone in Newcastle called Smith. The step forward promised by a data warehouse might be to find anyone in Newcastle who used to be a good customer, but whose spending had declined. Banks could use them to link together information about a customer's bank account, mortgage, credit cards and loans, and identify profitable customers rather than profitable accounts.

It appeared that to run Clubcard, Tesco needed a data warehouse. Each cardholder would be a complete record, and each shopping trip would update that record. The database would be able to show Tesco's marketers who were the cardholders of a particular age, or location, or store. Or it could show who shopped at what time, and how that compared with who shopped later in the day. It would show the effect of rival stores opening nearby, on which customers. Eventually, it might be able to identify what 'lifestyle' a particular customer had by profiling what he or she bought, and put him or her in a segment of similar people.

However, the process of considering such a warehouse for Tesco revealed the same problems that were shared by so many similar projects around the world. It was becoming apparent to even the most enthusiastic IT departments that data warehousing created unique problems. Harrison says:

> At that time I went with some of our IT specialists to see the Teradata data warehouse that Wal-Mart used to manage its huge product sales volumes. What was clear was that this technology hadn't been effectively used by anyone for holding and manipulating customer data. I chose dunnhumby for our needs because the staff could talk the language of business. Many of their competitors at that time were bearded sandal wearers, and I knew they weren't going to be a match for our business.

Data warehousing showed the ability of data to solve business problems. In practice, it often showed the inability of Harrison's 'sandal wearers' to solve retail problems efficiently. In reality, data warehouses had seven deadly problems that meant large stores of customer data were nothing like small ones.

1. Format

The data from so many different sources are never in a common format. An example for Tesco was the problem of integrating the transactional records from the 57 recently acquired William Low stores, which used different point of sale systems. *This raised the question: what was the simplest way to give Tesco's data a common denominator?*

2. Time

Time is data's enemy – a warehouse is a depository of historical information. The older it gets, the less relevant it is to what is happening in the business now. So if it takes six months to organize data and reach conclusions, you are already out of date. In some businesses, this might not matter that much. In retail, it does. *The decision to be made is: how quickly do the data need to be organized and available to be valuable as business information?*

3. Scale

Big isn't always beautiful in data terms. All data are, in theory, relevant, so in a warehouse approach all data have to be stored, all the time. After all, you don't know exactly what is relevant until you look, and you can't look at data that you don't hold. Analysing ever-increasing volumes of data means ever-growing capacity to store them, and multiplying the computing memory and processing power to handle them. You might even come up against the upper boundary of what is possible using the original software tools. Capturing and storing customer shopping data is a huge undertaking. For example, the data warehouse that housed all of the Sainsbury's Reward card data six months after launch had already grown to three terabytes of data – as much as 1.5 million paperback books. *The challenge to Clubcard is: are all the data useful all of the time?*

4. Quality

Bad data mean inaccurate measurement and can lead to wrong decisions. Take for example the sort of data produced by customer surveys. One might ask: 'Do you think your loyalty card is a useful way to earn a valuable discount?' Another might ask: 'Would you prefer a loyalty card or lower prices?' The likely results from the phrasing of the questions will be very different. Yet both could be presented as measures of whether shoppers like loyalty cards, and would provide an inconsistent picture from analysis, providing a skewed view of the real situation. Data warehouses are indiscriminate. They have to combine data with inbuilt bias, data from different sources, data with small errors, perhaps data that are wholly incorrect. Being able to manage the cumulative errors in this process, and give an accurate assessment of the risk that the result of an enquiry is wrong, is a subtle process. It is further complicated by an exaggerated respect for technology: the idea that because a computer worked it out, it must be right. *The question for Clubcard is: what is the best balance between quantity and quality?*

5. Cost

For every £1 spent building a data warehouse – purchasing the software, computers and storage – analyst Ovum calculates that companies spend £4 putting data into it. This running cost never goes away. The burden of IT can trap a company into a situation where it cannot afford to continue a project – even though it will never achieve a return on its investment if it does not. Computer company Tandem conducted research in 1997 into the ongoing problems that data warehouse projects were experiencing, and found that the biggest issue for companies was that they could not identify a return on their investment. How could they ever be sure it was working? How could they measure whether it had begun to pay for itself? By 1998, Ovum reported that more than two-thirds of large data warehouse projects had failed. *Tesco had to clearly define and measure Clubcard's projected return on investment.*

6. Culture

Creating and managing a data warehouse cuts across many disciplines in a company. Many projects fail because of turf wars – who should drive it? IT or marketing? *The Clubcard challenge was to have a simple reporting line for data management.*

7. Corporate ego

Data warehouse projects are by definition big and expensive. They tend to take on a life of their own, encouraging technical innovation for its own sake. In February 1997, Dale Kutnick, chief executive of market researcher Meta Group, dismissed most of the systems that had been built to extract information from customer loyalty programmes as copycat exercises without a clear direction. 'It's "me too" stuff. As soon as one does it, they all have to. This type of technological innovation is the worst kind,' he said. The warning to the Clubcard team was obvious.

When it came to collecting customer data, size was important – if Tesco did not have enough data from a wide enough range of its customers, it could not model their behaviour, and it couldn't apply that model to a large enough proportion of its customers. To make Clubcard relevant and compelling for the vast majority of Tesco customers, it had to be big in scale and ambition. *But in looking at the pitfalls of data warehousing it became clear that size was not everything.*

MAKING A WAREHOUSE WORK

Datamarts

From the increasingly apparent failures of data warehousing came a new idea: the 'datamart'. Just as Tesco had developed into a chain of town superstores from a heritage of running successful town centre convenience stores, so some companies were finding that starting small was often the best route to success with their customer data. The designers of datamarts took pragmatic decisions on data, time and resources and made compromises: they created smaller active stores of data by sacrificing detail, rejecting 'irrelevant' data, or creating a miniature data warehouse to solve a subset of problems, for example choosing to look only at one group of customers. Datamarts could proliferate, or grow with time, or stay as they were. They weren't perfect, but they contained cost and risk and they worked.

Independently, Clubcard's first data analysts discovered this pragmatic route. They looked at what technical capacity Tesco had, scoped out the most pressing requirements of the business, and tailored the database system around that. This was data realism, not idealism, at work.

They based their solution on the operational online transaction processing (OLTP) systems that ran the stores' tills. OLTP systems are designed to process as little information as is necessary, as fast as possible, while data warehouses are about getting rich information, and letting it sit there while it is analysed. The project team decided that there had to be a trade-off. Trying to capture vastly more information at the point of sale would mean radically upgrading the OLTP systems that kept the Tesco tills functioning, which in retail IT terms would be about as big a project as could be. The potential disruption of trade was of course a concern.

Capturing only 'summary' information would reduce the detail of the picture and accuracy of what could be deduced. It meant that some information would have to be guessed, or simply ignored. This was the trade-off that was demanded.

Cutting data down to size

The Clubcard team decided on a less ambitious project to change data to information. If dunnhumby could set up a series of tests to analyse customer behaviour, and if they could look at the results of those tests among specific groups of customers, they could learn something powerful about how people shopped.

In effect, they decided not to use the data to answer every question about every customer, but to answer some of the biggest questions about most customers. Harrison insisted that all the analysis had a sales focus. 'How would we present the data so that it answered a real business problem? If the data was "interesting", that didn't cut it. But adding more sales by doing something new – that did.'

If it was to use these results to direct its activity, and analyse the results from that, it would create a cycle of continuous improvement. The data were not just a way of deciding what to do next, they were a way of finding out if what you did worked.

There are few things to measure in a supermarket. There is price, there is the range of goods, there are promotions and offers, and there are store formats. With that relatively restricted menu, the analysts simply had to break out the data it needed to test a series of hypotheses. In 1995, that meant recording the customer ID, the total basket size and time the customer visited, and the amount spent in each department. This was all that the Tesco till systems could measure at the time.

dunnhumby also made a practical decision on timing: it didn't need, and could not cope with data delivered every day. Once a week was enough. Even so, the volume of this information was still far too great to analyse quickly. There were 15 departments, and each spend in each department in every store, represented in pounds and pence, would take five digits. Multiply by millions of baskets, and far too much data were coming in the weekly delivery.

dunnhumby created a statistician's trick to compress the volume of data by approximately 75 per cent. It built software that represented the spend in each department as a two-digit number between 01 and 99 – an approx-imately measured proportion of the basket total. Imagine dropping a packet of M&Ms onto a chessboard. A chessboard has 64 squares; so if you want to pick up one quarter of the chocolates, pick up those that cover any 16 squares. It might not be an exact measure, but it will be close enough.

So even the spend in each department was not recorded to the nearest penny. Insisting on using the exact sum was an example of unnecessary precision: the cumulative error, even when doing this over millions of baskets, would not seriously affect the confidence with which the analysts could measure the spend in each department.

What mattered?

Immediately, the effect of this pragmatic approach to the use of data became apparent, not least the living proof of the famous Pareto prin-ciple. As all marketing students know, this states that the top 20 per cent of customers deliver 80 per cent of the value to the company. Essentially customers are not of equal economic value, only the minority contribute significantly to profit, while the majority deliver mass to a business. By analysing customer behaviour over time through the use of Clubcard, Tesco found that in any single store, the top-spending 100 customers were as valuable as the bottom 4,000.

This dramatically illustrated the disproportionate impact on each store's performance of the most valuable and loyal few. As an insight it led to the decision to run the invitation-only Clubcard events in major stores, as a way to thank the store's best customers. Clubcard had brought it home to Tesco's senior management that this massively important minority of customers had been shopping the aisles for years before anyone recognized the size of their value to Tesco. They might have switched supermarkets, and Tesco would not have had the means of talking directly to them to win them back.

Life-stage segmentation

Without the means in the early stages to analyse an individual's shopping choices by item, the best and most common sense way to start segmenting shoppers was by 'life stage'. One piece of information that Clubcard immediately provided via the application form was the age group of the cardholder, so it was relatively simple to create meaningful customer segments based on the age and family make-up of the household. No one at Tesco would have claimed at the time that this was a perfect way to find common interests between customers – 'young adults' for example has to combine a wide range of attitudes, behaviours and priorities. But it was a useful start, and it gave a benchmark to measure the effectiveness of the Clubcard offer and its promotions. Segmentation by life stage can avoid simple errors – for example, offering coupons for Coca Cola to tea-drinking pensioners.

The listening data bank

By using data to 'listen' to customers, it became possible to understand findings that would usually be considered an error. Rather than asking the question 'What are they doing?', the Clubcard team found it more useful to ask 'Why are they doing it?'

A simple example was the early insight given by de-duping – that is, the process where data are analysed to show where multiple records seem to belong to the same person, or the same house. It's a basic process of database management, which isn't usually given much attention. In 1996, Clubcard files showed a large number of dupes with different names, at the same address. By asking 'Why?' Tesco had the insight: different members of the same family were holding cards, because they shared the shopping. At its simplest, both partners held a card. To which the response had to be: give them the chance to associate the points, and the data, from both cards as one record. Tesco could view what was being bought for the household – and the household would achieve a higher value reward every quarter.

Even when listening to bad news, Tesco could use Clubcard to 'ask questions' of its customers, and find out what would motivate them to change their behaviour. As the country was gripped with fear over the health risk of BSE in meat, Tesco was able to look at the effect on the meat department spend for its cardholders. Using this, the card was the basis for an experiment: different stores tried different price reductions on their meat. Using Clubcard data, Tesco could quickly find out the price its shoppers were willing to pay, and which shoppers could not be tempted back.

Street fighting with data

Even at this basic level, it became very clear to the marketers of Tesco that data analysis could help them in the store-to-store competition at local level. By closely reviewing and comparing each store's performance on various criteria it was possible to see opportunities to capitalize on and weaknesses to address. Between February 1995 and June 1996, the process of interrogating available data led to EHS producing 200 local direct mail campaigns in support of individual stores.

The analysis also established that the stores with the highest Clubcard penetration were least affected by competitors' attacks. So it was straightforward to create a table of Clubcard penetration per store: and in 65 stores, refits and new formats were advertised to the keenest Tesco shoppers using direct mail.

WHAT TESCO LEARNT ABOUT DATA

Working with dunnhumby, Tesco learnt as it went along. Perhaps it was good that it didn't know what 'mistakes' it was making at the time, or its early data processing might not have been so successful. Instead of building the largest data store it could, pragmatism ruled, and the goal was to build the smallest store of data that would give useful information. Call it a data warehouse or a datamart, it doesn't matter. It was a useable resource to understand better what customers did, and a predictor of what they might do in the future.

Pragmatism

Tesco started not from 'What would we like to do?' but from 'What can we realistically do, and will it make a profit?' It reasoned that any new information was progress – and built from there. It didn't agonize over information it couldn't extract at first, or hold up the process until it could get information. Instead, it asked questions that it could answer, and found that there were surprisingly many of them.

Progression

It built on each new discovery. Indeed, its early breakthroughs – for example, identifying its most profitable customer profile – drove its later research in profitable and useful directions. While the early systems were sometimes awkwardly stitched together, they formed a basis from which better data could evolve at a later date.

Approximation

The analysts were not precious with the data – and found that made the difference between sinking and swimming. From the start they mixed local and national analysis, and drove local and national mailings.

Learning

Clubcard wasn't just about passively observing trends, it was a massive laboratory of customer behaviour. Retailers had always experimented with price and range to see what worked – now Tesco could measure exactly what worked in any store. When it was doing something wrong, it knew in days. When it was doing something right, it could implement it nationwide in weeks.

Defence

Now Tesco could quickly identify its lapsed shoppers, or the shoppers who ignored certain departments, it could incentivize them. It found ways to defend itself against competitive store openings.

Segmentation

Collecting users into segments gave Tesco the opportunity to target its vouchers and coupons at people who really wanted them. Redemption rates for coupons varied between 3 per cent (the sort of rate Tesco might expect for a pre-Clubcard, completely untargeted mailing) and 70 per cent. But as it became better at modelling the behaviour of its customers, within a year the target was set at an unprecedented 20 per cent redemption rate. By the end of 1996, even before it could know any individual product that Clubcard users bought, Tesco was finally saying 'Thank you' in something like a personal way.

In 1996, Tesco crossed a bridge. Previously it had used data when it was possible and available. Now it had data for almost every occasion. Because it didn't have the means to compare who drank Coke against who drank Pepsi, it was forced to concentrate on bigger, broader questions. Even at this stage, Clubcard data had been an influential adviser for every major Tesco initiative.

Marketing director Simon Uwins says:

> As a company we have moved from being intuitive to being analytical. This is a much more complicated business than it used to be. We don't forget our intuition, but better data lead to better thinking, and our data give us the confidence to ask the right questions. You can have all the data you want, but the key is to use them to ask the right questions.

7

Four Christmases a year

- ▶ The Banana Man of Worcester
- ▶ To mail, or not to mail?
- ▶ Auditing the Clubcard statement
- ▶ Licensed to print money
- ▶ The 'Quarterly me'
- ▶ What Tesco learnt about mail

THE BANANA MAN OF WORCESTER

What sort of a person buys almost half a tonne of bananas as their weekly supermarket shop? In January 1997, physicist Phil Calcott, age 28, answered that question. Bananas being his favourite fruit, he was pleased to see extra Clubcard points were being awarded on each 3 lb bunch at Tesco. The bananas cost £1.17. The 25 Clubcard points were worth £1.25, at the exchange rate of the time.

You don't get to be a government-employed scientist without being able to calculate that at this rate the value you get back from Clubcard exceeds the cost of buying the bananas. Phil asked his local store in

Worcester to load his car with bananas, swiped his Clubcard, and after popping back the next day (his Peugeot 205 would only carry 460 lb of fruit at one time), racked up a banana bill of £367.38. His house contained 942 lb of bananas at one point. 'At one stage my living room was stacked from floor to ceiling with 25 cases containing around 3,000 bananas,' he said. So, having earned 7,850 points on his Clubcard, he set about giving the bananas away.

'I've always fancied standing on the street and seeing people's reactions when you give them something for free,' he told *The Times*. 'By the time I finished, queues were building up. Children in the street now shout "banana man" whenever they see me... I am waiting for Tesco to do a special offer on pineapples because I am rather partial to them.'

'We thought he had gone bananas,' said Tesco's local customer services manager Helen Williams. So did the press. The *Sun* printed a picture of him, buried in bananas. The *Independent* ran a concerned editorial on the amount of petrol and work it took to buy the bananas, warning that 'there is no such thing as a free lunch'.

The Banana Man of Worcester's gesture did not go unrewarded: when he opened his Clubcard statement in February 1997, he had vouchers that gave him £392.50 – a profit on the deal of £25.12.

While few Tesco shoppers have the delight of earning as much as £400 in Clubcard 'money' four times a year, the millions of reward-carrying Clubcard mailings that are sent out by Tesco each quarter are greeted with consistent enthusiasm by shoppers, even after 11 years of Clubcard's existence. In fact the Clubcard quarterly mailing has a credible claim to be one of the most effective direct mailing programmes ever devised.

Four times a year the programme creates an incremental sales effect that is comparable to the sales bump most retailers only experience at Easter or Christmas. So far Clubcard has rewarded customers with well over £1 billion of cashback, for them to spend on whatever they wish from Tesco. This generosity is not Tesco altruism, as this is a mailing that pays for itself every time it goes out.

As well as the cash to members in the form of Clubcard vouchers, each mailing pack contains discounts on individual products targeted at specific groups of consumers. These product coupons achieve redemption rates as high as 70 per cent in some instances. Direct marketing response rates rarely climb above single-figure percentages.

TO MAIL, OR NOT TO MAIL?

In launching Clubcard nationwide, Tesco turned itself into one of Europe's biggest users of direct mail overnight. Why did it not prefer to take the cheaper route, and give the discount to customers at the checkout?

Don't be part of the wallpaper

The decision was made very early on in the planning sessions, before Clubcard was even tested. As Grant Harrison remembers:

> Our project team and the guys from EHS scoped out various options for communicating with customers and delivering the Clubcard rewards. I had looked at various retail schemes around the world and what struck me was the poor perception of loyalty programmes that just gave benefit at the point of sale. Whether it was coupons or preferential prices or instant discount, the danger is that the benefit becomes part of the wallpaper. It costs the business a fortune to put the cash back into customer purses but customers take it for granted and so do staff. They certainly don't get enthusiastic about pushing the benefits of membership, it's another humdrum transaction. With a scheme based on rewards-on-demand you may get an increase in behavioural loyalty but it won't go any further; there's no opportunity to extend emotional loyalty. Terry Hunt called it the 'loyalty cul-de-sac'.

The team decided to look to the established retail calendar and integrate Clubcard into it. Successful stores use events through the year to concentrate the minds and energy of staff and customers on particular product ranges or promotions – Easter eggs, summer barbecues, Back to School, Halloween treats. Why not use the same thinking with the loyalty programme? Why not save up all the rewards earned by millions of customers and pay it out in four seasonal waves, delivered direct to their home along with targeted offers and information to encourage customers to come back into the store and spend their bonus?

That way the customers can anticipate a regular 'Thank you' package from Tesco courtesy of their Clubcard membership, the store managers can prepare themselves by stocking up on all the products that are featured in the in-pack promotions, and the staff can concentrate their efforts over a short period, helping customers use their Clubcard vouchers and coupons and encouraging non-members to join Clubcard and benefit next time round.

That was the best way, the team believed, to keep Clubcard a chosen rather than a given: an active benefit rather than a passive feature. And that thinking led Tesco to transform from being one of the country's biggest TV advertisers into one of its biggest direct mailers.

Big mailing, big leap of faith

For all the sound logic that backed the decision to use direct mail, the first quarterly Clubcard statement mailing was still a case of gritting Tesco's collective teeth and hoping for the best.

Today, the sales and business impact of the multi-million mailing can be accurately predicted and response rates modelled to the nearest decimal point, while the results are minutely observed, recorded and learnt from. This is now direct mail that customers complain about when they haven't received a copy.

During each mailing cycle the Tesco call centre at Dundee handles thousands of enquiries from Clubcard members, worried that they have missed out on their reward mailing. The regular tracking research consistently suggests that customers perceive the quarterly mailing from Tesco Clubcard not as 'junk mail', but as personal mail, not unlike a savings statement from their bank or a newsletter from their social club.

But all this became clear later. In spring 1995, mailing 5 million Tesco customer households was an expensive leap of faith.

You only value what you measure

Tesco insisted on meticulous testing and measurement in the mailing from day one. By monitoring the performance of every aspect of the mailing Tesco is able to fine-tune the offers and information sent to different segments of customers. In the first mailings the ability to segment was quite crude, but even at this level the technique of cutting the database into groups of shared interest or life stage brought valuable results.

By 1996 an internal report to the Tesco board expressed delight that:

> they [the mailings] are generating a significant sales impact both for the company overall and for individual product lines featured in the couponing programme... The statements are a competitive advantage that have not been recognized by other operators who give rewards to their customers at the till.

The leap of faith had clearly paid off.

The determination to gain maximum benefit from this newly discovered sales-generating medium led the Tesco marketers to strive for better targeting with every mailing. Although the communication to each cardholder remained simple, the operational complexity of the programme mushroomed. Even as early as August 1996, with the fifth statement mailing campaign, there were 1,800 variations of the 'standard' statement, with 100 different letter texts targeting different customer segments, preferences and local details. By February 1999, the mass customization of the mailing had risen to 145,000 versions. Today, Tesco sends out between 8 and 9 million mailings. The dream of one-to-one marketing is now limited only by the differences in behaviour of Tesco customers.

The hole in the basket

Much of the effort went into improving the targeting of the product-specific coupons. In the very first statement mailing it was one-size fits all, with only one set of six coupons offered to everyone. Soon the tracking research started to unearth a new source of customer aggravation – irrelevance. Customers complained that if Tesco were monitoring what they bought, why was it sending them irrelevant coupons? Two or three out of the six coupons might be usable – but that was no longer good enough. It was undermining the perceived value of Clubcard.

Today, four coupons are for goods that the shoppers already buy, two are for related items. The two bonus coupons are not just for products that Tesco has a surplus of – as Jack Cohen might have done. They are to fill the 'hole in the basket'. The bonus coupons are chosen using an analysis that shows that the customer has a high propensity to buy a product (that is, other similar customers buy it regularly), but so far that customer has not tried it.

AUDITING THE CLUBCARD STATEMENT

One of the responsibilities of the Customer Insight Unit at Tesco is to measure the business performance of the Clubcard quarterly statement mailing.

This measurement regime started in an ad hoc way, but two years after Clubcard launched, and around the time that Sainsbury's was starting to build a comparable membership base for the Reward card, Tesco acknowledged the importance of the task by recruiting at a senior level. 'When I arrived, I tried to work out what we should encourage people to logically buy next,' says the director of strategy Laura Wade-Gery, explaining her role, from 1997, as 'targeted marketing director'. As the complexity of the segmentation that Tesco created increased, so did the number of opportunities to measure the statement's performance. Wade-Gery continues:

> We needed to agree, what were we looking for this quarter? What questions did we need to answer? Because by simply staring at the data, all you get is confused. The statement is vital as a learning tool, but needs to be analysed with care. We tried to develop useful segmentations that actually told you something useful, rather than old people ate prunes, which wasn't a helpful observation.

Another Clubcard principle is that it is no good knowing something if you can't do anything useful with the information. The team only asked questions of Clubcard when the answers would help them do something better for customers. As Wade-Gery explains:

> Some other organizations have a great deal of customer data but don't have the philosophy of being customer-orientated. So their marketing departments get nowhere because they can tell you masses about their customers, but no one is fundamentally interested in doing anything about it. Banks are the classic example.

As part of their learning process the Customer Insight Unit instituted an analysis and research programme that measures key aspects and highlights areas for improvement. In advance of the next quarter's statement, the Clubcard team is briefed on the findings from the previous campaign. There are two essential aspects that the Customer Insight people track: results and trends.

1. Results

Clubcard has been developed on the principle that there is no such thing as complete success or total failure. Everything that happens is an opportunity to learn and everything that goes wrong contains the germ of future success. The main success criterion is return on investment (ROI). From the first mailing Tesco has been able to measure the ROI of the statement mailing to the nearest £100,000 from sales value during the period of anything up to £7 billion. This is calculated from:

- the value of vouchers sent out;
- the total cost to Tesco of the vouchers and money-off coupons redeemed;
- the like-for-like sales uplift that resulted;
- the regional variations;
- the customer segment variations;
- the take-up rates of the different product coupons.

2. Trends

In addition to a snapshot of each mailing's performance the Customer Insight Unit looks at emerging trends in customer behaviour to create a moving picture of Tesco's business. For example, Tesco monitors the lapse rate among new cardholders, seeing whether those who don't receive a reward in their first mailing tend to stop using the card in the second period (the answer seems to be yes – but only a very small reward is needed for them to carry on with the programme). Or they will analyse the behaviour of customers who tend not to use the discount coupons sent to them, assessing whether this is a constant or a fluctuating trend. They look at the effect of TV advertising on in-store response rates by region to better inform the media strategy, as well as the variations between lifestyle segments – which helps them increase the relevance of product offers in the future.

This assessment of effects and trends through the Clubcard statement mailing is easily the biggest ongoing mass observation survey of the UK's supermarket shopping behaviour.

LICENSED TO PRINT MONEY

The secret of Sherwood Park

In the Nottingham suburb of Annesley, 10 miles north of the city, lies the glamorously named Sherwood Park, a rather inappropriate name for a collection of large industrial sheds. One of the largest buildings is home to Polestar Digital, which since the first Clubcard mailing has been responsible for the millions of statements that Tesco sends out.

The four statement mailings are the high spot in the calendar for the print team who are dedicated to the Tesco account, but every week there are smaller tactical mailings – for example to one store, or one group of customers such as the Baby and Toddler Club. In all, Tesco mails more than 50 million packs a year. It prints 160 million Tesco price news leaflets.

From a relatively tiny run of 300,000 statements in spring 1995 with only one version, the production challenge has steadily grown so that today the task is to print with total accuracy and security more than 12 million statements, four times a year – with potentially every pack customized to the individual household (although in reality there are around 4 million variations because there are fewer distinct types of customer behaviour than there are ways to customize a statement).

The Clubcard statement, the world's largest mailing of its kind, is time critical. It's not just that Tesco's 700 stores have been specifically prepared and stocked to cope with the increased demand it creates, but others have to gear up for the scale of the operation. The Post Office, for one: on the peak days of the mailing, the Clubcard statement represents 6 per cent of all the mail sent in the UK.

The virtual organization

To manage the operation a number of disparate organizations have to combine seamlessly for a few weeks to form a 'virtual' Clubcard organization. From Tesco, the Clubcard team is booked into a local hotel along with colleagues from EHS Brann who have designed and planned the statement. dunnhumby's representatives bring the mailing data on 20 spools of tape, packed into a cardboard box, as the volume of data is too huge to make it economical to send it electronically. (For security purposes, the process has risk management built in. One set of tapes travels North on the A1, the other on the M1.) Two of this ad hoc committee are responsible for the correct barcoding and legal accuracy of the words used in the mailing. Through Wednesday, Thursday and Friday of the print week they will check every word, every logo and every design element – and if not every record, they will be responsible for any last-minute changes (for example, Clubcard holders who have died, or have requested no more mailings, or phoney names flagged by bespoke joke name suppression software). This isn't just a fact-checking exercise: it's also part of the audit trail. Ultimately Tesco head office will have an accurate check of how many vouchers it has issued, in effect how much 'money' it has put into circulation, cross-checked against the print records. This is as much a banking as a retail exercise.

The statement printing process occupies 125 people for 16 days, taking 80 per cent of the capacity of the printing operation, working round the clock in three eight-hour shifts. It brings together envelopes that are printed in Madrid, letterheads that are printed in Leeds and inserts that can be printed just about anywhere in Europe.

The fuel driving the whole production process is the customer data, allowing each mail pack to be tailored to be as relevant as possible to each cardholder, quickly and inexpensively. In short, the Clubcard statement mailing is the perfect example of the power of technology to mass customize. In a world where 90 per cent of IT projects run late, this is an example of the other 10 per cent.

Security measures

With so much Tesco 'cash' being distributed through the post, security is a major consideration. In an age when colour photocopiers and desktop publishing have made forgery so easy with just a few thousand pounds of equipment, the Tesco statement mailings have had to adopt many print security features. Inspect a recent Tesco statement and you will see that the paper is embossed, perforated and watermarked with a series of designs developed to make forgery difficult and detection easier. The face value side of the vouchers is unphotocopiable. Each coupon and voucher has the customer's name, alongside its own serial number and barcode, traceable to the cardholder. There is even a tiny perforation around the letter T of Tesco. It is always possible to counterfeit any legal tender but these measures are intended to make it more expensive to try than the benefit a forger could obtain.

Distribution challenges

Having been printed, the statements are folded (using machines that work at a rate of 16,000 an hour), stuffed and glued (8,000 an hour) and packed into bags and metal cages. Forty-four cages get packed into each of the Post Office trucks that are used to carry away the complete mailing campaign. Despite the vast numbers, the statements have to be individually identifiable, so that in an emergency any package can be pulled out at any time before delivery. The code number that identifies any statement also makes it possible to be flexible over the order in which they are processed: Polestar doesn't know until 48 hours beforehand which statements it will be loading onto those trucks.

The Clubcard quarterly statement mailing is a major operational and commercial commitment for Tesco. As well as a proven sales opportunity, each statement carries substantial risk. The projected uplift in sales, so vital to the stores' annual sales performance, could be undermined by a statement that is a week late, contains the wrong information or offers, sends miscalculated rewards, or features inaccurate barcodes. If Clubcard offers Tesco the chance to replicate the sales effect of Christmas four times a year, then Santa's helpers need to make sure Christmas comes on time.

THE 'QUARTERLY ME'

One of the landmarks that Tesco established almost by accident came as a result of the quarterly mailing. Could it use the basic results of its segmentation to create the world's first personalised magazine? *Clubcard Magazine* – known as the 'Quarterly me' – could be delivered with the statement, and would have targeted features and coupons. The majority of its features would be general information on its new products, initiatives in the stores, helpful tips like recipes and health advice, which were common to most customers. But a significant portion of the Tesco magazine could be targeted. Shoppers on a budget would not be bombarded with long features about premium-priced food. Young shoppers had different priorities to senior citizens: Tesco could recognize that.

It was an excellent idea, but a tough one to make work. First, the odd shape of the mailing meant that *Clubcard Magazine* was square, much to the irritation of advertisers whose copy was formatted for rectangular pages. Second, the magazine was limited to 30 pages, or the cost of posting it would have been prohibitive.

Even so, to make *Clubcard Magazine* profitable the cost of advertising in it had to be huge – a magazine with a print run of 8.5 million was, at the time, easily the largest-circulation magazine in the UK. '[We were] competing with national magazines who sell their advertising for between £5,000 and £7,000 a page,' says *Clubcard Magazine* publisher Sarah Wyse, who works at contract publisher Forward Publishing. She was asking advertisers for up to £37,000 for a page.

How could they do it? In media sales size matters – so being able to reach half the households in the country certainly helped. But *Clubcard Magazine* had more than scale. First, it had an element of targeting. While print costs meant that the segmentation was rough and ready, offering five editions divided by life stage, it was better than nothing. Perhaps more important, advertisers could directly measure the results of their advertising once a quarter using Clubcard. 'We could prove there was a short-term or a long-term effect of advertising,' says Wyse, 'In the usual way that advertising is bought and sold, it wouldn't work.'

The effects varied widely, with sales uplifts anything between 1 per cent and – for one brand of toilet tissue – 27 per cent. Wyse had no explanation for why a single piece of advertising created such a dramatic uplift, but she could demonstrate that it was *Clubcard Magazine* that did it.

Win some, lose some

After a brief trial in 1995, the first fully-fledged issue of *Clubcard Magazine* was sent out with the statements in May 1996. Originally the five categories: students, young adults, older adults, families and over-60s were based on the customer data offered at sign-up. Just as with the Student Clubcard, the student edition didn't last long. The readers were hard to reach editorially, and they kept moving house. And after one year, it became obvious that segmenting the magazine at Christmas was a waste of money. As Wyse points out, many of us have a common experience at Christmas, and tend to share our shopping habits.

For seven years, *Clubcard Magazine* delivered a one-of-a-kind experience for readers and advertisers. During that time, supermarket magazines burst to prominence in the UK, and by 2003, 8 out of the 10 highest-circulation magazines in the UK were published by brands. The Association of Publishing Agencies calculated in 2003 that 114 million consumer magazines were published in the UK, and half of all adults read a supermarket magazine.

For a while, *Clubcard Magazine* worked well, despite its crude segmentation, but eventually its impact diminished. 'We discovered that only 20 per cent read the magazine, and it was in danger of being a junk mail,' says Simon Uwins, UK director of marketing. If the magazine was seen as junk, it might undermine Clubcard. So Tesco did what it always does when it finds something isn't working: it stops doing it. In 2003 it killed off its 'Quarterly me', and introduced a free magazine by the till that customers could pick up if they wanted it. The inevitable conclusion is that if the segmentation is too crude to deliver an obvious benefit, a higher-quality unsegmented product is better for both Tesco and its customers.

'I suppose you could say that by not doing something,' Uwins jokes, 'we enhanced the quality of what we do do.'

WHAT TESCO LEARNT ABOUT MAIL

The need to get into direct mail on such a large scale was simply a function of the programme's design – but the lessons that Tesco has learnt along the way have allowed the company to maximize return on a major marketing investment.

Talk, listen and learn

The quarterly direct mail programme gives Tesco the opportunity to sustain a regular 'conversation' with customers. As each mailing becomes more targeted and informed by individual data, then what Tesco says should get more and more relevant. Customers talk back to Tesco by responding to offers, redeeming coupons, joining special interest clubs, entering prize draws, etc. Each response is an opportunity to learn, refine and improve.

Give people what they want

Having opened a channel of communication, Tesco has to act on what people are saying. If coupon redemption by a certain customer segment is low, then don't repeat the offer; find something they will respond to. When brands market by averages rather than individual need, the temptation can be to market customers into submission, no matter how resistant they are. For example, by producing targeted versions of *Clubcard Magazine*, or producing special mailings for vegetarians, Tesco learnt that the more relevant the brand is the more responsive customers are – and the less profligate the business needs to be with discounts and offers.

Constantly experiment

By taking small groups and testing ideas and offers with them in the mailing, Tesco takes a lot of the risk out of innovative marketing. The Clubcard mailing gives it a chance to experiment with propositions on a scaleable but discreet basis. In many ways the mailing is now the brand's marketing laboratory.

Measure

How is the programme working? What's doing well, what isn't? Where does the mailing make Tesco money, where is the unnecessary cost? What can we improve? By methodically tracking and auditing the performance of the mailing every three months on a number of levels of customer response (from redemption to attitude), Tesco gets clear guidance on what needs to be done next. The answers are expressed in cash and percentage points. There are direct comparisons over time. Every significant figure can be measured to answer the question, are we doing the right thing for customers?

Remember who the mailing is for

The mailing is supposed to be for the benefit of the person whose name is on the envelope. A mailing might be commercially successful, but ultimately it may detract from what Tesco is trying to do. The experience of *Clubcard Magazine* showed that just because the method of communication was once valuable, it would not always be welcomed by the majority of customers; and just because it may deliver immediate financial returns for advertisers, it may not be helping shoppers, or long term, helping create loyalty. If that's the case, the commercial success is undermining the value of the entire mailing, and hurting the customer relationship.

Review then predict

The statement may have become the UK's most responsive direct mail campaign, but that can't be taken for granted. As a retailer measured against the store performance of its competitors, Tesco needs to sustain its like-for-like sales effectiveness. Through meticulous planning of the statement mailing's contents (localized sales messages, promotional offers and product-specific couponing) Tesco tries to future-proof the Clubcard effect. This planning has to go hand in hand with stock control and store logistics, so that any demand created by the mailing is properly satisfied in the stores. Timing is everything – but the analysis of results from previous campaigns enables Tesco to predict what will occur next with ever-improving accuracy.

Make it fun

The Clubcard quarterly mailing is a seasonal gift from Tesco to customers, a present containing good news and money to spend. The mailing is informative but always with the emphasis on entertainment. Research shows that a Clubcard member values his or her statement mailing because it is personal, genuinely a 'quarterly me'.

8

You are what you eat

- ▶ Five years of work
- ▶ Five problems for the data to solve
- ▶ The loyalty cube
- ▶ Discovering that you are what you eat
- ▶ Baskets become Buckets
- ▶ Buckets become Lifestyles

FIVE YEARS OF WORK

'You intellectually know that a programme like Clubcard has great power,' says Richard Brasher, today the Tesco director in charge of all its non-food business. 'But the difference between knowing that you could do something, and finding out that you can, is five years of work.'

In 1997, Brasher, then Tesco operations marketing director, and his Clubcard team began those five years of work. In two years since rollout Tesco had successfully recruited the majority of its regular customers into Clubcard – around four out of every five pounds spent at Tesco was identifiable to a Clubcard holder. Tesco had refined Clubcard to maintain public interest and customer participation. It continued to create excitement and controversy in the press, and had lifted sales on a tactical basis. Four times a year, the statement mailing recreated the Christmas sales effect, and the redemption of product coupons was at levels that Tesco could barely have dreamt of before Clubcard. To sustain the momentum, and build on it, meant a new strategy. It was time to start serious work on the data.

Already a lot of progress had been made establishing a platform to manage and harvest customer data. Customers were being segmented by life stage and sent offers, messages and magazines based on those segments. The sales potential was becoming clearer, thanks to the basic behavioural categorization work by recency, frequency and value (RFV). Customers could be identified by the store they used, down to the particular departments they did or did not shop in.

FIVE PROBLEMS FOR THE DATA TO SOLVE

By early 1997 though, Tesco's satisfaction at a job well done was giving way to frustration. It knew that as a corporate asset the data promised more than was being delivered. Now that Sainsbury's had finally responded with its Reward card, the pressure was on to maintain the massive lead that Clubcard had achieved for Tesco. The next challenge for Clubcard data lay beyond marketing communications. There were fundamental business decisions that Tesco had to make, that could be made with greater confidence if the data could be made to reveal more of the real customer behaviour behind them. There were five main business problems that Tesco needed to address.

1. Price sensitivity

How could the Clubcard data help Tesco set competitive pricing levels that generated significant impact on sales and improved the perception of competitive pricing among customers, but without damaging the business performance of Tesco?

Tesco aims to match or preferably beat its rival supermarkets on price. About 20 years ago, food purchases represented half of the average household's annual expenditure. Today it represents around a third. Food inflation has, broadly speaking, stopped. Asda (and its parent Wal-Mart) had then and still has the reputation for being the cheapest. Its Asda Price Promise campaign was widely known, and liked, by customers. At Tesco, the Unbeatable Value campaign did not achieve as much impact when it was launched in September 1996, despite a Tesco promise that customers who found one of the 600 Unbeatable Value products cheaper elsewhere would get a refund of twice the difference. (Sainsbury's had reacted with its Autumn Value promotion the following week, but that also struggled against Asda Price Promise.) The danger was setting off a price war that would have serious implications for Tesco's business and indeed the whole food retail sector. The City hated the price wars, the ultimate zero-sum game. When one chain slashed prices of baked beans to a loss-making few pence, the others could simply follow, and so everyone makes a loss, with no one enjoying a competitive advantage. Back in 1993, supermarket chain Gateway had started its Price Check promotion, which was credited with being the first of the 1990s price wars. In the 12 months that followed, in a generally buoyant stock market, the market capitalization of the food sector dropped by 45 per cent.

The Tesco board wanted to win the price battle, but it also wanted to get more impact for the money it invested – in short it wanted to create a more efficient, strategic mechanism for price reduction. Brasher and his team believed that if they could understand which of their millions of customers cared most about discounts, and also which products and commodities they most wanted to see discounted, they could fight the battle as fiercely as any rival but on their own terms, investing in price cuts where the money would work hardest. Then it would be a sustainable customer proposition, not merely a short-term promotion. The answer, Tesco was certain, lay in the Clubcard data.

2. Ranging for customers

How could Clubcard help the commercial teams modify their product ranges to gain maximum appeal to specific groups of customers? The dream was to ensure that the entire product range on sale at each store (up to 45,000 lines) accurately represented, in selection and proportion, what the customers who shopped there wanted to buy. Even now, the range on offer in a particular store is mainly governed by its physical format (square-footage, shape and facilities like access or car parking). Much less attention is given to the preferences of the people who shop there. The customers are generally defined in terms of national or at best regional averages and treated like national averages. Tesco knew that was wrong and wanted to do something about it. It wanted to de-average its offers to customers, and that meant designing its offers more specifically to local requirements. The marketing team also knew that if they could get a clearer picture of the tastes of each store's constituency, they could profitably fill more of the 'holes' in their customers' baskets.

3. Range creation

Could Clubcard data help Tesco lead, rather than respond to, emerging customer tastes? The food team at Tesco wanted to introduce new ranges targeted at the growing number of customers who had specific dietary demands and preferences – gourmets, organic food buyers, food allergy sufferers, dieters or healthy eaters. Tesco own-label products had a significant market share among its shoppers. Tesco had been the first to introduce 'Value' lines, offering basic items at low prices. Now it wanted to develop an equal reputation for a wider range of specialist food – gourmet ready meals for example. But who would buy them, what did they buy now and how big was the opportunity?

4. Promotions

Promotions have been on supermarket shelves since consumer brands emerged in the 1900s. We are all used to seeing '20 per cent off', 'buy one get one free' (known in the trade as BOGOF) and other discounts. Historically, the measure of success for these promotions has been sales. Clubcard might give new insights. Perhaps customers only buy the brand when it is on promotion, or some 'cherry pick' offers across the store. Some might stock up when their favourite brand is promoted. Do some customers not change their behaviour at all?

5. Competitive attack

How could Tesco use Clubcard data not only as a defensive resource protecting and growing its current customer base, but also as an offensive weapon against its supermarket rivals, gaining competitive advantage? By being first, Clubcard told Tesco who its customers were, and also who they weren't, knowledge that brands like Sainsbury's had yet to build. Hence the new challenge to the data specialists was to turn the data outwards to the threats and opportunities posed by competitors.

The segmentation models already devised were too blunt as instruments to contribute to this analysis. To take the next step as a knowledge-rich company, Tesco would have to create a new picture of its customers from the transactional data it was collecting.

The common denominator of these challenges was the need for better-quality knowledge of customers. The data analysts knew they had to create robust new groupings of customers, new ways to identify and predict behaviour, and a new shared language for the Tesco business that could be easily used and understood to describe customers. Segmenting by crude geodemographics, RFV and life stage, and collecting data only at store department level were useful but too bland and unfocused for this work. For example, using those measures, it was virtually impossible to distinguish between the purchasers of competitive brands, or to identify which shoppers were buying on price and which were buying on quality. At this stage Clubcard told Tesco broadly 'who, what, when and how much', but not 'why'. Why did customers make certain decisions, and what did that usefully reveal about the differences that existed between customers?

The first step was to create a useful measure of loyalty. This was developed not just for Tesco but also for a number of dunnhumby clients at the time.

THE LOYALTY CUBE

Imagine that all a company's customers can be placed at some point in a three-dimensional cube, such as the one shown in Figure 8.1. Their location in that cube suggests what sort of actions would be appropriate to earn their lifelong loyalty.

Contribution

The first axis of the cube has to be the customer's profitability today. Some very loyal customers make a very low contribution to company profits. For example, at Tesco, a pensioner who cooks from scratch may be incredibly loyal but unprofitable, as margins on basic staples like milk, bread, flour and sugar are low. A customer who pops in a couple of

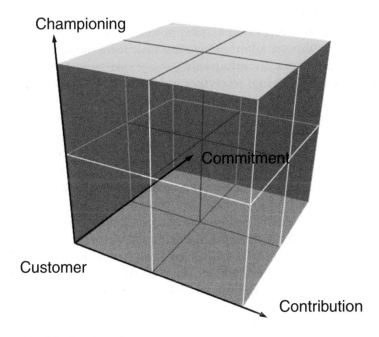

Figure 8.1   The loyalty cube

times a week for a prepared meal at a premium price, plus a good bottle of wine, is much more profitable, but probably less loyal to the brand. Contribution does not, in Tesco's model, reflect loyalty – Terry Leahy's concept of the scheme was to encourage loyalty, not just profitability.

Should more profitable customers be the main focus of a loyalty programme? Not necessarily. They may take more rewards from it. Yet it may not be possible to influence their behaviour a great deal, other than to stop them defecting.

Commitment

The second axis measures future value. This contains two elements: the first is how likely that customer is to remain a customer, because a defecting customer has no financial value in the future. Some customers may defect for perfectly good reasons: for example, a family might move house, and there isn't a local Tesco in the new area.

Other customers who may be about to leave can be saved by a loyalty programme. Perhaps they have not realized what other benefits the company offers. For example, Tesco targets customers who never buy wine – perhaps they have not looked at the range recently, and prefer to go elsewhere on the untried assumption that 'the off-licence is better there'.

It also measures 'headroom'. This is the potential for the customer to be more valuable in future, provided you do everything possible to demonstrate value in that headroom. Customers who are already buying as much as possible from you have little headroom. For example, a customer may simply not have any way to spend more on food at Tesco; Tesco might be already providing nearly all their daily needs. Trying to incentivize more spending on food is wasted effort. For customers with little headroom, new complementary areas become much more important, such as new departments in a store. For example, expanding health and beauty or clothing departments will extend headroom. Developing new businesses such as launching financial services or going online become ways of extending headroom.

Headroom is vital to a mature loyalty scheme like Clubcard. Most people who are going to join Clubcard have already done so, so the effect of the card has to be to change behaviour among existing customers, not to act as a recruiter to the programme. Finding shoppers who don't buy wine, clothing, financial services or use the internet, but who might be amenable to doing so, is extremely important.

Championing

Customers with little headroom can act in a third dimension on the cube: as an ambassador for the brand. This is where the idea that loyalty programme members are 'members of the brand' comes to life. If they see value in a programme, they will recommend it. If they are getting an obvious benefit from it, then that benefit will become an aspiration for their friends and associates.

Championing the brand like this can be as simple as word of mouth. A customer's use as an ambassador can have two peaks: the first is initially, when a programme is launched. This was extremely apparent when Sainsbury's launched its Reward card in the wake of Clubcard. There is a large crossover of shoppers, and there had been a lot of positive media coverage for Clubcard, meaning that Sainsbury's could reach the same recruitment level in much less time. This was before the

day-to-day benefits of the Reward card, which were financially approximately the same as the other cards on the market, were apparent to
customers. Cardholders were overwhelmingly positive about the idea
of loyalty cards – and so flocked to own another one.

The second peak is when those customers act as mentors, in effect
being a trusted advocate of the brand. As we will see, more than half of
Tesco customers who join the Baby Club do so when their mother enrols
them. The daughter may not even be a regular Tesco shopper – yet the
Tesco brand is sold to her as a partner. It brings new people to the brand.
Championing is a way that customers say 'Thank you' to Tesco once
Tesco has said 'Thank you' to them.

The long-term value of a low-value customer may be in recruiting
higher-value customers. Some customers may be low-value
customers, but have great potential as champions. That is the second
peak in championing activity: passing on your long-term opinion.
Older sisters may tell younger brothers. Neighbours who regularly get
money off their holidays pass on the secret. Organic vegetable buyers
who give a successful dinner party may tell their friends where they
bought the ingredients.

DISCOVERING THAT YOU ARE WHAT YOU EAT

Applying the principles

The first order of business in 1997 was for the Clubcard core team –
participants from Tesco, dunnhumby and EHS – to brainstorm the
problems. The conclusion was that the difference between customers
existed in each shopper's trolley: the choices, the brands, the preferences, the priorities and the trade-offs in managing a grocery budget.

The shopping basket could tell a lot about two dimensions of the
loyalty cube. First, it could quantify contribution, simply by looking at
the profit margins on the goods each customer chose. Second, by
assessing the calories in the shopping basket, it could measure the
headroom dimension. Just how much of a customer's food needs does
Tesco provide?

Previously the analysis had segmented customers using RFV and life
stages, or analysed the response rates of individual marketing
programmes and mailings. That did not require that every single item
was collated and analysed. At the beginning Tesco's till technology

simply could not provide the data. In 1997, for the first time, a sample of customer data was polled from every store. This was based on one customer in 10, whose data were processed in detail and became the archetype for the other 90 per cent.

Applying Clubcard data to decisions as critical as a national pricing strategy required a much more meticulous approach. There was no alternative to looking at every item a customer bought – every customer, every basket, every visit. As the 18th century gastronome Jean Anthelme Brillat-Savarin said, 'Tell me what you eat, and I shall tell you what you are.' It's a judgement we all make of others when we are waiting in the supermarket queue. Whether we are thinking, 'I wish I had seen that', 'That looks adventurous', or simply, 'I'm glad I'm not at their house for dinner', we find it easy to construct a life for our fellow shoppers at the checkout, knowing little about them but the contents of one trolley.

At dunnhumby, the analysts believed that this game could become a business discipline.

A mountain of data

One obvious hurdle to overcome is that analysing one trolley is never enough. A busy weekend with relatives visiting, a rare dinner party, a child's birthday, a shopping trip for some special indulgences, can all give a skewed view. A single shopping trip is not a robust guide to the normal life of that household. The analysis had to take into account many shopping trips, regularly tracked.

Second, that mountain of data that would have to be analysed and modelled took Tesco to the limit of its IT capability. By recording every item purchased by 10 million cardholders, on average visiting once a week and buying 40 items, means coping with 1,600 million new items of data a month.

Third, what do the shopping patterns that this analysis revealed actually signify? How could Tesco associate meaning with the customer's decision to purchase particular products, or combinations of brands? Getting this wrong would mean that all the conclusions reached from combining those items would be wrong too.

For early experiments, the analysts used a sample from the 10 per cent. This sample, representing 1 per cent of shopping trips, was already used to quickly estimate general customer response to coupon offers in the statement mailing. Now it was to be used to try and model the customer from the shopping basket.

The first step was to decide how products might describe a customer. Some examples: from the 45,000 items that Tesco sells (in retail parlance, they are known as stock keeping units or SKUs) which ones can we say most appeal to customers making judgements on an 'environmentally friendly' basis? Which choices are most attractive if you are short of cash but looking to get the most nutritional quality? Which win out for customers who shop once a month in bulk? Which items indicate that the shopper is liable to seek out and try new things?

The same product may have very different meanings for different groups of customers, because Tesco customers represent a broad spectrum of wealth. An inexpensive pack of butter might be the main brand of choice for one household trying to stretch a budget, but might only be used for baking and cooking in another home.

These choices and trade-offs lead to more rounded customer profiles, based on statistically valid but also intuitive assumptions. And these assumptions had to be relentlessly tested and coded before the trolleys could 'speak' truthfully. It meant crossing the bridge from knowing 'what', to deducing 'why', because when Tesco knew better the 'why', it could offer new products, ranges or prices to customers in ways that would encourage customers to think 'why not?'

Fourth – but vitally – how could Tesco collect and transmit these data? In 1995 the data team had built a system to work with department-based data (bakery, fresh meat, crisps and confectionery, for example), because at the outset that was all they had. Tesco's IT systems were not built to supply any more detail. They had managed to make this an advantage – less data meant quicker analysis at lower cost. There are 15 departments but there are 45,000 different items in a store. The move to item-based analysis magnified the level of detail by a factor of 3,000 on this measurement alone.

The year's work on the 1 per cent of customers had taught the team a lot. For example, if recording all 45,000 SKUs was initially too big a challenge, why not move to an interim stage and analyse the majority of sales? Out of the 45,000 lines, 8,500 accounted for 90 per cent of sales. Working with that number would inevitably be quicker and easier, and common sense suggested that it could yield almost as much insight as if the other 36,500 lower-sales-contributing lines were also included.

A project team from dunnhumby and Tesco was put together to work on the project. Meanwhile Tesco's IT department was testing a new generation EPOS system at 20 of its stores, capable of automatically giving for the first time full itemized checkout data for every Clubcard holder.

BASKETS BECOME BUCKETS

Redefining the question

The best data analysts are not like most people. They are mathematicians, of course, but they are also creative thinkers. When they look at a seemingly insurmountable problem they are at their happiest. They think: if we can't answer that question, how can we redefine the question so that we can answer it? There is always a solution.

In this case, the redefinition was as much linguistic as numeric. The data experts pondered the problem of analysing a basket, and between them, they invented the 'Bucket'. The Bucket was an unglamorous term for any significant combination of products that appeared from the make-up of a customer's regular shopping baskets. Each Bucket was defined initially by a 'marker', a high-volume product that had a particular attribute. It might typify indulgence, or thrift, or indicate the tendency to buy in bulk.

The analysts then looked at the 1 per cent sample for the other 8,500 items, searching for those items that were bought more often than would be expected in combination with one of the most purchased 'marker' products. Even on 8,500 items, this is a massive analytical task. There are just over 36 million pairs of items to identify and quantify. They did this by picking clusters of products that might be bought for a shared reason, or from shared taste – and this created 80 Buckets.

Tesco was no longer sifting through 45,000 items, or even 8,500, searching for patterns that identified groups of shoppers. Now it was seeking out the mix of each shopper's behaviour using 80 Buckets. Each customer's Bucket score was used as a measure to signify how he or she liked to shop. Buckets were simple and practical. They were still approximations, but far more accurate and defining than the previous segmentation models. And they had a huge advantage: they could be measured without an expensive IT upgrade for every checkout in every Tesco store.

The till walker

Buckets could be identified thanks to another inspired discovery. The analysts realized they could use a new source of data automatically generated by the checkouts – an audit trail, created by Tesco tills, called the 'till walker'. The till walker is a simple list generated by the barcode scanner, designed to eliminate fraud. Working with the IT department they instructed the till walker to also look for the specific products in any of the 80 Buckets, then every time a key item was scanned, it would link that Clubcard member with the appropriate Bucket. The combination of which shoppers bought from which Buckets, and how many items in those Buckets they bought, gave the first insight into their shopping preferences.

The team analysed each customer based on how many items they put into each Bucket. They collected the data in four-week cycles, over 12 weeks in all. Then it was time to make order from the chaos.

The technique they used is called 'cluster analysis'. This is a common statistical method of grouping customers with similar profiles over a number of variables. Putting the data into three dimensions, you can place the score in three Buckets as a point inside a cube. If those three Buckets suggest a type of customer, then we would see similar shopping patterns. We see that pattern as a cluster of points beginning to appear: a bright blob in the graph. But dunnhumby had 80 Buckets. It was effectively looking for clusters in an 80-dimensional space. You can't draw it, but mathematically you can see it. And to Tesco's delight, when it looked at the 12 weeks of data it had processed, the clusters became clear.

How many records?

We have seen how Tesco had avoided the pitfalls of spending millions to build a data warehouse. It was the vogue in large organizations to spend huge amounts of money on new computer systems designed to bring together data from a host of separate systems.

The analysts had one more hurdle to cross. They had successfully applied the clustering techniques to the 1 per cent sample of data. Now it was time to apply the process to all 10 million customers across the 80 measures. Cluster analysis is particularly computer-intensive: it takes billions of calculations to analyse 10 million records.

The work on the 1 per cent suggested computer processing time measured in months for the whole 10 million. At the time, dunnhumby's computer had cost a little over £1.2 million. Software suppliers could not help. Perhaps it was time for a massive upgrade. But the Clubcard team would never be able to justify this type of expenditure, which would fundamentally change the economics of Clubcard. There had to be another way. The cluster analysis process was dissected and another innovative solution found: cluster analysis would come first, on a sample. It would then be reapplied to the full data set. The result was almost as accurate, and took a few days instead of a few months.

Today, using 100 per cent of shopping data for every customer, the team's computer technology still costs a fraction of many competitors' data warehouses, but supports over 100 regular analysis users.

BUCKETS BECOME LIFESTYLES

Different customers, different needs

These clusters could then become the segments Tesco would use, as long as they stood up to the scrutiny of real-life retailers. Did they make any sort of sense? The apocryphal story, a sort of urban myth of data analysis, is about the retailer who looked at some analysis of transactional data and found that a lot of shopping baskets contained both beer and nappies. It makes sense when explained as the normal choices of new fathers shopping for the two essentials in their new lives. The beer-and-nappies correlation is the 'what' (not a very useful insight on its own). The link to fatherhood is the 'why', and an insight a retailer can work with.

Equally, through cluster analysis Tesco had used its Buckets to sort out the 'what'. Now it had to interpret the clusters to divine the 'why'. If there was no logical social reason for the clusters to occur, then the process was useless, too random to inform future decisions. Since human beings seldom behave randomly on a consistent basis, the result would probably also be wrong. To the team's excitement, when they examined the list of products in each cluster, they seemed to make sense. They were distinctive, and they told a story: some clusters bought a lot of high-value, prepared products. Another shopped for ingredients and value foods. Another was obviously buying convenience food for a family.

The team settled on 27 different clusters, which became its first customer segments. This was given the catchy title of 'Tesco Lifestyles'. To test their discovery the data team pulled out the results of old marketing campaigns, analysed on an RFV basis, and reran the data. They saw that by matching the right lifestyle to the right offer, performance would have doubled, trebled and in some cases quadrupled if the selection of customers had been made on the new basis, compared to the results achieved with the original segmentation model.

Lifestyles inside Tesco

The Clubcard team knew that Lifestyles was only the beginning of the process of segmenting Tesco customers. The Lifestyle segments weren't the ultimate model: they could be further refined. But the results suggested that this was a big step forward in the use of transactional data to drive sales. It reinforced Tesco's competitive advantage and for Tesco that was good enough.

For the business, Tesco Lifestyles proved its worth. Coupons targeted by lifestyle in the Clubcard statement mailing doubled the redemption rates achieved in the first mailings. In the short term this would cost Tesco money, as the higher the redemption the higher the sales subsidy from Tesco. But they had proven the power of this method of segmentation.

The insights started to flow in. For example, after the November 1997 statement, Tesco saw a disquieting result from the mailing. 'Loyal Low Spenders' were least likely to redeem their discount coupons, yet 'Can't Stay Aways' and 'Weekly Shoppers', the other most loyal groups, were most likely to use them. What did this tell? Perhaps, Tesco reasoned, the amount a shopper had to spend to be able to use a coupon was too high to be appropriate to the Loyal Low Spenders, with their small but regular shopping trips.

'We have not succeeded in correctly targeting this group and rewarding their loyalty,' Tesco could now admit in its internal analysis – because across the other 'loyal' segments, coupon redemption was as high as 82 per cent. As a group Loyal Low Spenders were a major contributor to Tesco profits, despite their cost-conscious shopping trips. Immediately, Tesco set about improving its offer to this group. Tesco Lifestyles worked because it helped suggest solutions to problems that Tesco previously didn't know it had.

Defining customer segments in this way also gave Tesco the means to personify groups of customers clearly. The descriptive names they gave to the Tesco Lifestyle categories were more than just a shorthand or marketing gimmick. They were coined to make the segments come alive in the minds of Tesco staff at every level, from the board to the checkout. For example, it's hard to put a face to the name 'Young Adults' – one of the original life-stage segments – because the differences between young adults in their spending habits, their tastes, likes and dislikes far outweigh the similarities. Young adults have only one shared characteristic: their age, which tells us little about what they tend to buy.

As a retailer Tesco found it a lot easier to picture the individuals who made up groupings like 'High Spending Superstore Families', and go from there to think of ways to encourage them to consolidate more of their spend at Tesco. It's a grouping that has meaning. You can picture them. It helps managers in the business think about helping real people, with real-life needs.

When Buckets became Lifestyles, Tesco made a change: for the first time, its data analysis could describe groups of customers that staff in the stores could relate to. It had peered into our shopping baskets, and made sense of what it saw.

9

Lifestyles become habits

- ▶ Using all the data
- ▶ The Rolling Ball
- ▶ Shopping Habits
- ▶ Big Brother
- ▶ Segments at work

USING ALL THE DATA

According to Sir Terry Leahy:

> What creates loyalty is how much we understand your life and what we do about it that helps your life. If you wanted to, you could just use data to make customers do what you want them to do, you 're just using it as a tool to sell more things to them. You could approach it that way. We never wanted to do that. Our competitors had all the details of what their customers bought too, but if you don't have the vision as a retailer that you are doing this to understand customers better, and deepen that relationship, you're always going to wonder why you're making the effort.

Buckets had worked: the Tesco Lifestyles segmentation dominated Clubcard marketing until the end of 1998.

If the original data strategy of using 10 per cent of the data was the equivalent of turning the data tap on, segmenting by Lifestyles had turned up the flow considerably. Finally, after a total upgrade of its IT system, Tesco was ready to analyse all the data on every visit by every shopper at every store.

Taking in all that customer data really was like drinking from a fire hose, but because it had waited an extra two years, Tesco now – at least in theory – had the capacity to drink. It was a challenge that would take almost two years and a number of false starts and revisions to master.

The problem with Lifestyles

Lifestyles was not perfect, as Tesco had acknowledged from the start. There was a hole in the idea of Buckets. One weakness was that a few of the product Buckets did not seem to help decide which customers were in which clusters. Intuitively, the combination of products in these Buckets seemed important to the team, but they didn't define clusters clearly. If a product Bucket is going to define you, it should be a significant part of your shop, and not all the 80 Buckets were equally important. Also, two or three Lifestyles looked like regional variations of similar patterns.

Even with 10 million customers to talk to, the size of some of the 27 Lifestyle segments was proving to be too small to address effectively. The danger is that customer segmentation becomes absurd. Tesco could theoretically create 10 million Lifestyle segments of one household each, but there isn't an affordable way to communicate with those customers at that level. Until every home is constantly linked through digital media, that one-to-one dream remains a dream. Also, segments allow management to hold a 'picture' of a customer in their heads. Too many, and there is no picture. Without the picture, as Tim Mason says, 'Who are they running the business for?'

So the trick would be to create new customer groupings that were large enough to be cost-efficient to use, but with a richness of common interest to be truly meaningful as a way to picture customers. If the segmentation could be remodelled to tease out new larger groups, but with equally strong identifying characteristics, then the Clubcard data would work harder. The data boffins had to start again.

People describe products

'Why not turn Lifestyles upside down?' they reasoned. Take each product, and attach to it a series of appropriate attributes, describing what that product implicitly represented to Tesco customers. Then by scoring those attributes for each customer based on their consistent shopping behaviour, and building those scores into an aggregate measurement per individual, a series of clusters should appear that would create entirely new segments. The Buckets suggested many of the key dimensions of what motivated customers to shop in certain ways; for example, there was a 'Snacking and Lunch Box' Bucket.

The team started by eliminating non-foods (the peculiarly inexact term that food retailers use for anything they sell that we cannot eat), because the availability of stock varied widely from store to store. They then set about imagining 50 things that our shopping baskets might say about customers. What does it mean if we buy a lot of ready meals? A lot of fresh produce? No meat? Do we like to try out new products, or exotic ingredients? Are we motivated by price promotions?

Measuring customers on a number of these criteria could start to create distinct profiles. The team believed that such analysis would reveal distinct patterns in shopping, so that it might be possible to identify the busy urban couple who shopped for ready meals but loved to be adventurous and spend a little extra. Or the health-conscious shopper who buys fresh fruit and vegetables, and avoids red meat but sometimes eats chicken. Or indeed any one of the distinct shopping characters we all see in our local supermarket, and think, 'I know who you are'. We often recognize a mirror image of ourselves when we look at someone else's basket.

Tesco felt more comfortable with this approach – but it wasn't going to be easy. The approach the team took involved incorporating two fundamentals of attitudinal research, used for half a century but never before applied to 45,000 items of grocery: for data boffins, Likert and Osgood are heroic figures. Even if the rest of us have never heard of them, we know their work – the Likert scale and Osgood's Semantic Differential Procedures. Not though, generally speaking, two concepts on the lips of every supermarket employee.

Likert and Osgood

Renis Likert's scales, first seen in 1932, are probably familiar to all of us, even if we have never heard the name. Every time we fill in a survey and decide whether we are very satisfied, quite satisfied, quite dissatisfied or very dissatisfied, when we are rating our experiences in a hotel or our appreciation of an in-flight meal, we are using the Likert scale. In this case, the two ends of the scale are satisfaction and dissatisfaction. A scale might also start at zero and go to 10, when we're asked, for example, 'How exciting was the film you just saw?'

In the 1950s, Charles Osgood's Semantic Differential Procedures created a breakthrough in how we are able to measure more abstract or judgemental concepts. What do we mean by 'honesty' or 'optimism'? With a particular politician, how do we evaluate what we call his or her 'principles' with what we would deem 'intransigence'? In a supermarket, what is the essential difference in our minds between 'cheapness' and 'value'?

Osgood created a way to score concepts as a series of Likert scales. In experiments, subjects are given a car, for example, and a variety of adjectives to describe it. They could rate each adjective on a seven-point scale, rating between fast and slow, good and bad, and others. Using the scores for all of these attributes, an Osgood profile becomes a map of the connotations for the product or concept.

So this was the new insight that drove the next stage in Clubcard segmentation: that each product we buy says something about us, and by scoring it in this way, it can build a picture of what attitudes and beliefs drive our behaviour. At least, what drives it while we are in the supermarket. Osgood profiles had another advantage: they produced numerical scores, and numbers can be worked on by using computer analysis. By creating 20 scales on which to judge the attributes of every product in the store, it could then create 20 numerical measures. Turning numbers into insight was becoming a Clubcard speciality.

But what scales to choose? 'Low fat' against 'high fat', 'big carton' against 'small carton', 'needs preparation' against 'ready to eat', and 'low price' against 'high price' are just a few of the two-tailed Likert scales that they ended up choosing. There were also single-tailed measures, such as 'Is it a promotion?' and 'Is it a major brand product?' With 20 scales agreed as a way of grading every product on its shelves, all that the team had to do was to produce the Osgood profiles. That is, 45,000 Osgood profiles, one for every product from anchovies to asparagus, whisky to washing powder. But judging 45,000 products on 20 different scales would mean agreement on 1.2 million individual ratings before the segmentation could be used. That was simply not credible. There had to be a simpler way to make this approach work.

THE ROLLING BALL

What does someone with a degree in physics and a postgraduate degree in marketing do? That was the decision facing Giles Pavey in the early 1990s. He tried market research:

It had marketing which I was interested in, and numbers that I was good at. But what I didn't like was that you would test to see which of two designs people liked best, and you know what the answer will be before you start. It's going to be the more expensive one. The market research would come back, and the people that commissioned it would more or less go with what they had already decided anyway.

He tried retail auditing, where the sales data on particular products are aggregated from a number of retailers, and sold back to the suppliers:

This was a lot better for me, because it was real data. The trouble is, when a sales promotion is running, the sales figures might jump by a factor of three during the promotion. What you don't know is, have you brought a lot of new users to the product, or is it the same lot of people buying three times as much? If we have managed to get people to trade up, will they just trade back down?

That's when Pavey came to work at dunnhumby on the Clubcard team. And as he says, it immediately gave him the best of both worlds. 'It is 100 per cent correct data, you can see what individuals are doing, rather than just a total set of store sales, it is rich data – and it's an insightful way of looking at customer behaviour.'

A million decisions

It's also how he came to be working on the project looking to evolve Tesco Lifestyles. The realization that there were 1.2 million Likert Scales to be completed if the new approach to segmentation was going to work appealed to Pavey's scientific rigour. But the problems posed in trying to create the second generation of Lifestyles seemed too much like a nightmarish slog. That is, unless you are a data analyst, the sort of person who sees an insoluble problem – and redefines it as a problem that can be solved. For Pavey and his fellow analysts, it was the opportunity to do something entirely fresh, the opportunity to do a more rigorous segmentation project than anyone had attempted in the UK before. This was where Pavey's physics met his marketing experience: taking the real world and abstracting it to a set of fundamental laws.

Some of the 1.2 million decisions would be easy to make: it's not hard to decide if a product is 'own label' or not. Others were much harder. No one, as far as we know, had ever tried to distinguish how 'adventurous' every product in a supermarket is. Tinned fish probably isn't; extra virgin olive oil is. Is brie adventurous? How adventurous is it? More than decaffeinated coffee? Less than a red pepper?

They set about devising a way to allocate attributes for every item. The process created was known as the Rolling Ball. To create a Rolling Ball categorization, Pavey and his team started with a small set of products that definitely have the quality you seek: so if you want to find out which products are adventurous, start with extra virgin olive oil and ingredients for Malaysian curries, and see which customers bought those products.

Then look at what else these customers have in their shopping basket. Discard items that show up in everyone's basket (bananas or milk, for example), and keep looking, building bigger and bigger groups of products. When can the process stop? This is where the rolling ball idea came in.

The products that are picked up early will have a high 'adventurous' rating. As the ball gets bigger, those ratings are probably lower, and certainly less reliable. So how to stop the ball? Well, the basic idea was that each of the major attributes were large dips in a huge surface. When the ball starts to roll into an adjacent hole, then the ball should stop. For example, you might start off trying to predict adventurous products, but after 400 or 500 products are coded, you start to find a lot of products that are more 'fresh' than 'adventurous', and so the ball has started to roll down an adjacent hole. The mathematics to solve this problem were challenging, but the method created groups of products that intuitively seem right.

Eventually, the rolling ball process produced an effective grading mechanism for all 20 attributes for every product, based on the contents of 10 million shoppers' baskets and trolleys, checked, amended and approved by a panel of three analysts.

To create these sets of attributes, scored and allocated to each product, took the team three months of hard work. What Tesco had now was the raw material for segmentation that very few retailers in the world were capable of producing. They were now able to use these 20 scores to create clusters of shoppers with shared motivations and preferences.

Testing the segments

This was not the end of the journey. It's possible to segment in ways that ultimately are artificial – segmentations created simply because they represent a statistically elegant and measurable difference between two groups of customers. For example: is someone who buys organic produce when possible, who lives in Wales, going to be different from someone who buys organic produce and lives in Scotland? Just because we can measure where the person lives doesn't necessarily make the difference useful when it comes to profiling them as a potential customer.

The new Tesco Lifestyle segmentation was based entirely around what people did, not who they were. It was a clean break from the past. The new customer segments would be revealed by feeding the customer data that Tesco collected into this new model. Customers would define the segments, not simply slot into them.

The first thing the team found was that creating a robust set of segments would take another six months of data crunching. The Rolling Ball categorization short-circuited the process of giving attributes to all of the products Tesco sold, but it didn't give an instant answer to the ultimate test: sales effectiveness. 'We got something that we believed was 90 per cent there, but whether that 10 per cent would give us problems when we tested the segments we created across the whole business was a concern,' says Pavey. 'That's why we had to go into such fine detail.'

As with the Buckets concept, the Clubcard data team had created a multi-dimensional space in which to spot customer clusters. By looking for similarities in behaviour across all 20 dimensions, they could isolate clusters of data, one by one, and interrogate them. Cluster analysis is partly deterministic: there is a risk that you see only what you are looking for. It was important to ensure that the results both created groups that had an internal logic, a reason to exist, and existed mathematically, not simply in the eye of the seeker.

The first set of clusters, the most obvious, catered for a large number of customers with easy-to-spot characteristics, characteristics that would score very high or low on a few of the 20 attributes. They also had a clear, logical focus that could be described easily. For example, customers might have a tendency to buy the cheapest products in every category – they were in a self-defining sense, 'shoppers on a budget'. Others might consistently demonstrate they have expensive tastes, but no time to cook, so they bought a lot of top-of-the-range prepared food.

But Clubcard provided much more data than that produced by customers' grocery choices. Tesco had other criteria to test the validity of each of the emerging clusters, making sure they were identifying genuine interest groups, not just marketing-led confections bound together with false logic. So when each cluster was isolated it was tested by other factors – for example, how often did they typically shop, and when? What magazines did they read?

Making sense of segments

Each time a cluster became apparent, fewer shoppers remained lost in 20-dimensional space. After six months, 13 well-defined and tested groups had been identified. But the 14th made no sense. 'We weren't happy with a group of people who had fairly traditional taste, and were driven by convenience. They weren't our traditional time-poor, food-rich convenience food buyers,' explains Pavey. 'They bought only mainstream convenience foods. We could not understand who they were.'

The reason they couldn't understand who these customers were is that the cluster contained two groups. If those two groups were measured using different types of data, they might break apart. The team researched who might be in this group and they used the extra data that Clubcard had provided not to show that this cluster had a logic – it didn't – but that it contained two highly similar clusters, both of which had their own logic. The behaviour that distinguished the groups was not the products they bought, but the family types, frequency and time of shopping.

The theory was that two subsets existed inside this cluster. Subset one comprised young people in shared accommodation who didn't know how to cook and didn't really care. Subset two was made up of families with traditional taste who love using their microwaves.

The data came to the rescue. First, the team looked at the time people shopped – and found that the family groups often shopped late at night, suggesting that many were shift-workers. Then they looked at the magazines that the remaining shoppers in the segment liked to buy at Tesco and found a lot of hobby magazines typically bought by young adults, for example computer magazines. On their own, neither of these yardsticks would create a segment, but they helped reinforce the reasoning behind it. To make the segmentation work well, an extra segmentation was born, 'Shopping Habits', which used not just what people bought, but when people shopped.

SHOPPING HABITS

The team had created a series of groups that had a strong internal logic, a size that made them worth addressing, and were defined by the contents of their Tesco shopping baskets. Most importantly for Tesco, those clusters gave them some solid clues about the aspirations of different groups of shoppers. By creating these segments, Tesco could better profile the needs of the majority of its shoppers.

The Shopping Habits approach to analysis created a series of groups almost naturally, rather than the groups generating assumptions of shopping habits. Of course there is no single right answer in this work. If Tesco had started with different criteria for defining shopping behaviour, or if the 20 attributes given to the 20,000 products in the Tesco range had been slightly different, then the segments might well have turned out differently, and many shoppers would have found themselves (unknowingly) categorized in a different way. After all, the Lifestyles approach created a completely different set of groups, which had also worked for the business – just not as efficiently.

Segmenting with confidence

Shopping Habits has proved to be very useful to Tesco. This analysis tool helps the business better understand what different types of customers might want to buy from Tesco that they currently don't, not just what they are currently buying. If it isn't the only answer, then Shopping Habits is certainly the best answer currently available. Any segmentation is artificial, because everyone is different. But 'best' in this context means 'most useful'.

The Shopping Habits categories were developed using a combination of mathematical rigour, creative analysis and old-fashioned retail nous. They created a new way for Tesco to present itself to particular customers that made the brand more relevant to their daily lives. They provided information about what customers want and don't want from Tesco that could be acted on. And they can be used to answer day-to-day questions that the business needs to ask, without resorting to the retailer's medical complaint: 'gut feeling'. If something looks odd in the data, Tesco is now much more confident that it isn't a freak measurement effect, but a significant clue to customer behaviour. 'Previously, if something looked surprisingly interesting,' says Pavey, 'I normally suspected it to be wrong.'

Data trumped gut feel in the launch of the Tesco 'Finest' range. The company introduced it in stores where it thought that it had its most 'upscale' customers. Sales were a disappointment. So Tesco removed the range, and re-merchandized it in shops where Clubcard identified the largest number of customers with a 'Finest' lifestyle, to create the sales impact it wanted.

The potential rewards of getting the analysis right are spectacular. For example, the analysis showed that one segment of regular, loyal shoppers regularly shopped in 12 out of the 16 Tesco store departments. If each of its members could be encouraged to shop in the other four just once in every three-month period, then Tesco calculated that the additional revenue would be worth £1.8 billion. Segmentation works, not through spectacular changes in customer behaviour, but by encouraging fractional changes in the way shoppers shop. Every little does indeed help.

BIG BROTHER

One of the consistent problems with loyalty programmes is that while customers are enthusiastic about participation in the process, when confronted with the volume of data that the company running the scheme has collected, they are less comfortable. One of the effects of data protection legislation is that any of us can request a copy of the information that any company holds on us, at any time. For loyalty data, the information can run to many pages.

For a society that values individual privacy and equates the holding of files of personal data with organizations like the secret police, the risk that a supermarket's loyalty scheme will be seen as a threat, not an advantage, is real. Simon Davies, the founder of pressure group Privacy International, says:

> There are many people who don't consider the downside of loyalty schemes. Loyalty cards work on the face of it, but to get discounts, you have to accept the imposition of a loyalty card, and consent to give up your personal data. That consent is a fraud, it's a bit like slavery to your supermarket.

Any supermarket that tries to 'enslave' its customers, rather than reward them, won't be able to run a scheme in the long term because participation in the scheme will dwindle. For Tesco, the defence against the charge that it is acting like Big Brother is two-pronged. First, it defines clearly what will be done with the data collected – and what will not be done with it. Second, it reinforces the usefulness of data by using them for easily understood benefits.

The Clubcard Customer Charter

In Chapter 2 we looked at the charter as the manifestation of the loyalty 'contract'. Created on the first anniversary of Clubcard's launch, it defines clearly and in plain English what Clubcard does.

It tells customers that Tesco uses the data to send a statement and vouchers to their home. It tells them Tesco will send offers 'on things that may be of interest to you... And of course we want to make sure any coupons you receive are for products you'd actually want.'

It also says what Clubcard does not do: 'Your personal details will not be disclosed to any other company unless it is necessary for the operation of the Clubcard scheme... if at any time you would like your details taken off the database, we will do so immediately.' You can also request that no offers are sent, using a free phone number.

Using its power for good, not evil

Alongside the core work of producing segments that Tesco can use to target offers more effectively, Tesco has also been able to use Clubcard data to create a number of 'social' benefits for shoppers – working against any perception that providing data to Tesco is a one-sided deal.

An example is the work done in targeting price cuts at the customers who needed them most (see the previous chapter). There are more specific examples too:

- The 'Free From' range, developed for allergy sufferers, is bought by a small proportion of customers. Clubcard data tracks who is buying it, how committed those buyers are – and the results make a strong case for continuing to invest in the range.
- Committed organic shoppers sometimes have to buy non-organic, simply because Tesco does not offer an organic alternative for every product in the shop. By looking at customer segments that value organic produce, and seeing which non-organic products they also buy, it has been able to extend the range by prioritizing the organic alternatives that are needed most.
- Tesco has introduced 7,000 local products, by using Clubcard data to see where customers were choosing a locally produced alternative.

SEGMENTS AT WORK

Tesco has made a long, hard journey in its understanding, analysis and use of data, from a basic recency, frequency and value (RFV) model, to life-stage categorization, through Lifestyle to Shopping Habits segments. But it has been a journey that has consistently created value for the business along the way and taught Tesco how to make customer segments helpful and relevant.

A segment has to be identifiable

That's for every customer. Using the data available, you have to be able to allocate a segment to all of your customers. If it doesn't point every customer to one, and only one, segment, then the segmentation isn't working.

A segment must be viable

It has to be large enough to make it economical as a business-generating tool. It might be possible to identify thousands of microsegments using the quality of data that Clubcard collects. Those segments may be elegant constructs, but if they are not genuinely useful, or more accurately, useable, for the business – which means that the customer gets an improved offer and the retailer gets an improved return – then the data experts are simply showing off. A viable segment has quantifiable value – that is, it must be possible to market products and services to that segment that will make it worthwhile. Tesco probably has hundreds of thousands of anglers as customers. But the cost and effort of identifying them would be wasted, because Tesco doesn't sell anything in particular that anglers would want more than non-anglers.

A segment must be distinctive

It has to have characteristics that make it clearly different to other segments, and those characteristics must have meaning when the segments are used for the purpose intended.

One-to-one marketing

It is often considered that the ultimate goal of segmentation is 'one-to-one' marketing. The experience of Tesco Clubcard suggests not. Single-person segments are arguably distinctive, in as much as only one person qualifies to be in each one, but they are definitely not viable – the cost of marketing to them outweighs the benefit. They are also not distinctive within the practical world that Tesco inhabits. We are all individuals, but when it comes to our shopping habits we have a lot more in common with many other customers than we have significant differences.

It's discovering similarity that makes segmentation such a powerful business tool. This is another reason why one-to-one marketing is a false goal: because we inhabit a segment of thousands does not mean that we cannot have a dialogue with Tesco that reflects our particular needs. The Clubcard statement that Tesco shoppers receive each quarter is driven by the segmentation; each is individually tailored to each shopper's needs. It is as close as one-to-one for most practical purposes, but still driven by broad business decisions.

Segmentation is always imperfect, nobody would claim otherwise. It requires approximation, but increasingly intelligent and informed approximation. The skill is in accurately assessing what is technically possible at the time, and using that to create robust segments that yield useable customer insights in days rather than months. Any segmentation strategy in the retail world has to be practical, scaleable and replicable. It has to produce results cheaply enough, quickly enough and flexibly enough to be useful in the existing conditions of the business.

As Terry Leahy says, this is not just a sales tool. Segmentation has deepened the relationship between Tesco and its customers, and puts Clubcard data into the decision-making progress at every stage. 'Most loyalty programmes in the UK failed because the business management assumed that they were something that their marketing people did,' says Peter Wray, managing director of loyalty marketing consultancy pgw, and formerly European Manager for BP's retail customer loyalty programmes. 'Tesco was different.'

10

Launching a bank

- ► Clubcard Plus
- ► Outbanking the banks
- ► The bank of Tesco
- ► Sainsbury's bites back
- ► A new way of banking
- ► The Clubcard effect in a new business

CLUBCARD PLUS

When former Tesco chairman Lord MacLaurin came to write his autobiography, he saved his harshest words of criticism not for the old guard of Tesco management that he successfully ousted in the 1970s, or for the retail competitors that he fought to outwit in the 1980s. He directed some of his most withering remarks at the high street banks:

> For too long, banks had patronised their customers. For too long they had opened their doors at 9.30 and closed them again at 3.00. For too long they had worked a five day week, careless of the fact they were closed at precisely the time when so many people needed them.

By the time Clubcard was rolled out nationwide, MacLaurin had personal experience of this antithesis of good retailing. Since 1986, MacLaurin had been a non-executive director of NatWest, aghast at what he perceived as management's indifference to its customers. If MacLaurin thought that Tesco could do better, Clubcard soon gave him the opportunity to test out that assumption.

Doing the bank's job

Richard Brasher, who in 1996 was running Tesco marketing on a day-to-day basis, says:

> We didn't know an awful lot about banking, but we knew as much about banking as the banks knew about customer service. And we knew a lot more about customer service than they did. We thought we had a chance to be successful at doing part of their job.

While Sainsbury's had been planning the launch in June 1996 of its Reward card, the response to Tesco Clubcard, Tesco had been secretly preparing its own response: a completely new loyalty product. The introduction of Clubcard Plus ('the only card you will ever need at Tesco') beat the Reward card by a week.

The idea for Clubcard Plus came from listening to customers. Since the launch of Clubcard a new view was frequently aired, particularly by those customers who were getting the most benefit out of Clubcard membership. Why couldn't they use their Clubcard not just to earn points, but also to pay for their shopping? Tim Mason, group marketing director, recalls members of the panels asking, 'I can pay with every other card in my wallet, why not yours?'

In the first Clubcard research, Tesco looked at several loyalty schemes in the United States and Europe that set a high entry commitment for customers, on the assumption that the more commitment asked initially, the higher the commitment that customers show to the scheme once they join. We all know the difference between our attitude to a health club that we pay an annual membership subscription for and one that we can pay for as we go. We take the former more seriously than the latter. Inevitably high-commitment customer schemes tend to attract fewer customers, but can be a very successful retail loyalty model.

The Clubcard team was intrigued by the programme run by the ICA supermarket chain in Scandinavia. It ran a members' discount scheme where shoppers were obliged to pay money into an ongoing 'current account' with the store in order to qualify for the discounts they got back. The scheme, like many of the basic mechanics of loyalty marketing, was at least a century old. The precedent for the idea was a variation on the universal 'Christmas Club', inviting shoppers to pay in a small amount every week to get discounted goods at the end of the year. This wasn't the all-embracing concept that Tesco was looking for in its mainstream loyalty programme, but was an interesting idea that intrigued the Clubcard team. It re-emerged when Clubcard's focus shifted to payment cards.

Once again, Tim Mason brought together his Clubcard pioneer team with EHS and dunnhumby to brainstorm all the options. Should it be a Visa or Mastercard? Should it be an option account of the sort offered by Marks & Spencer or Debenhams? Should it offer extended credit, or shorter checkout queues, or double or treble Clubcard points?

They tested combinations of features and benefits on customers, along with creative treatments and propositions. Customer reaction was positive – but there was a problem. The conventional cards were boring. After the success of Tesco Clubcard, the Tesco board wanted to innovate, and to grab the spotlight from Sainsbury's Reward card.

Pre-paid loyalty

The development team took a fresh look at the model set by ICA. Instead of introducing a store card, with a fixed credit limit and charging high interest, why not turn convention on its head with a pre-payment card that let the customers set their own limits and actually paid interest on the balance while the account was in credit? This offered an extra advantage: there would be no problem assessing customers on their credit-worthiness, as they only had access to their own money, so there was no problem with rejecting applicants. There was no APR charge to make Clubcard look stingy. Clubcard Plus would become an interest-paying savings account instead. This looked more like 'Every little helps'.

The Clubcard Plus model agreed by the board was a 'stored value' account. Tesco shoppers who applied were invited to set up a monthly direct debit from their current account to their Clubcard Plus account. The amount deposited was calculated on the average shopping bill. Customers were encouraged to set this on the high side, so that they earned interest while they were in credit. There was a modest overdraft facility built in, but the commercial risk to Tesco of this arrangement was tiny. The benefit to customers, on the other hand, looked very attractive.

They would get more loyalty points, double the normal rate on every purchase made on the new card, and their money would earn interest – 5 per cent gross a year – while it was on deposit. At this rate of interest customers with their money in a building society would potentially earn more by turning over their cash to Tesco than letting it stay where it was.

In return, Tesco believed it would get an increased level of commitment from the most loyal cardholders: they have effectively consolidated their grocery shopping in advance. It was not, at this stage, a deliberate plan to launch a new bank. In reality, the experience of creating Clubcard Plus was the first step on the road to creating Tesco Personal Finance (TPF), the brand's proprietary banking service.

OUTBANKING THE BANKS

A serious commitment

The first problem: launching Tesco Clubcard Plus would be against the law. Under the British legal system, if Tesco wanted to set up a payment card system that involved the equivalent of an interest-paying savings account it couldn't simply act like a bank, it had to be a bank. Or at the very least it had to form a partnership with an organization that had a banking licence.

The next major challenge was on more familiar territory – what should Tesco ask its customers to do, and what should it offer them? Asking customers to commit up to £800 a month was ambitious. It was hard enough, as the UK banks and building societies had discovered, to encourage a regular saver to change his or her choice of financial institution. Customer inertia had arguably kept some banks going, despite showing little or no customer focus – Tesco's worst nightmare would be if its customers simply did not take it seriously as a place to 'invest' their cash, even if that cash was already set aside for their grocery shopping.

Personal financial security was another critical issue that Tesco had to answer. It had to be able to promise customers that Clubcard Plus would be as secure, or more secure, than traditional payment cards, as card fraud quickly gravitates to any device seen as a 'weak link' in any payment system (for example, the explosion of credit card fraud on the internet during the dot-com boom). In addition, once it had resolved these simple issues, the Tesco marketers had to recreate the energy around the Clubcard launch just 16 months before.

Not surprisingly, with Lord MacLaurin's non-executive directorship at the bank, NatWest was Tesco's first choice as its banking partner to create Clubcard Plus.

A whole new ball game

Clubcard Plus was a radical concept, but this was a time of growing radicalism in financial services thinking. In 1996, the industry was experimenting with a number of 'stored value' bank cards – also known rather glamorously as 'electronic purses' – that were predicted to replace loose change for most of our day-to-day transactions. The most famous was called Mondex, created by NatWest and the Midland Bank, with the backing of 17 other banks across the world. Mondex was being trialled in a number of small shops in Swindon, with 13,000 residents using the card. Cardholders would charge it with money from their bank accounts using the local bank ATM, and then use that 'stored value' to pay for anything from as modest a purchase as a newspaper to as significant as a new car.

Visa was experimenting with its own 'Visa Cash' initiative, which worked in a similar way. The summer of 1996 saw 12 major trials of Visa Cash, most importantly at the Olympic games in Atlanta, where visitors used the cards 200,000 times, making £670 million of purchases. Elsewhere, smaller local initiatives were being used as methods for paying for parking or road tolls. There was even speculation that BT would apply for a banking licence so that its phone cards, at that time available in every corner shop, could be used as a form of currency – for example, they could have been used to pay at automated dispensing or ticket machines. So Clubcard Plus, which may seem an eccentric product today, was then part of what was thought to be the innovative next wave of non-cash payment products.

Tesco didn't foresee at the time of developing Clubcard Plus that the UK would experience an explosion in people's use of debit cards – using their bank cards for cheque-less payments that were automatically debited from their current account. By 1997, debit card use had outstripped credit card use: 1.5 billion debit card transactions compared with 1.1 billion credit card transactions took place that year. But by 2001 that trend had become even more exaggerated with 2.7 billion debit card transactions made, compared with only 1.5 million credit card transactions. For the first time, the British were more likely to pay with a debit card than a cheque. The effect of this revolution in debit card usage proved fatal for the electronic purse concept. Today nine out of 10 adults carry a debit card: and that has effectively swallowed the market for a general bank-issued 'stored value' card like Mondex. It would even create an insurmountable barrier to the growth of Clubcard Plus.

Clubcard Plus eventually proved to be one of a kind – a stored value card successfully launched nationwide. But in 1996 it looked likely to be the first of a new wave of retail loyalty models. A feature on the BBC's 'Pound for Pound' programme explained at the time how it made shopping more convenient. Its message to consumers was that Clubcard Plus was the beginning of 'a whole new ball game'.

Clubcard Plus's advantage

Clubcard Plus had a huge advantage over conventional savings accounts. Because it was designed primarily to support store sales performance rather than become a stand-alone profit centre, it could offer a much more generous package of benefits to customers than a bank could. Tesco could reinforce and grow trade from some of its most valuable and committed customers. This meant increasing their spend as they consolidated their shopping in more departments at Tesco. Clubcard Plus also gave Tesco the opportunity to attract new customers or grow occasional purchasers who might be attracted to save with Tesco by the best market interest rate, while double loyalty points would encourage them to become regular Tesco store shoppers.

To entice customers to this radical new loyalty card concept the terms for Clubcard Plus were generous. The minimum qualifying spend to earn double the normal rate of Clubcard points was set at £5, not £10. There was no joining fee. Even though the credit-risk to Tesco was negligible, it decided to be selective in who was invited to take out Clubcard Plus. One million customers from the 8 million households then on the database were mailed, chosen by credit scoring and their keenness to take up Tesco offers. This was the first time that Tesco might be in the position of having to refuse customers access to a product, so it was careful to target affluent credit-worthy customers to minimize the number of rejections. The overdraft facility that cardholders were offered was equivalent to one month's direct debit payment, with the interest rate they would pay fixed at 9 per cent (again, deliberately pitched lower than bank interest rates). This low interest facility was guaranteed until the end of the year. Cardholders would also have instant access to the funds they had deposited into their Clubcard Plus account from NatWest Servicetills.

Lessons learnt from the launch of the basic Clubcard were also applied to Clubcard Plus. Staff were told early, and encouraged to 'sell' the card. This time, Clubcard Plus was launched first to Tesco employees, two weeks before the public launch. Those two weeks meant that Tesco staff would find out how to use the card, so they could pass on the information to shoppers when it launched nationally. They also had the opportunity to experience processing transactions so that any systems glitches would be highlighted with minimum risk of embarrassment to Tesco.

An instant hit

Among the first wave of Tesco customers invited to trade up to Clubcard Plus, it was an instant success. By August 1996, 60,000 had signed up. Card usage was encouraging too, rising to 57,000 transactions per week (so on average, every cardholder was shopping every week, well beyond the average). The value of deposits on Clubcard Plus accounts amounted to a rolling total of around £10 million, or about £170 in credit per cardholder. And the way that Clubcard Plus cardholders behaved at Tesco was extraordinary – on average they were increasing their spend at Tesco by £4 a week.

Clubcard Plus worked. Tesco had shown that it could extend its ambitions and launch and administer a payment variant of its loyalty card. It had also proved that the Tesco brand was elastic enough to appeal to customers in a very different sector, indeed it seemed that Tesco was potentially more appealing as a financial services provider than the bank brands that had been in business for decades.

Newspaper money pages were soon encouraging their readers to use Clubcard Plus as a category-leading instant access savings account, to hoover up interest that was typically 20 times better than they were getting at their building society or high street bank. 'It is worth a look even if you mostly shop elsewhere!' urged the women's lifestyle magazine *Best*, helping to recruit affluent non-Tesco shoppers to the Tesco brand.

In August 1996, just two months after the launch of Clubcard Plus, retail consultancy Hyperion was already speculating that Tesco Clubcard was becoming a better indicator of customers' credit status than conventional means. As its chief executive David Birch told *The*

Grocer, 'Proof that someone is a regular big spender at particular stores may prove more valuable than traditional credit searches.'

Tesco certainly had growing confidence in its ability to carve a slice from the UK financial services market. It set an ambitious goal: to sign up 600,000 Clubcard Plus accounts by the end of 1997 – about one in 10 of the active Clubcard households at that point. Tesco even appointed its first director of financial services, a concept that only a few years before would have sounded absurd. It was now thinking beyond Clubcard Plus to the next wave of financial services products.

THE BANK OF TESCO

A short-lived triumph

In 1997 Clubcard Plus reached its 600,000-membership target. The Evans Hunt Scott direct marketing campaign was a success: it was that year's Marketing Society 'Product of the Year'. It had sustained the momentum of the larger Clubcard project by demonstrating further innovation and ambition while competitors were still struggling to make conventional loyalty schemes work. It had proved that Tesco was a credible brand in financial services. In many ways it was a resounding success. But it was a short-lived triumph.

Tesco management quickly came to realize that despite impressive first year gains, Clubcard Plus could never be big enough to fend off the banks' debit cards, and could never reach a scale that would justify the systems and processing costs that a one-of-a-kind payment product creates. Ultimately all stored value cards were made redundant by the growth of debit cards, which are today routinely used for cashless transactions, even for small sums. Shoppers were already carrying a bank ATM card, so using that card to pay for groceries was convenient and easy to understand for them. Clubcard Plus was not designed to be used outside Tesco, and the method of replenishing it by direct debit from an existing bank account meant that it did not have the flexibility of a debit card. Today, you can't apply for a Clubcard Plus – just as you can't use a Mondex card in Swindon, or find a Visa Cash card in every purse and wallet. Unlike Mondex and Visa Cash, however, thousands of Tesco Clubcard Plus shoppers still use their cards every week.

Nonetheless Clubcard Plus was enough of a success that the Tesco board was determined to continue its push into financial services. It also realized that to expand into financial services further, Tesco needed two things: a banking partner it believed could create a successful long-term joint venture, and a portfolio of financial services products that would appeal to Tesco customers and that would ultimately be profitable in their own right. Clubcard Plus no longer fulfilled that role, and neither did NatWest.

NatWest out, RBS in

As Lord MacLaurin recalls:

> It was the success of the [Clubcard Plus] scheme that encouraged Tesco to look more closely at the whole complex issue of financial services... We approached NatWest to see if it might be interested in an extension of the original scheme. The meeting was held at [NatWest headquarters at] Lothbury, and I took a team to meet [NatWest chairman] Bob Alexander and his people to talk through the whole idea. Our pitch was quite simple... I for one thought it was an offer they couldn't refuse. But I was wrong.

NatWest declined to get involved. One sticking point, as suspected by MacLaurin, was what he called a 'lingering prejudice against trade' – that while Clubcard Plus was an interesting promotional gimmick, there was no belief that mere grocers knew how to administer financial services, and that NatWest's reputation would suffer by association. The underlying problem, however, might have had more to do with fear. If the nation's most successful retailer, with its trusted brand and access to millions of customers every week, could make a success of its bank, the prospects for a high street banking giant like NatWest looked gloomy. They would be competing for the same groups of customers, but these were customers that, through Clubcard, Tesco knew a lot about, while NatWest, with its process-centric approach, knew next to nothing about them. Either way, NatWest saw Tesco's push into financial services as a lose-lose situation.

So Tesco had to look for a new partner, and it found one in the Royal Bank of Scotland. It was an ideal fit. The RBS had a long track record of innovation (in 1728 it had offered the first ever overdraft, and other firsts included the first hire purchase scheme and the first bank savings stamp) and its management team was widely regarded as bold, open and approachable. It was experienced in successful joint ventures and opening new markets, having 10 years previously bought in to Direct

Line Insurance. It also at that time had fewer current account holders than the big names in UK retail banking, with less than 3 per cent market share in England or Wales, where Tesco was most dominant. So it did not fear that a successful banking offer from Tesco would cannibalize its own business – which was principally focused north of the border and accounted for 40 per cent of the retail banking market in Scotland.

For instinctive retailers like Tesco, which had built its business on 'getting it right for the customer', RBS offered more important, if less tangible assets. Unlike most of the other UK retail banks, RBS had a 'try anything' culture that mirrored Tesco's approach to opportunity. The hectic pace of innovation that Tesco had set with Clubcard did not seem to frighten the team at RBS. In the United States, RBS was experienced at providing joint venture banking with supermarkets through its subsidiary Citizens Bank, a company it had acquired in 1988, and which had been transformed from a fusty 160-year-old institution to a modern, diversified financial services provider. A surprised *Daily Telegraph* reporter conveyed the shocking truth about Citizens Bank's in-store activities at the time: 'Staff adopt a more casual dress code and regularly capitalize on the supermarket theme, distributing related freebies. They have been known even to dress up as supermarket produce to advertise their presence.' Not, perhaps, the image that NatWest sought.

One thing was certain: RBS harboured no prejudice against trade.

A joint venture

On 13 February 1997, almost exactly two years after it launched Clubcard, Tesco announced that it was going to create a joint venture with RBS, with each party owning half of what was to be called Tesco Personal Finance (TPF). NatWest put a brave face on it. 'Our involvement with Tesco on Clubcard Plus has been entirely complementary to our plans,' said Tim Jones, the bank's managing director of retail banking services, 'but its move to provide a broad range of financial products does not fit with our strategy.'

NatWest was less prepared perhaps for the news from Tesco that the 'entirely complementary' part of the project was almost over too. Because Tesco could not keep two banking partners, NatWest was to lose the Clubcard Plus contract in May, only 11 months after the company signed it.

This was not the end for Clubcard Plus – but it was the end of its growth. Clubcard Plus would not form part of the core strategy for TPF.

It was a hybrid financial product, with a split purpose: store loyalty and payment choice. It had uncertain long-term profitability and while popular did not have the mass appeal of conventional financial services products. As Mason puts it:

> With the benefit of hindsight, we might have been better even at that stage to have launched a credit card rather than an innovative shopping product, which is popular with people who hold it but is individual and different. It's a struggle to get a lot of people to hold a card like that, because they think, 'I've lived all this time and never needed one, so why do I need it now?'

The partners agreed to maintain the current Clubcard Plus membership base, but processing and member support would be hard to integrate into the RBS call centres and support structure onto which Tesco was piggybacking. So when the Clubcard Plus account changed hands, applications were closed. Tesco has, however, stayed loyal to its existing cardholders. Seven years later, there are still 150,000 Clubcard Plus users earning double loyalty points for their purchases, almost all of whom can be counted among the most loyal Tesco shoppers. (One of the most committed Clubcard Plus fans today is Mason himself, who always shops using it.)

The lasting benefit of Clubcard Plus, however, extended beyond the 600,000 Tesco customers who joined, to over 1 million customers who now use Tesco to look after part of their financial needs. It was the major first step that Tesco made towards becoming a retail bank in the UK, paving the way to creating TPF.

It revealed just how Tesco was respected as a brand and that Tesco had irreversibly left behind its 'pile 'em high, sell 'em cheap' retail past. It was no longer just 'trade'.

SAINSBURY'S BITES BACK

Losing first-mover advantage

Tesco developed its financial services strategy from Clubcard. Sainsbury's took a different route and took a lead with the launch of Sainsbury's Bank in February 1997. It had barely begun building its customer data warehouse from the transactions recorded on the Reward card, launched in November 1996, when it announced that it would offer financial services in a joint initiative with the Bank of Scotland, a partner selected using similar logic to the Tesco deal with RBS.

Sainsbury's had been looking at financial services as early as June 1996, when deputy chief executive Dino Adriano had told analysts that the company would also be launching a payment card and 'certain financial services'. Indeed, both Sainsbury's and Tesco seemed to have looked once more to the Co-op chain for inspiration. The Co-op had long been running in-store 'Handy Banks' for its customers, who were accustomed to seeing the Co-op as a safe home for their money.

Sainsbury's Bank was conceived and designed as a telephone bank, in contrast to the original Tesco concept that offered banking support staff available in every major store. Sainsbury's wanted a rapid launch and none of the structural hassles – and expense – that would result from housing banking staff in a space-constrained supermarket. Lower overheads, it reasoned, would enable it to offer more competitive rates to customers, balancing out any perceived lack of service.

It was given extra impetus to announce the new launch by a profits warning in early 1997. In mid-February, only one week after Tesco and RBS had announced their partnership, Sainsbury's Bank went live, promoted in 244 stores, with a bold prediction from the company that it would recover 60 per cent of the predicted £20 million profits shortfall with this new venture.

Sainsbury's Bank started by offering two Visa card variants, which offered interest rates of between 14.7 per cent and 18.5 per cent – lower than the rates offered by high street banks, but well above the new generation of 'discount' credit cards from issuers like MBNA and Capital One. Its unique selling point was the offer of double Reward points on every transaction in Sainsbury's and anywhere else in the world. Customers who switched their credit card debts to their Visa cards were also offered Reward points as an incentive. Two savings accounts followed, offering different returns based on the minimum investment. It promised competitive personal loans, mortgages, and home and motor insurance.

If anyone at Tesco privately doubted that customers would accept financial services from their local supermarket, they had only to look to their rival for reassurance. In the first two months after launch, 10,000 customers a week started accounts with Sainsbury's bank. By the end of April 1997, the bank had 100,000 account holders and £100 million in deposits.

Clubcard to the rescue

This time Tesco hadn't got there ahead of the market. Sainsbury's had grabbed the first-mover advantage. But Tesco still had its Clubcard customer data. To give TPF every chance of success, the transactional data recorded by Clubcard would be invaluable. Until now Tesco had used the insights and focus that Clubcard produced to defend itself from competitors, to increase shopping frequency and to stretch into marketing new grocery lines and some non-food products, or to increase usage of its petrol stations. This was interesting and new but safe, store-based. Using this new relationship with customers to market an entirely new brand in a completely different sector would test whether Clubcard was truly building a customer relationship with Tesco. Would customers thank Tesco for the invitation to get more value, or object to their grocer's presumption?

There was also the uncomfortable matter of what Tesco was legally allowed to use its customer data for. As TPF was a joint venture with another corporate entity altogether, RBS, it was effectively a different company. There are well-defined restrictions on how Tesco could use its own customer data to support its own bank. If it stepped over those limits, Tesco would not only be breaking its contract with its customers, it could be breaking the law.

Protecting privacy

Chronologically speaking, the Data Protection Act of 1984 wasn't written that long ago, but in business terms it legislated for a different era. The authors had not envisaged a time when millions of customers would freely engage in a membership programme that involved allowing their supermarket to analyse their purchases from tens of thousands of options. It also didn't take into account the emergence of brands that had the strength to burst out of their original sector and launch things like credit cards. By 1997 it was clear that car manufacturers would sell holiday loans, phone companies would offer mail order and supermarkets would even offer personal banking.

'Tesco's banking operations are already running into trouble,' warned *The Grocer* in the summer of 1997. Around 20 Tesco Clubcard users had objected to the Data Protection Registrar (today renamed the Information Commissioner) after receiving their latest Tesco Clubcard statement mailing. The July mailing included an insert giving details of the forthcoming launch of the TPF credit card. The question that the Registrar had to decide was: was this an abuse of personal data?

The foundation of the 1984 Data Protection Act, subsequently strengthened in 1998 to align with more rigorous European legislation, is that customer data can only be used for the purpose under which they are collected. For example, if a retailer collects data in order to offer rewards to its customers, it could not sell or give those data to a telephone company or a government agency without the customer's permission, no matter how good the offer from the third party was, or what social benefit the third party claimed it wished to produce. Beyond the EU, and in the United States particularly, there is a much more liberal interpretation of data protection based more on self-regulation.

Under the 1984 Act, companies approached the Data Protection Registrar, declared their intentions, and volunteered to abide by the law. Under the 1998 Act, this was strengthened massively: companies are subject to the law, whether they know they are breaking it or not, and can be fined heavily for disregarding it.

One of the more amusing consequences of the Act was that when the UK Ministry of Agriculture, Fisheries and Foods announced that the supermarket multiples were keen to work closely with it in January 1999 to monitor customer purchases of genetically modified food, all the major supermarkets denied this was true – because even if they had wanted to share their loyalty card data with the government, they would have been breaking the law in doing so.

A clear policy

Tesco was aware of its duties under the Act and internally had a firm policy of always interpreting it in favour of the customers' right to privacy. It reasoned that the integrity of its brand must never be undermined by bad practice. So from early 1995, the company had made it clear it would not disclose customer information to third parties without express permission from each individual Clubcard member. Tesco has always been well within its rights to disclose averaged, non-personalized data – for example the proportion of its customers preferring one brand of toothpaste to another, or which products are unpopular among shoppers on a budget or pensioners in the South of England. But these are accurate market insights based on aggregate information, not individual insights based on personal data.

The policy on using Clubcard data to mail Tesco customers was very clear: only Tesco-sponsored communication would be sent. The packs might include offers from manufacturers and supplier brands, but the communication's provenance would always be Tesco. 'We will not send junk mail,' said the Clubcard Customer Charter, launched the same day as Clubcard Plus:

> Every quarter we will send updates of the number of Clubcard points collected, together with Clubcard coupons and a Clubcard magazine, as we currently do for all Clubcard customers... We are registered under the Data Protection Act and will comply with it fully. We do not pass on our customer names and addresses to any other company, save in connection with the management and administration of the Clubcard Plus account.

Under the terms of the Data Protection Act, Tesco could justifiably send mail to selected customers to advertise its new range of financial services products. The risk was to brand perception, and not legal compliance. Would the good image of Tesco elevate customers' perceptions of financial services, or would the relatively poor image of financial services detract from customers' perceptions of Tesco?

In reality, Tesco was not 'running into trouble' – it had not broken any laws. But by sending a mailing to its customers entitled 'Changes to how we use your Clubcard information' Tesco had alarmed some of them. As was its habit, the Data Protection Registrar asked Tesco to meet it in the second week of August 1997 to explain its intentions. Tesco afterwards reassured the press that they had 'resolved their differences'. Clubcard mailings carried TPF marketing, as did the Clubcard magazines. But individual data did not – and still do not – flow from Tesco Clubcard to TPF's marketers.

A NEW WAY OF BANKING

Five months after Sainsbury's bank debuted so successfully in the UK supermarket sector, it was joined by TPF. Tesco and RBS each committed £25 million to the new venture, with the promise to 'create a new way of banking'. On 23 July 1997, Tesco launched its Visa credit card (offering an APR of 16.9 per cent interest, with an introductory rate of 12.9 per cent for six months). Travel insurance and loans were to follow, with a high-interest-paying savings account designed to appeal to current

Clubcard Plus members as well as the broader saving public. By the end of the month, TPF promised to open customer service centres in every large branch.

Points for savers

Once again Clubcard provided one of the key differentiators for the new range. It wasn't just the comparatively attractive (for the time) interest rate that accelerated growth for the new Tesco Visa card offer: TPF was also offering Clubcard points, one for every £2 spent on any purchases on the card anywhere in the world. The pulling power of the Clubcard currency was proven once again, but created some strange anomalies.

A Tesco Visa card customer who spent £100 a week at Asda would earn 50 per cent of the Clubcard points that a cash customer spending the same amount at Tesco would! Of course, the majority of customers who took up the new credit card realized that if they shopped at Tesco, and paid by Tesco Visa card, they would get 50 per cent extra back – earning points from their credit card balance, and points for the value of the shopping.

In the ongoing publicity war between the major supermarkets it was inevitable that Sainsbury's chose the day before the launch of TPF to offer its first mortgage to the public, achieving another first in the sector. By autumn 1997 Tesco, Sainsbury's and Safeway had fully functioning loyalty card schemes with the majority of each brands' customers participating. In addition all three now offered a range of financial services products to tie-in customers even closer to the brands. It was clear that the major losers would be high street banks and building societies, which had long neglected to improve the value they were offering their customers. Supermarket banking in general was looking a very attractive alternative to hundreds of thousands of people.

There was evidence that despite the first-mover success of Sainsbury's Bank, it had not attracted away too many of Tesco's potential financial services customers. On 22 September, Tesco launched its savings account, offering a best-in-class 6.5 per cent interest. In just four weeks 150,000 Tesco shoppers had invested as much as £5,000 each in this account. Ironically for the established financial services players, it was the billions of pounds that had been gifted to shoppers in windfalls as their building societies demutualized that helped boost the take-up of the new offerings from the supermarket brands. These windfall payments were looking for new homes, savings accounts paying high interest rates – and supermarket banks offered the leading interest rates in the country, as analysts warned that demutualized banks would offer less attractive rates in future.

In the first weeks, every newspaper personal finance column was recommending one or more of the supermarket savings products. The new accounts were designed to operate on retail rather than traditional banking margins. Terry Leahy, who had ascended to the job of chief executive just before TPF was launched in February, emphasized that the new bank was more about making customers happy and the business energized than maximizing profit margins:

> We hope that it will develop the offer to the customer, by setting new standards in terms of convenience, simplicity and value, and out of those things will generate some good demand and [we will] make some money out of it in the long haul. Everybody at Tesco is more excited about the next few years than at any time in their career here.

Too many customers

TPF benefited from another massive structural advantage thanks to its supermarket parent: it could be promoted for free in the most cost-efficient mass medium of them all, the aisles of the store. Leaflets were offered at the checkout to apply. It was soon very clear that Tesco could acquire new credit card or loans customers through the in-store channel at a fraction of the cost of conventional recruitment media like the national press or standard direct mail. The conditions for growing TPF looked favourable, but it was not all good news.

When it came to the launch of the new Tesco savings account, customer demand swiftly outstripped TPF's capacity to respond. Within the first few weeks, 150,000 Tesco shoppers had applied and sent in their investment cheques, but the new joint venture bank simply could not process the cash influx in time. By late October, the then TPF chief executive Derek Sach had to apologize to the market and promise investors that their interest would be backdated, as shoppers were forced to wait several weeks for their savings accounts to be opened.

The scale of demand for a Tesco initiative had exceeded all expectations – but this time there was a serious shortfall in customer service that could have caused long-term problems for the brand, had it not acted quickly.

Today, TPF is the largest issuer of Clubcard points outside the grocery business. It still offers one point for every £2 on its credit card. By combining the strengths of joint venture partnership with competitive products, and cost-effective in-store recruitment with smart customer service, and adding in the value of Clubcard points, TPF is now an established bank and a successful business. In the financial year ending in 2005, it could announce that 1.7 million customers carried a Tesco credit card, that 1.4 million motorists trusted Tesco car insurance and that 300,000 customers have bought instant breakdown insurance at a Tesco supermarket till.

TPF backs the concept of 'Every little helps' – it doesn't issue a credit card without making an affordability check, for example, to minimize credit problems.

It has also more than realized Leahy's ambition to 'make money eventually'. In the year to 2005, TPF made profits of £202 million, of which £101 million went to Tesco.

THE CLUBCARD EFFECT IN A NEW BUSINESS

Ultimately, NatWest could be forgiven for being wary of the combination of Tesco, Clubcard and banking. 'We advertise less, but we have other ways of telling people we are there for them,' says Tesco's Tim Mason. 'We recruit financial services customers using our physical assets, brand recognition and loyalty. It costs us one-fifth the cost to any conventional financial services company.'

Clubcard has contributed significantly to the birth, growth and enduring success of TPF. Through the evolution of Clubcard Plus it demonstrated the customer demand, brand credibility and management capability for Tesco to offer financial services products. Through the intelligent application of transactional data, Clubcard enabled Tesco to target the right financial services products to the right customers at the right time. Through the quarterly statement mailing Clubcard provided TPF with one of the most cost-efficient recruitment media known in the retail finance business. And through the use of Clubcard points as an integral benefit of TPF products, Clubcard provided a widely valued currency that gave TPF a clear competitive edge.

The brand loyalty of a customer who shops at Tesco stores, using a Tesco credit card to pay at the checkout, before driving a Tesco-insured car back to a Tesco-insured home is multiplied. Those customers frequently receive Tesco vouchers worth £50 or more in the quarterly statement mailing. By stretching the Tesco brand to a completely different business, the loyalty contract between company and customer becomes more beneficial to both sides.

After being rejected by NatWest, Lord MacLaurin speculated that 'Maybe one of these days you will find Tesco bidding for the National Westminster Bank.' It didn't have to. In March 2000 NatWest was bought by the Royal Bank of Scotland, Tesco's banking partner.

11

Babies, beauty and wine

- ▶ Strengthening the bond
- ▶ The inner circle
- ▶ Baby Club
- ▶ Clubcard pizza
- ▶ What Tesco learnt about 'sub-clubs'

STRENGTHENING THE BOND

When some of its shoppers spend more than others, Tesco could look at it two ways. It could congratulate itself on the valuable customers, or it could try and find out what was causing the lower-spending group not to spend more. An early example of how Tesco took the approach that its glass was half empty opened up a new way of looking at one significant group of customers – and ultimately led to a significant change in the way Tesco communicated to them.

A hole in the basket

In 1996, when the Tesco Clubcard team was looking into the shopping habits of young families with babies, it discovered a useful potential source of revenue: families with young children who shopped for childcare products among their health and beauty spend at Tesco spent appreciably more at the store than 'look-alike' families who didn't. So a family with infant children and with a similar shopping basket in every other respect, but who never considered Tesco the place to buy things for their baby, was significantly less valuable to Tesco than a family who was happy to do their baby's shopping at their supermarket.

On one hand, this was good news: Clubcard had helped Tesco identify a group of shoppers who were consolidating their health and beauty shopping – not traditionally a supermarket speciality – into a Tesco shopping trip. On the other hand, this was worrying news. Why, Tesco asked, would many new parents, perhaps the UK's busiest super-market shoppers, choose not to buy their baby products at Tesco, when the stores carried the full range of products and brands they wanted to buy? With the mother and baby market worth £2 billion a year in the UK, Tesco was missing a sizeable sales opportunity.

Twenty per cent more

Overwhelmingly, the families who chose not to buy their baby products at Tesco preferred instead to do it at the UK's largest chain of pharmacists – Boots the Chemist. And this was despite the fact that Boots was often 20 per cent more expensive for key products compared to the Tesco equivalent. These visits to Boots had an effect on Tesco more significant than the lost sales on baby essentials. A mother who shopped for one or two baby items at her local Boots would often as not fill her shopping basket with general products, such as shampoo or razor blades, which had nothing to do with her baby's needs. Boots had for several years been broadening its range, transforming from a traditional chemist to a retailer of all health and beauty products, and in the process had cut a bigger slice of the household budget.

What drove normally cost-conscious Tesco shopping families to go to another retailer to pay higher prices than they needed to? It hardly made sense. In every other category, where a multiple retailer like Tesco offered customers a 20 per cent price advantage – or anything like it –

the purchasing trend would swerve significantly towards the supermarket and away from the higher-price high street specialist. The clearest example is the decline in market share suffered by independent grocers and off-licences, generally attributed to the big price differential between the smaller format shop and the out-of-town superstore.

A rational bond

Missing out on its proportionate share of a £2 billion market was one problem. But it was a symptom of something else. In asking customers 'Why?' Tesco discovered something about its relationship with them. The strong bond that the Tesco brand had always had with loyal customers, a bond reinforced by Clubcard and further demonstrated by the success of Tesco Personal Finance (TPF), was very rational. The emotional bond was much weaker.

When asked about their attitudes to shopping for newborn babies, the members of the regular customer panels told Tesco that their views of retail brands changed. Bringing up a baby brought out different priorities and preferences, especially when the baby was the firstborn. These young family shoppers were delighted to define their relationship with Tesco around their grocery needs, and they were confident in developing that relationship to include wines, books, socks, videos, even microwave ovens. They were even happy to consider widening Tesco's relevance to their lives in terms of good-value financial services.

But trusting Tesco to offer the best for a newborn baby? For many that was a much bigger step. The authority of the Boots brand in this area of need was based on its history, its expertise and its cornerstone status on Britain's high streets. Boots was unwilling to discount, not only because it did not have the business size to compete on price, but also because it knew it had the pedigree that allowed it to command a premium price, to say, 'There are some things money cannot buy.'

Of course, the mother-and-baby market was not simply a two-way fight between Tesco and Boots. There were discounters both in the supermarket business (Asda) and the high street pharmacy business (Superdrug) that could compete fiercely on price in the health and beauty market. Safeway had long been focusing its customer acquisition strategy on young families, offering them baby-changing facilities for example, and skewing its promotions to attract them. In the late 1990s Sainsbury's was also driving hard into a category that offered a large potential market with high-spending customers, and saw the chance to develop new businesses – most importantly, pharmacy – that customers valued and needed, and that would secure higher margins than groceries.

Tesco the chemist

Tesco was determined to assert itself. How could it appeal to customers who were unconvinced by its relevance in this area, and emotionally predisposed to the authority of Boots? Clubcard had helped define the challenge, but Clubcard alone could not do the job. This was not simply a case of targeting discounts through the Clubcard mailings, because price was not the problem. Customer feedback told Tesco that mothers were looking for emotional security.

Boots gains a new advantage

To add to the pressure, Boots was trialling its own loyalty programme in late 1995 and through 1996 – the Advantage card. Eventually launched in September 1997, the card was an immediate success. The scheme's positioning of 'treat yourself' was a perfect summary of the reasons why customers, women in the main, were drawn to Boots for their health and beauty purchases over the supermarket rivals. The Boots trials ran in East Anglia and the South West, with around 200,000 shoppers actively using the card. Advantage-linked sales accounted for 40 per cent of sales in the trial shops. The like-for-like sales uplift for the trial amounted to an impressive 4 per cent, which when rolled out nationally would make the card's dividend to loyal customers self-funding, while delivering top line growth, according to Boots's own calculations, by April 1999.

The evidence was that the new entrant into the loyalty market was likely to be a success with mass appeal. So there was going to be a huge overlap between the Advantage card and Clubcard membership, perhaps more significant than the crossover between the Tesco and Sainsbury's schemes. What is more, with its premium pricing and higher margins, Boots was able to inflate the exchange rate of its promotional 'currency'. Advantage Card was offering a massive 4 per cent payback to Boots customers. And although Tesco had discovered in its early trials that the exchange value of Clubcard points made little difference to the participation of most of its customers, later experience showed that a valuable minority of the most loyal customers were far more aware of the exchange value of the programme's rewards. The launch of TPF, in particular, revealed a growing segment of 'points chasers' who modified their shopping behaviour to gain a significantly greater number of points.

In the loyalty poker game with Boots, Tesco was constrained by its competitive margins. The Clubcard team could never contemplate offering a reward value greater than 1 per cent; without price increases it would be financially impossible. Boots had raised the stakes and was unlikely to be beaten by the conventional Clubcard 'Thank you' alone.

Boots Advantage card outperformed all expectations and was to become profit-enhancing by the end of the 1997/98 financial year. Tesco quickly recognized this as a far more serious rival to Clubcard than Sainsbury's Reward card. The Advantage card was a strong defensive tool for Boots, arguably more generous in its payback to customers than Clubcard. If Tesco was going to persuade a significant number of its own customers to switch their baby care spend from their local Boots to their Tesco store they would have to add something very different to their proposition to succeed.

THE INNER CIRCLE

Outgun or outsmart?

A traditional retailer's tactic would have been to throw money at the problem, spraying deep discount offers at as many of the target audience as possible, both in store and through door-to-door leafleting, in the hope that some of the segment would get the message and shift allegiance on a discount pricing basis. It might have worked temporarily, creating a blip in sales performance for the category. But it would definitely have cannibalized Tesco's profits, as the majority of customers outside the target audience – many of whom were perfectly happy to buy their health and beauty products from Tesco – would also enjoy the discount bonanza.

Thanks to Clubcard, Tesco knew what long-term effect discount coupons had on customer behaviour. It also knew that it would not be enough in itself to effect the scale of change it was aiming to achieve. It concentrated instead on interrogating the reasons why this group of shoppers preferred Boots. And the answer came down to a simple insight: young mothers, particularly first-time parents, trusted Boots as a source of expert help and advice. For many Britons at this life stage, Boots was in their 'inner circle'.

From rational to emotional

The concept of the 'inner circle' had been core to Tesco thinking since the launch of Clubcard. The idea is similar to the 'Favorites' list of websites on your PC. Bewildered by so much choice in the world, consumers generally edit their possibilities and maintain their own manageable menu of brands that they trust. 'Anyone who knows about these things knows the need for brands to develop emotional commitment with those customers, and the need for those services to be personalized to them,' is how Tim Mason explains the challenge to those seeking inner circle status among customers.

Mason's 'bright young things' in the marketing department knew all about the inner circle ideal. Grant Harrison, at the time heading up the Clubcard project team, had set the goal of putting Tesco in customers' 'inner circle' as one of the founding principles of Clubcard. In many ways and for many customers it was working. The launch of TPF for example was 'about being on the inside, helping the customer deal with the outside world,' he said.

To establish Tesco's right to have inner circle status for young families would require improvements on a number of fronts. Guaranteeing in-store baby-changing facilities in all stores would help. Giving greater prominence to the in-store pharmacies, with trained pharmacists on hand to give advice, would be another important development. Safeway, strategically targeting young families as its main source of growth, was even experimenting with in-store crèches.

But Tesco had other means to make a difference to this customer segment. It had deeper customer knowledge than any of its rivals. And it had a membership relationship with its customers that was proven in establishing new behaviour from them.

The thinking, therefore, was to build on the Clubcard effect. In addition to the generic Clubcard programme, which was designed to appeal democratically to all 10 million members, why not create a smaller, more targeted club specifically for customers at a very special and challenging life stage? It would use the successful medium of personalized direct mail, and use the Clubcard idiom of saying 'Thank you' to members in a relevant and value-adding way. And it would be very clearly for mothers expecting a child, or families with young babies. The aim was to create for the first time the degree of trust in Tesco that Boots enjoyed with this group – enough trust to put Tesco in their 'inner circle' of brands for baby care. Once inside the circle Tesco could compete strongly on price, range and convenience with its main rival.

BABY CLUB

A new type of loyalty programme

In late 1996, Tesco insiders Elliott Weider, Sarah Baldock and Helen Godley were appointed by marketing director Richard Brasher as the first project team to run Tesco Baby Club. Their task was to create a new Clubcard proposition that would gain the trust of these unconvinced shoppers. What was needed was a new type of loyalty offer: one that was true to the principles and the methods of Clubcard and piggy-backed its infrastructure, but which had its own strengths. Working with planners from Evans Hunt Scott and Forward Publishing, the project gave birth to Tesco Baby Club.

The project team recognized that Tesco Baby Club had to reach the parts that Clubcard did not. Weider explains:

> Clubcard is a functional scheme. Customers come into the store, spend a pound, get a point, and then get prizes. What we were trying to do was to create an emotional attachment with Tesco. Do customers really like us? We didn't know. We wanted to create a sense of what we would call emotional loyalty, create goodwill… show we really care for our most loyal customers, we look after them. That is what these clubs are all about.

The focus was on showing empathy with the aspirations of young mums. 'When Baby Club was talked about internally, they were careful to talk about a new mother, think what she would be going through, rather than try to bombard her with marketing information. It was exactly the right approach,' says an ex-Tesco staffer who worked on the launch, now a customer relationship management (CRM) consultant.

Baby Club was essentially a group within the greater Clubcard programme, and it established the precedent for further focused offerings. Anyone who wasn't currently a Clubcard member was free to join Baby Club – but as part of their membership, they were automatically enrolled in Clubcard.

Baby Club worked on many of the same loyalty principles as Clubcard:

- It was an opt-in relationship. Shoppers were invited to apply for benefits rather than Tesco just sending them offers based on current data – for example by looking for antenatal-related products in the shopping basket, and automatically enrolling them in the club. Pregnant women (or, as it often turned out, their mothers) could call, and register with their name, address and the due date of the baby. 'Leaflets, inserts in other magazines – and the mailing, that is how we get people to join. We don't strong-arm customers into Baby Club, it's a very soft sell,' says Weider.
- It had a single tier of membership. All expectant mothers were equal, no matter how much they already shopped at Tesco. Non-Clubcard holders got the same initial benefits.
- It was centred on the Tesco store, and aimed to create a relationship with the Tesco brand, not allowing Baby Club to become a distinct brand in its own right.
- It offered customers value-adding benefits primarily through Tesco's medium of choice for personalized contact: direct mail.

But it also had some differences:

- There was no minimum spend to qualify (at this time, Clubcard members still had to spend at least £5 in-store for their shopping basket to qualify for points).
- To get her first Baby Club mailing, a mother-to-be might not have ever visited Tesco. Loyal Clubcard members were encouraged to recruit family members and friends to Baby Club.
- The benefits of membership were presented as more to do with help than with monetary rewards. Research showed that inexperienced first-time mothers in particular feel a great need for information and expert advice during this intense personal experience. They look to objective sources for this as they prepare for birth and the early months of caring for their baby. So Tesco Baby Club brought together respected health experts and friendly GPs to provide valuable, easy-to-follow information at each of the key stages of pregnancy and early motherhood. This was the core of Baby Club's perceived value, while money-off product coupons were offered as

the bonuses of membership, there to make it easier to get the right things from the store.

- The membership of Baby Club was time-specific. While overall Tesco had the mission to earn lifetime loyalty from customers, this proposition could only add value during pregnancy and the first two years of a baby's life. This meant that Baby Club had a far tougher job in maintaining a high level of relevance. The basic Clubcard maintains a pretty constant membership base over the years. By definition, the membership of Baby Club would refresh completely every two and a half years.

- The Baby Club's communications were based with as much precision as possible on life stage, not spend or shopping habits. Before the birth, the mailings concentrated on preparing the parents-to-be, with suitably targeted product offers. Straight after the birth, the advice concentrated on tips to help with the newborn baby, and the coupons would incentivize products that were most useful at that time – for looking after baby and indulging mum.

- The Baby Club mailings had to be dispatched in a sequence that fitted with the due date of the mother to be, rather than seasonally. So its mailing cycle was independent of the main Clubcard mailing. Over the course of their membership, mothers were sent seven major mailings, plus a number of tactical mailshots that gave them very specific offers in-store.

An active choice

Baby Club was a move to introduce active choice into Clubcard. To generate goodwill among a very specific audience, Tesco was prepared to invest a lot more into the relationship than it knew it could normally afford. It was prepared to give a generous gift to build loyalty. 'Clubcard is inevitably a conditional scheme: you do this, and we give you that,' Weider says. 'We wanted to make the relationship in Baby Club unconditional. Sign up for something with us, here is something for nothing, and we hope that you will stay with us.'

It was risky. The offer might be welcomed, but would Tesco's unconditional generosity be repaid in kind by customers consolidating their spend in an under-performing category? 'It was a big commitment,' Weider remembers. 'Once you have started a club, you can't easily stop it.'

Would extra mailings risk the balance of goodwill among Clubcard members already regularly mailed by Tesco? Weider says:

> It's a real pitfall of clubs like this, they could just become yet another mailing programme. We have always been ultra-careful with Clubcard. You need to strike the right balance. Once or twice a month, people will value what we send them. Put the Clubcard logo on the front and people genuinely value it, but only as long as we are strict about what we send them.

Baby Club mailings would offer high-value information as their principal customer benefit – the sort of information that new parents need, but don't know exactly where to get. Authoritative, responsible advice on the baby's health, diet and development would be more important than promotions. Information that had no direct sales message was also going to be a key feature: how to get your baby to sleep soundly at night, what times to feed – all written by people who were independent specialists in the field.

The everlasting partwork

The task to produce the content was a natural for another of Tesco's long-term partners, Forward Publishing, the contract publishers who had already created *Clubcard Magazine*. When invited to view Tesco research panels, the company's publishing director Sarah Wyse was shocked at how adamant Tesco mums were that they would go to its main healthcare rival. 'I watched hours of customer research and still found it difficult to understand. But often their mothers would just tell them to go to Boots, and the midwife would too. We lost them the moment they got pregnant.'

Forward Publishing had previous experience working on mother-and-baby magazines, so it knew the challenges Tesco would have to meet. 'Mother and baby publishing is very broad as a topic, it takes a reader from pregnancy all the way through to two years old. But a woman's needs and interests change radically from one end of that spectrum to the other' Wyse says. So the project team decided to take a segmented approach to the challenge, breaking the information into the key stages. That meant asking for the due date of the baby, and providing the right sequence of relevant information around that date:

It meant we were able to mail Baby Club members at exactly the right moment. When the child starts eating solid food, you can mail to tell the parents all the things they want to know, how the child might not like certain foods and why, for example. And, of course, you can tell them all the things they might need to buy – and provide coupons for them.

The result was a new publishing concept: the everlasting partwork. As each issue of the Baby Club information pack is devoted to a specific age and therefore development stage, the content doesn't need to change dramatically over time. Every six months it is revised and updated, to keep the content novel and the design fresh, but it is essentially the same programme. The sequence of magazines is driven by the customer's agenda, rather than when the publishing schedule dictates she should have it.

An example is the pre-natal pack. Holding up a cheerfully coloured pack, Wyse says:

When you are just about to give birth, one week before your due date, this arrives with a letter. The letter and coupons take the personalization and targeting as far as we can, just like the Clubcard statement mailing. We are not claiming this is a coffee table publication to be treasured forever. It has a specific life for the following three months until the next issue arrives.

A healthy bouncing success

The Clubcard team was given two years to make Baby Club generate a profit. There was a financial risk. The invitation to join the club was sweetened with £150-worth of money-off coupons for every member. Although most of this was funded by the supplier brands that wanted prominence in the communications to customers, Tesco was also committing promotional budget to subsidize the offers. With the press coverage and word-of-mouth recommendations, this was potentially a huge outlay in discounts. If Tesco's generosity were not matched with higher sales from the members, the value running into tens of millions of pounds would all be heading towards the customer, with little return.

With Clubcard, Tesco had the means to measure precisely the sales impact of a variant like Baby Club. By monitoring short-term coupon redemption rates and then tracking the ongoing transactional activity of the members across all store departments, they could calculate precisely the return on investment. Tesco staff worried that there may be a promotional blip, with discount chasing but no sustained sales effect.

The results were spectacular, eclipsing any other innovation that led from Clubcard. Inside its first two critical years, 37 per cent of all British parents-to-be joined. Tesco was building a valued and valuable relationship with two out of every five expectant mothers. Tesco's market analysis revealed that, thanks to Baby Club, the company had increased its share of the mother and baby market to almost 24 per cent – a proportion that was now larger than its share of the total grocery market. Baby Club made Tesco a force in the health and beauty sector, and beyond that the members of Baby Club outspent their peer group by £40 million a year in total.

It was not just a case of reinforcing the commitment of current loyal customers, either. The tracking research showed that a third of the new-to-Tesco shoppers who enrolled in the Baby Club remained loyal to Tesco after their membership of Baby Club elapsed. This programme was deepening the relationship that Tesco enjoyed with this valuable young family segment, and broadening it too.

Clubs catch on

Not surprisingly, other retailers were quick to launch their own initiatives. On 6 March 1998, Boots launched 'Mother & Baby at Home', mailing 500,000 catalogues to Advantage cardholders who were buying baby products – its first marketing promotion based on the data it had collected from the Advantage card. The catalogue contained 1,500 products that could be ordered by mail or on the phone, and were delivered to the door. Richard Homes, then the director of marketing at Boots the Chemists, said:

> We expect Mother & Baby at Home to be the first in a series of targeted initiatives which will take Boots closer to our most important customers. In an increasingly competitive market we can only succeed if we offer customers the type of shopping which exactly meets their changing needs.

Sainsbury's had beaten Boots by three months with its own response to the Tesco Baby Club. The '0–5 Club' was launched in January 1998, offering £100 of discounts to joiners. While it was designed to serve a larger age range than Baby Club, this proved to offer both an advantage (the chance to capture a larger share of young families more quickly and cheaply than a baby-only strategy) and a serious disadvantage too. As Tesco knew very well from its customer research groups, the needs, interests and priorities of a first-time mother with a newborn baby are very different to those of a confident mother with a 5-year-old child at playschool. The ability to deliver relevant information is diluted by trying to appeal to more mums. Nonetheless, in the first year the 0–5 Club attracted 250,000 members, and has performed well enough to survive the replacement of Sainsbury's Reward card by the Nectar programme.

Baby Club fired Tesco with enthusiasm. What other life-stage groups or special interest areas could Tesco target with the 'sub-club' approach (the generic term coined by EHS) and add to the Clubcard portfolio? Unexpectedly, given the massive success Baby Club had experienced, Tesco's answer was more than one – but not many more.

CLUBCARD PIZZA

Tim Mason challenged the Clubcard team, led by marketing director Richard Brasher, to find other ways to replicate the extraordinary success of Baby Club. Conventional retailer instinct would be to rush into areas like pet care, gourmet foods or green living, where a clearly defined subset of products had an equally defined and large customer base who might be persuaded to join a special interest club.

Resisting gut feel

The Clubcard team was now adept at interrogating the customer data and listening to customers in groups to back up gut feelings. Before making any rash moves, a new club concept had to answer some questions:

- Was there a clear customer need that was being fulfilled? Or was this mainly a convenient tactic for Tesco's commercial advantage?
- Was there a strong case for supplier brands to contribute to running costs through offers and advertising? Were there appropriate brand partners?
- Was there a significant opportunity to increase customer share in the category? Tesco had a lot of ground to make up in baby care. Was that the same for pet food, for example?
- Would this add substantially to the emotional equity of Clubcard, and therefore the Tesco brand?
- Could it be the best in class? Or would it only be a me-too?

If Baby Club was going to be joined by a range of other sub-clubs it was important to be clear about their relationship with their own parent, Clubcard. How would all these ideas fit together?

Terry Hunt created an analogy for this: imagine a pizza and the selection of toppings in a pizza parlour. Clubcard is designed to appeal to all customers, it is the universal loyalty contract that Tesco offered to regular shoppers. So Clubcard is the essential bread base with tomato and mozzarella. Baby Club and the other sub-clubs would be the toppings on the menu. Clubcard members could choose from a range of ways to personalize their membership according to their tastes and life-stage. This offered a way that Clubcard could avoid becoming a 'given', gradually taken for granted as a normal part of day-to-day shopping, and regain the status of a 'chosen': personal, timely and relevant.

Using these criteria, the shortlist became a shorter list. The interest areas with strongest customer appeal and a sound business case were: toddlers (mums with 3–5-year-old children), kids (families with 5–8-year-olds), wine, and health and beauty.

Keeping promises – Kids Club

This is the Tesco Kids Club 'code of conduct':

1. We promise that all Tesco material will have been approved by our parents panel to ensure suitability.
2. We promise not to advertise prices to children or advertise products that could cause unnecessary pester power.
3. We promise not to send coupons or money-off promotions directly to your child. Any coupons will come addressed to you, the parent/guardian (sealed separately within your child's mailing) so you can use them without being pestered by your child.

The sub-club strategy increased the pressure on Tesco to declare its principles. Through these programmes Tesco was presenting itself as the champion of customers' special interests: it needed to show it could be trusted.

Baby Club set the precedent by offering a reliable source of easy-to-understand, timely advice to families with infants, prepared by medical experts. If the Kids Club, aimed not just at the parents but also at 5–8-year-old children, was to make a similar impact it would need the same degree of authority – but authority of a different kind. Tesco

From humble beginnings… the original
Tesco Clubcard. (Agency: EHS Brann)

The first Tesco Clubcard statement mailing,
now one of the world's most profitable
mailing programmes.
(Agency: EHS Brann)

Tesco's internal magazine for February 1995 celebrates the launch of Clubcard. On the left, marketing director Tim Mason; on the right, the chief executive at the time, Sir Ian (now Lord) MacLaurin.
(Source: Tesco archive)

A night out at Tesco! Exclusive Clubcard evenings were very popular.
(Agency: EHS Brann)

Tesco *Clubcard Magazine* was Europe's biggest circulation general interest magazine.
(Publisher: Forward)

Student Clubcard – great take-up, great gags, but not great for business.
(Agency: EHS Brann)

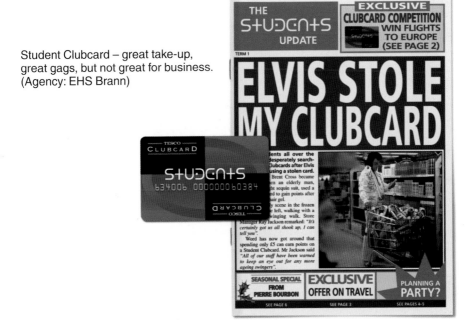

Tesco MasterCard allows customers to earn points wherever they spend their money.
(Agency: advantage)

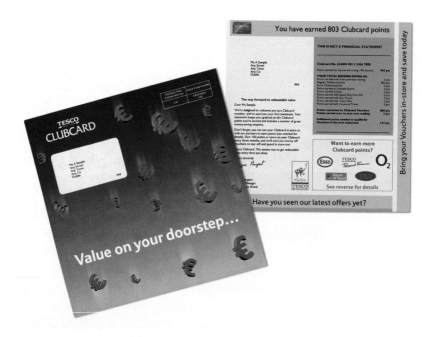

Tesco Ireland was the first overseas market to introduce Clubcard.
(Agency: EHS Brann)

In South Korea, the Familycard, which is used with around 80 per cent of sales, also offers coupons that can be redeemed at 'Culture Centres' for education classes.
(Source: Tesco)

There are now more than 500 town centre Tesco Express stores – almost half of Tesco UK locations. These convenience stores offer a challenge to Tesco: will shoppers use Clubcard for small purchases?
(Source: Tesco)

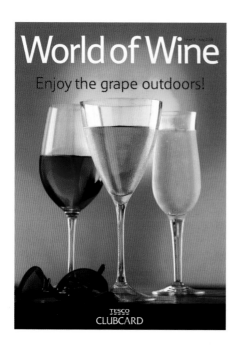

Every litre helps – Tesco Clubcard World of Wine has over 250,000 high spending members. (Agency: EHS Brann)

Tesco Clubcard is the 'Every Little Helps' promise in action. (Agency: EHS Brann)

The Dot-com bubble that didn't burst – Tesco.com benefited from Clubcard data.
(Agency: EHS Brann)

A gift to home movers courtesy of Tesco Clubcard.
(Agency: EHS Brann)

Issuing Clubcards as key fobs helped to boost usage – significantly among men.
(Agency: EHS Brann)

The redesigned Tesco welcome pack, created in 2003, is easier to understand so
that users can take advantage of offers such as Clubcard Deals.
(Agency: EHS Brann)

had to convince parents that it could be trusted to communicate directly with their children in a fun but responsible way, 'This was a risk, talking directly to children,' Weider, who was leading the Tesco project looking into sub-clubs, admits. 'Not selling to them, talking to them. Our research showed that parents trusted us to do that.' More than that, if Kids Club was going to work it had to convince the most demanding audience of all, the children themselves.

Weider and EHS brainstormed the options for Kids Club. They quickly concluded that to be the best retail club for this age group it would have to impress the child first, and reassure mum next. This was helped by the results of focus groups that showed that mums wanted Tesco to understand that they were busy – and wanted Tesco to give things to do direct to their children, not to them.

Kids would not take seriously anything that wasn't truly for them, the team decided. The project team researched various offerings from building societies and publishers aimed at this age group, and too often the kids found the content of the clubs patronizing, earnest or just plain wrong. Children told Tesco they wanted something with playground kudos. They wanted content that connects with the things they enjoy on TV or in the cinema. They wanted what is authentic among their peer group.

Tesco wasn't really a brand that kids felt they 'owned'. But Disney was. Hence the brand partnership that was forged to create Tesco Kids Club. With Tesco appealing to the parents and Disney the brand for the children, Kids Club had two strong brands, but that meant Kids Club also had to find a way to talk to two audiences at once. With the Disney tie-up, finding enough content to entertain and inform children wasn't a problem. But the project team had to use direct media to recruit members, while ensuring that everything they sent was appropriate.

As parents were the cardholders, Tesco could simply rely on them to sign up on behalf of their children. The Kids Club website would be accessible from the parent's computer and the club mailings, including a Disney comic and free gift, would be addressed to the kids. A separate mailing was enclosed addressing the parent, with any sales promotional material safely sealed and separate from the content for children.

Avoiding 'pester power'

Tesco recruited a 'parents panel' to review everything before it gets to the members. Weider explains:

> It's a group of teachers based in Somerset. They check everything we send out before it goes. Probably 99 times out of 100, we get it right. There are times when we make mistakes, but we listen and learn. One thing we soon learnt was that we had to resist Kids Club becoming a sales mechanic.

On the other hand, there had to be a clear opportunity for sales benefit from Kids Club to justify this Tesco venture. Weider describes this as 'encouraging interaction between the parent and the child,' and whether that's as simple as the young club member giving the envelope of offer coupons to his or her parent, or mentioning a few key brand names so that kids know about them, there is what Tesco calls a 'very soft sell'.

Weider stresses constantly that Kids Club is not intended to encourage 'pester power', but acknowledges it's hard to get the balance right. 'When we first sent out the Kids Club packs, we really played the selling side down,' he recalls. 'That made parents more suspicious: they asked, "Why are you doing this if you are not trying to sell us something?"'

The compromise is that sections in the comic are 'sponsored' by suppliers. The transparency of the club is reinforced by Tesco asking permission in the marketing process. This has some surprising results, showing how Tesco is trusted to act responsibly: when signing up for Kids Club, parents are asked what they would allow Tesco to offer to their children. Almost 70 per cent gave permission for Tesco to send free samples direct to their kids.

How many more clubs?

Tesco's growing confidence in talking appropriately to customers with special interests quickly led to new clubs for well-defined groups: The Baby Club was first joined by a Toddler Club (the two were later amalgamated into, not surprisingly, the 'Baby and Toddler' Club). Tesco also launched a Healthy Living club which recognized health conscious shoppers, and the World of Wine which catered for shoppers who wanted to learn more about their favourite tipple. Although the later clubs did not match the 450,000 rolling membership total of Baby Club – they were not set up with those targets in mind – all have contributed to growing their categories, and all had six-figure memberships by the end of 2003. Only one substantial target remained: the Tesco Food Club, one which had perhaps the greatest potential of all. The Food Club was to be launched as part of a massive revamp of Clubcard – which we will cover in more detail later – which boosted memberships of every one of the existing clubs as well.

Nevertheless, the other clubs consistently met or exceeded their performance targets. For example, the Toddler Club, launched in May 2001, had an initial target of 150,000 members. By August, it had 200,000: two out of three of its members had joined after being members of the Baby Club. That, for Mason, is a demonstration of the true value of Clubcard:

> I think marketing people use the expression 'emotional attachment' in too free a way. It can be misinterpreted. When I talk about it I don't mean, cut them in half and they'll have 'Tesco' written through the middle of them. I mean that people have an emotional bond to Tesco in that they feel we are on their side. That we look out for their interests, don't patronize them or take them for granted. And most important, we deliver on our promises. It's the sort of customer thinking that says, 'Tesco has always done all right by me.' On one hand that sounds rather dull. But it is actually massively valuable. It is, in fact, branding.

WHAT TESCO LEARNT ABOUT 'SUB-CLUBS'

Identify real emotional needs

In researching a variety of subject areas that might become Clubcard sub-clubs, Tesco has learnt that there are not very many that have emotional resonance. 'We're all very busy,' Tim Mason says. 'You are only going to give mind space to a Tesco Club when the information is valuable enough. Time is everyone's scarce resource. That will always be the limiting factor.' A special interest area has to evoke sustained enthusiasm among potential members to warrant the effort of a separate membership programme. An example is the Wine Club: customers didn't want lots of information about wine, they told Tesco, they wanted to be able to try new fine wines. So Tesco pre-selected five 'corkers' a month, and using coupons, encouraged members to try them at a discount. Says Mason:

> The only club that is worth running is one that satisfies a genuine consumer need, because actually, they are the only clubs that consumers are interested in. We could, for example, run a dieting club. It would actually do quite well, it's an aspect of people's lives that at certain times is very involving.

Ideas for other clubs, which may even represent a larger part of Tesco business, have been shelved because that degree of enthusiasm and interest is less apparent, or because the potential for involvement is not shared by prospective members who have disparate priorities and tastes.

For example, many customers choose organic foods – but focus groups showed this choice was based on a wide variety of motivations and priorities. It turns out that they have little in common as a group of individuals. A Tesco Organic Club was considered, but not pursued for this reason. In the end Tesco decided to appeal to customers choosing organic options for health reasons through the Healthy Living club.

Make a clear business case

There is no point creating an elegant proposition for a particular interest group if it does not have the capacity to deliver value to Tesco. There has to be a potentially large membership (at least 100,000 in Tesco's terms). And it must be credible that those customers will significantly enhance their shopping behaviour as a result of participating. A Tesco Pets Club, for example, would probably appeal to a wide audience, with a clear emotional commitment to the welfare of their pets. But as Tesco carries a limited range of pet supplies, and the potential for sales uplift is very small, the club would not be financially justifiable.

A sub-club is not just for Christmas

Once Tesco has invited customers to identify their particular interests and join a new club, that's a big commitment on both sides, one that will strongly affect a customer's goodwill towards the brand. While membership is a free gift, withdrawing membership would undoubtedly be damaging to customers' perceptions of Tesco. 'You don't want to develop a more special relationship with 150,000 consumers, then turn round to them and say, "tough",' says Mason.

Unconditional benefits are powerful

A member didn't have to be a current Tesco shopper to join Baby Club. She didn't have to shop her way into the club to earn the rewards of membership. This was a something-for-nothing offer to new mums, a gift from Tesco. But that unconditional gift proved very powerful. Tesco found that by offering a reward up-front it attracted large numbers of current and new customers, gained positive perceptions and influenced shopping behaviour in a valuable direction.

Be a 'chosen' not a 'given'

People value most what they actively choose. By making the sub-clubs an opt-in proposition, Tesco made sure that awareness was high from the outset. By asking customers to provide information about themselves, or seeking their permission to talk direct to their children, Tesco increases the strength of the loyalty contract. For those customers who take up the invitation, that deepens their connection to the Tesco brand.

Special interest creates a general effect

Remarkably, the Clubcard customer data show that the sales potential of this strategy isn't just restricted to the categories that the clubs represent. Mason says:

> We need to learn more about the economics of Clubs, but it's clear that active participation in clubs does change behaviour positively in other areas. You don't need to be Einstein to realize that if you are a member of the Wine Club, you might buy a bit more wine, not least because we give you some vouchers to help you do it. But if I say that being members of the Wine Club also leads to shoppers buying more fresh groceries, we can all agree that's very interesting. Why do they do it? Because they do. What we now know is clubs change behaviour.

12

A bigger deal

- ▶ Partners for Clubcard
- ▶ Solo, shared and outsourced
- ▶ The early Clubcard partnerships
- ▶ Clubcard Deals
- ▶ Broadening the offer

In August 2005, one Tesco customer bought 10,148 Birds Eye Beef Dinner frozen meals, in what the *Daily Mail* headlined 'The Great Roast Beef Stampede'. Canny Clubcard members had realized that by spending £1.95 on three meals, they would get a windfall of £1.50 worth of Clubcard points.

The trick was to convert the points into Clubcard Deals vouchers, redeemable on anything from free flights to magazine subscriptions, which effectively multiplied the value of the points by four. Word of this informal arbitrage scheme spread via word of mouth and internet bulletin boards – especially www.moneysavingexpert.com – and Tesco freezer cabinets were emptied of their beef dinners. The challenge to the customers was, what to do with all the frozen meals?

The controversy even featured in the letters page of *The Times*. 'Sir, your report pokes fun at the "pleas for recipe ideas" which have apparently been posted on websites,' wrote an indignant Tesco shopper on 7 September 2005, 'If you had read the posts more carefully you would have seen that a large section of people, including myself, have been buying the beef and redistributing it to shelters for the homeless and the Salvation Army.'

It seems that many shoppers were happy to give away their Birds Eye beef dinners because they already had banked the Clubcard points they craved. But who were these points chasers, and why were they craving them so much? To answer that, we have to visit Sussex.

PARTNERS FOR CLUBCARD

The headquarters of Clubcard Deals is typically Tesco. Five minutes from the main runway at Gatwick Airport, facing a six-lane highway and sitting next to the car park of the local Carpetright, it's an anonymous red brick office building. The interior is equally functional. There's nothing exceptional to see – unless you know what you are looking for, because Deals is a vital component of Clubcard's future.

On any one day the staff process £100,000 in Clubcard vouchers, and input the details that are passed to the central Clubcard database holding all the Clubcard membership account information. A bank of laser printers is in perpetual operation, printing the Clubcard Deals tokens that will be exchanged by Clubcard members to pay for branded package holidays, family days out, hotel stays or restaurant meals. This is the end result of a low-tech process, an orderly manual 'paper chase'. But at Clubcard Deals, a wholly owned subsidiary of Tesco, the Clubcard loyalty contract is being extended. Here, Tesco enhances its relationship with the brand's most committed customers.

As the director of the Deals business, Steve McArdle explains, for anything outside the Tesco supermarkets, his office controls Clubcard's 'earn and burn'. If a customer earns Tesco Clubcard points from a Beefeater restaurant or because Powergen supplies their electricity, or any of the other partners that now issue the Clubcard promotional currency to reinforce their own customer loyalty, the process of crediting that value to the Clubcard member's account is managed by Clubcard Deals. One of the Deals team's roles is to negotiate and manage Clubcard contracts with third-party retail or service industry partners, selling them points in bulk and processing them once they've been issued to customers. If a Clubcard member chooses to redeem Clubcard vouchers to pay for anything outside the range offered in-store – one of the Clubcard Deals that has been available since 1999 – it's a Deals voucher that makes it happen.

Boredom is our enemy

Since the novelty impact of Clubcard's launch died down, the Clubcard team has faced an ongoing challenge: to stop Clubcard becoming a bore. Carolyn Bradley, one of the original launch team for Tesco Clubcard, says:

> There has always been concern to keep Clubcard fresh, keep making it better, enabling customers to get more out of it, and keep them using it actively. We have always monitored in-store participation rates for Clubcard very closely, looking at whether people are redeeming vouchers at consistent levels, whether they are still presenting their cards at the checkout, measuring how many people opt out of receiving communication from us.

This isn't an academic exercise. Tracking a wide range of measures for Clubcard participation – behavioural patterns like the percentage of transactions identified by Clubcard, the percentage of sales value, the redemption rate of Clubcard vouchers and product coupons, the collection period before redemption, as well as what shoppers actually think about the card – is vital to understanding how the scheme is progressing. With every adult in the UK possessing on average three retail loyalty cards, a large number of those are not being used. They are failing in their only function.

It was to meet this challenge, and in particular to offer the most loyal, high-spending customers an involving new way to spend their membership dividend from Tesco, that the Clubcard Deals operation was conceived. Within the pages of the Deals brochure Clubcard members can choose travel, leisure and luxury deals. Rather than spending vouchers on some extras like wine or chocolates, or even paying for an entire week's groceries, customers can choose to redeem them for a discount on their holiday to Florida, a family visit to Legoland, a magazine subscription – even health insurance from HSA. 'All the deals we have done that involve partner brands or suppliers are about keeping Clubcard fresh, preventing the customer fatigue which would be a serious concern,' Bradley adds.

Today Deals is one of the largest sales agents for theme park tickets in the UK. It issues £31 million in vouchers every year to 1 million Clubcard holders. In 2002, Legoland Windsor opened, with a firework display, on one night exclusively for Tesco shoppers.

SOLO, SHARED AND OUTSOURCED

Before we see how Tesco Freetime has expanded Clubcard's reach and relevance, it is worth looking at the advantages and disadvantages of a retailer sharing its loyalty programme with partner brands.

Solo schemes

Advantages

A single-brand scheme is by far the simplest, and on the face of it the most logical model. After all, the purpose is to concentrate a customer's brand choice and build loyalty, not to encourage trading everywhere. A company invites its customers to join, rewards them for shopping regularly, gives them a reward, and the customers come back to spend it by shopping regularly.

The original model for Clubcard was a completely solo scheme. For Tesco it offered unambiguous control. It knew exactly how many Clubcard points it was issuing to whom; how and when those points were being redeemed; and what the sales effect was in its stores. It was always Tesco issuing the points and Tesco stores accepting the vouchers, with no brand confusion. The contract was between Tesco and its customers alone. As Mason put it at the launch: 'Clubcard is as much about Tesco showing loyalty to the customer as it is about the customer showing loyalty to Tesco.'

Disadvantages

If the advantages are mainly to do with control, the disadvantages are mainly to do with cost. A solo-brand programme has to be marketed, administered and financially justified by the brand alone. All the risk is carried by one business, as is all the burden of investing to keep the scheme attractive to customers. 'Standalone schemes can be effective in changing customer behaviour,' says Keith Mills, who runs the competing, non-standalone Nectar scheme of which Sainsbury's is a member, 'but it is expensive, and customers will not pay inflated prices for a loyalty scheme.' Only an organization that has a broad enough customer base to create the economy of scale needed will be able to dream of running a loyalty scheme on its own at no net cost – whether or not it manages the operational problems. Realistically, in the UK only the supermarkets have the breadth of retail base to achieve this scale.

Shared schemes

Advantages

For those brands less blessed than a supermarket with mass appeal, wide product range, high frequency of visit and high value of transactions, the disadvantages of a single-brand model will probably outweigh the advantages. The next option is some sort of brand cooperative programme, usually administered and led by one retailer – say a chain of petrol stations – but offering the opportunity to collect and spend points at a number of non-competing outlets or services.

An example is the 'Premier Points' scheme offered by BP and Argos. Premier Points could be collected at BP petrol stations, from the Choice Hotels Group, or through several power supply companies. They could be spent at Argos stores. The scheme was closed in September 2002, as it was rolled into the Nectar programme.

Peter Wray, formerly European Manager for BP Retail Customer Loyalty programmes, is still a fan of a cooperative approach to loyalty for most brands:

> Tesco can have the attitude that it is happy to work with partners, as long as things are done in the Tesco way. You risk in that case only attracting secondary brands. If you risk that, it is fine, but you had better make your loyalty scheme the best in the world, or it will fail.

Working in the Netherlands, where no retailer tried the single-brand model, influenced his view. 'Companies in the UK and US can often get too wrapped up in themselves, and forget the customer. There are far fewer examples of working together in the UK and the US than in the rest of Europe.'

By offering customers the chance to acquire points from a broader base of relevant brands, this approach creates more opportunities to increase the population of active customers, so a scheme has the potential to gain 'critical mass'. It also means there are more outlets and a better range of products on which keen points collectors can spend their rewards. Without the choice guaranteed by a supermarket, this model is more likely to retain their long-term participation than a restricted number of ways to spend a reward – for example, on more petrol.

Disadvantages

Schemes of this type have weaknesses too, though there are savings from sharing running costs. There is the imbalance of commitment from the participating brands; each retailer is restricted in its access to useable customer data; there is a lack of control over promotional activities; and there is the potential for inter-brand disputes. By widening the net to include different participating brands and then having to manage their ongoing expectations there are additional administration costs for the programme's main sponsor that can cancel out the savings from sharing the cost of the infrastructure.

Outsourced schemes

Advantages

Some brands go a step further: participation in an independent loyalty programme, combining a very wide range of brands as partners from specific sectors, but under the umbrella of an independent loyalty brand. Air Miles is an independently branded scheme, with countless companies over the years actively using the currency for acquisition and retention promotions. Today the most prominent example in the UK is Nectar, the latest creation of Air Miles inventor and loyalty marketing entrepreneur, Keith Mills.

Nectar, based on a successful Canadian loyalty programme that 70 per cent of Canadian households take part in, has a very appealing customer proposition for those who love to accumulate promotional currency: earn points quicker. Launched with a line up of founding partners including Sainsbury's (the supermarket ditched its Reward card in favour of Nectar), Barclaycard (the credit card sacrificed its Profiles scheme), BP (abandoning Premier Points) and Debenhams (the department store chain had previously relied on its account card base alone), the scheme was soon joined by Vodafone, Adams and Thresher as issuers of Nectar points.

The attraction to cardholders is clear. Because they have so many more outlets to earn points from, they can accrue enough to redeem on what they choose much faster than they would if they collected with just one brand. Nectar claims that it is possible to earn points on 40 per cent of your household spending if you directed that spending to one of its 17 sponsors. And because customers are potentially getting points from so many sources, they can credibly save for rewards of greater value – a long-haul return flight for example. 'As a customer, I get two, three or four times as much value from the same shopping experience as I did from a single-retailer loyalty card,' Mills says, 'In Canada, we have 110 retailers in the programme.'

Retailers can share the costs of recruitment, communications, data management, rewards and processing as well as pooling learning from the database. The partnership approach also provides a sophisticated loyalty marketing capability to smaller brands and organizations that could never build and sustain a significant programme alone. 'Sainsbury's is offering the same on loyalty as it was when it ran the Reward card,' says Mills. 'Customers are getting better value, and the operating costs are significantly less.'

Outsourced schemes also have the advantage for retailers that they are good models for customer acquisition. Because the pool of Nectar users will always contain shoppers who were strangers for each retailer, they can begin to use the scheme to attract those members to shop with them.

Finally, the outsourced model can appeal to many different types of shopper. 'Our objective is to put together such a broad base of places to collect and spend that no matter who you are, it's useful,' says Mills, who accepts that only between 10 and 15 per cent of Nectar members are 'points chasers'.

Disadvantages

There are disadvantages to the outsourcing model. First, there is the danger of a 'common market dilemma' in which there will be some brands that become net contributors of value back to customers (issuing more points value than is subsequently spent with their brand) and others who become net beneficiaries (attracting more of the scheme's value to be spent with their business than they issue in points themselves).

Then there is the question of 'loyal to what'? The experience of many participants in the Air Miles programme is that it appeals to a significant minority of people who are very loyal to Air Miles, but not to the brand that offers Air Miles. So they switch allegiance to wherever they can collect more of their promotional currency of choice. The risk is, for example, that by subsuming a retailer's loyalty marketing effort under an independently branded, multi-partner programme, the link between store and customer is not strengthened at all.

Will shoppers become more closely bound to Nectar than Sainsbury's? Would they stay with Sainsbury's if Nectar changed brands to, say, Morrison's, or go looking for points at Morrison's instead?

These structural problems mean that brand partners come and go. Evidence of this is that of the seven original participants in the UK's Nectar scheme, two of them, Barclaycard and Vodafone, have subsequently pulled out. They have been replaced by other brands, for example Ford, Hertz, TalkTalk and American Express (which issues a Nectar credit card).

In October 2004, before these departures, the *Mail on Sunday* reported anonymous Nectar sponsors who were disappointed that the promise of the Nectar concept had not carried through into measurable sales increases. 'We are certainly not in a rush to renew the contract,' said one; Nectar was 'not quite as exciting as we were led to believe it was going to be', added another. Barclaycard's explanation of why it decided to leave the scheme was that it was no longer of value to itself or its customers.

A related and equally fundamental problem is: who owns the data? Under data protection legislation the company responsible for the customer data is the brand that managed the original transaction. In the case of a partnership loyalty programme, the owner is Air Miles or Nectar or whatever scheme asked the customer to sign up and give personal details – not Sainsbury's, or Debenhams or any other participating brand. There will be protocols in place for data access, but the capability to interrogate the information, gain insights and understand opportunities, the major competitive advantage that Clubcard has given Tesco, will not be available to the same degree to any single member of an outsourced scheme.

Finally, there is the practical problem of getting various brands with very different agendas and priorities to cooperate. Promotions, campaigns and scheme changes have to be driven outside the partner organizations. This can lead to confusion for customers – for example, you might be able to earn points on the garage forecourt, but not in the shop if a non-participating retailer runs it. The chance to introduce tactical marketing initiatives swiftly is reduced and innovation limited, as decisions have to be agreed between member companies. 'You give up some control,' admits Mills. 'Nectar has to have rules.'

Tesco identifies this as the fundamental flaw in Nectar: it can never be 'bound in' to the business, because it can never completely share the objectives of a single participating retailer. There will always be some tension between what the retailer wants to achieve and what the loyalty scheme wants to achieve. For a retailer like Tesco, which makes earning the lifetime loyalty of its customers its first priority, outsourcing a scheme like this can never work. Mason asks the question: 'Is a loyalty scheme an integral part of your business, or something you just bolt on when it is convenient?'

THE EARLY CLUBCARD PARTNERSHIPS

Points for pints

'The Tesco Pubcard' was the headline in the *Sun*. 'Customers get points for pints.' On the evening of 7 January 1998, customers at the Slaters Inn public house in Dalkeith, the Rat and Parrot in Reading and Ye Olde Transporter in Sunderland, among others, found that their New Year pint of beer came with a 'Thank you' – provided they had brought their Tesco Clubcards. At the beginning of 1998, the supermarket started a three-month trial with brewer Scottish and Newcastle retail, which owned 2,600 pubs across the UK. Of those, 31 were selected to trial the scheme, targeted at 70,000 Clubcard members who lived within 15 minutes of the pubs in question.

Those 70,000 card holders – minus the ones that Clubcard data showed may well be teetotallers – were invited to try the scheme by direct mail, earning the standard pound-a-point benefit, and receiving vouchers for cut-price rounds of drinks and bar meals. In Sunderland, the patrons of pubs like Maggie Mays or the Mountain Daisy were also offered Clubcard application forms to test whether Tesco could encourage shoppers to sign up at the bar.

The idea of using Tesco Clubcard in your local pub was one of the more experimental brand partnership ideas that were trialled, but it failed to catch on. Too many male customers and not enough enthusiasm among bar staff were the two most probable reasons for a low take up. It was just one of many partnerships considered or trialled. From the beginning of Clubcard's story, Tesco received offers from other retailers and service brands that wanted to cooperate in the Clubcard scheme. The first of those, and a company that we will meet several times in the Clubcard story, was Air Miles.

An opportunity with Air Miles

It was not surprising that Air Miles would be interested in forging a trading alliance with its fledgling competitor back in 1995. When Clubcard launched, Air Miles was already well established, easily the UK's most popular loyalty programme. But its management team was quick to recognize the marketing power that Clubcard had the potential to unleash for Tesco. The Clubcard team were equally aware of the opportunities they were revealing.

They knew that Clubcard opened up a new channel of communication for Tesco with millions of ordinary households in the UK, a medium that had no equivalent. It could 'broadcast' marketing messages to an audience approximately the size of that enjoyed by a national commercial television channel, and simultaneously it could 'narrowcast' those messages to a subset of interested customers that could be measured in the tens of thousands – about the circulation of a specialist magazine. It offered interactive feedback from customers, via coupon redemption at the checkout as well as the helpline. It already had an integrated 'platform' – the personalized card, the mass-customized statement, the segmented *Clubcard Magazine,* direct mail campaigns, the coupons and vouchers and the call centre – long before the internet and other digital media could make that claim to media integration.

In short, Clubcard had instantly turned Tesco into a powerful media owner and customer relationship management tool. Air Miles (and others) saw how this would inevitably attract other brands that might become partners, in direct competition to Air Miles.

Air Miles had one distinct advantage over Clubcard – longevity. It had launched in 1988, and had several million avid collectors. It was, and still is, one of the best examples of lateral thinking in modern marketing. An empty airline seat means wasted revenue and depressed margins for an airline – as the plane still has to fly, it is a net cost. Yet the perceived value of an airline ticket, at least before the rise of the budget carriers and the troubled times that have hit the world's airlines, was very high. By creating a unique trading currency linked to flights, Air Miles could offer its airline partners a way to soak up spare capacity at a disguised discount rate, and so protect premium prices and profitability. The currency – Air Miles – was bought in advance by retailers who could then incentivize their customers to collect miles for a high-value reward, air travel, with Air Miles acting as the clearing centre and agent, matching supply and demand. As early as 1988 it had established partnerships with Shell and NatWest, which used the currency to incentivize customers to take up products and increase spend, giving Air Miles a larger base of collectors in return.

The question for Tesco was: would a similar link with Air Miles be beneficial? Air Miles came to Tesco to offer a partnership from a position of strength. It had a brand, an established 'earn and burn' process, and it could offer to tie up Clubcard with an existing family of non-competing brand partnerships overnight. From Air Miles' perspective, everybody benefited: Clubcard got accelerated scale and credibility, and Air Miles kept its number one position in loyalty. The Clubcard team considered the offer – and refused it.

The proposal from Air Miles had not intimidated them as much as crystallized their thinking. They decided that Clubcard was to be a 'gold standard' loyalty currency that would control its own destiny.

Loyal to what?

The most important question in the meetings to discuss the Air Miles tie-in was: 'Who owns the relationship with the customer?' There is no doubt today. 'Clubcard is a loyalty scheme designed by Tesco for Tesco customers for use within Tesco. It is a Tesco brand-building device and relationship tool. It is an extremely valuable part of Tesco,' says marketing director Tim Mason.

'Clubcard concentrates on Tesco customers,' says Tesco chief executive Sir Terry Leahy. 'There may be customers of these other businesses involved, but it is for Tesco customers.'

This didn't mean that Tesco would not cooperate with other partners. It just meant that Tesco would always be the boss of its own Clubcard medium. The Clubcard team knew that Clubcard was potentially a 'gold standard' already, capable of financially justifying itself. They wanted to grow the scheme for the benefit of Tesco's own shoppers and its own brand. They would invite other retailers to participate to broaden the Clubcard experience for customers, even to the extent of allowing partners to buy Clubcard points from Tesco and issue them to their own customers. But Tesco would only allow the points to be 'burned' in their stores.

Negotiations – if they could be called that – with prospective partners had two rules. Rule 1: many other businesses can issue Clubcard points to their customers. After all, Tesco customers want as many opportunities as possible to build up value on their account. Rule 2: only Tesco can redeem their value. Just as Air Miles exist to be spent on air travel and holidays, Clubcard points are there to be spent in Tesco.

Even on this basis, several major retailers were happy to surf on the wave of goodwill stirred up by the nation's most successful loyalty programme. Thomson Holidays, then the UK's biggest travel operator, signed up for six months from January 1996, and B&Q, the home DIY chain, signed a Clubcard contract in April 1996 and benefited from its promotional pulling power for more than two years.

B&Q was Clubcard's most successful early partner by some distance. In the first three months alone, the promotion recruited 126,000 new Clubcard holders, 30,000 of whom went on to use the Clubcard in Tesco. The company calculated that if only 5 per cent of them were new to Tesco, it would generate £6.6 million in sales.

The problem with partnerships

Other retailers took a different view. Sainsbury's decided to join forces with Air Miles in 1996, striking a deal that allowed customers to convert their points earned with the Reward card into Air Miles. Dozens of retail loyalty schemes sprang up, with the majority using points-redeeming partnerships to bolster them. Too often they were poor value: Texaco felt the need to revamp its Global Card's rewards – after someone calculated that to get a set of pans, you had to buy enough petrol to get to the moon and back.

In October 1996, the Consumers' Association (CA) published a critical report in its magazine *Which?* 'These deals are better than nothing,' said spokesman Andrew McIlwraith, 'but they all mean spending large amounts at one supermarket and do not justify shoppers going card crazy.' The report contrasted ways of spending the rewards customers earned when they spent £1,000, £2,000, £3,000 and even £10,000 in different supermarkets; the figures are shown in Table 12.1.

The CA pointed out that the average grocery spend a year was £2,900, which gave shoppers a standard reward of £29, but while other retailers offered a variety of ways to redeem the dividend, Tesco stuck doggedly to its policy of issuing only vouchers to be spent at Tesco, convinced that

Table 12.1 The Consumer's Association report into customers' spending of rewards (Source: *Daily Mail*, October 1996)

	£1,000	£2,000	£3,000	£10,000
Sainsburys	£5 each off four meals for two at Beefeater	£20 to charity of your choice	480 Air Miles – enough to fly to Paris and back	£100 off your BT bill
Safeway	Casio SA2 keyboard	Cordless kettle, day trip for two to France, plus children's video	Two for the price of one on a cruise to Spain, plus other offers	Six toasters or 12 trips to Paris for £57 each, or free cinema trips every week for 16 weeks
Somerfield	Set of glasses or designer phone at Argos	Cordless hairstylers	Exercise bike or personal organizer	£89 flying lesson, plus £11 gift
Tesco	£10 off shopping	£20 off shopping	£30 off shopping	£100 off shopping

in most cases, the problems of partnerships outweighed the advantages. That situation was shortly to change.

Momentum without headroom

In the words of Crawford Davidson, Director of Clubcard between 2001 and 2003, 'If the best you can offer is to save money off your normal supermarket bill, it's a pretty boring idea.' Remember the loyalty cube: one axis is 'headroom' – that is, how much extra business you can, as a retailer, expect to win. When that business has been largely won, the value of a loyalty scheme for that customer can dwindle, with disadvantages on both sides.

To interest customers in earning the vouchers, Tesco knows it has to motivate its shoppers to want to spend them. That might mean simply substituting money they would have spent anyway with vouchers. 'If they make 52 shopping trips a year and we subsidize four of them, I have no problem with that,' as Mason says. Better though to give them something more exciting to spend their vouchers on. That motivation to burn means a motivation to earn.

Tesco was thanking these excellent customers, but potentially the Clubcard vouchers were substituting normal spend, not encouraging new behaviour. Steve McArdle at Clubcard Deals concurs:

> Families are the customers who spend most in Tesco, but we found that we were not fulfilling their needs. They were getting a pound a point in the store, we were giving vouchers and they would save up, come back once a quarter and take it off their shopping. It was not very involving, and not a great thank you.

The basic Clubcard programme had reached its limits with the brand's best customers.

CLUBCARD DEALS

Fairness, not equality

One of the virtues of the Clubcard programme had always been its simplicity. As Sir Terry Leahy asserts, Clubcard's inclusiveness, its one-tier simplicity, was one of its main advantages:

> In 1995, Sainsbury's was further ahead in trialling a card. They had it in more stores, but complicated things for themselves by looking at too many discount rates and we had the advantage that we had a very simple offer, easily understood. That's the power of a simple promise.

At Tesco, there were no Gold Card customers who could get special privileges in the stores like shorter checkout queues, personal assistants or better prices. This would run counter to the principles of the brand and the values of the company: for Tesco there can never be such a thing as a 'better' customer. But there are undeniably more valuable ones.

Pure equality in a commercial environment does have its drawbacks. Recognizing and rewarding the most loyal shoppers only in proportion to the value they give to the company is commercially a questionable idea. A one-size-fits-all scheme is fine at the beginning of a programme to get it established with as many customers as possible, but companies inevitably want to invest more with better-value customers. 'Having only one level of rewards looks like fairness,' says Peter Wray, managing director of loyalty consultancy pgw Ltd, 'but in practice it is reverse discrimination. You are over-compensating your least valuable customers. As a shareholder I would question that, and as a customer, I'd shout, "That's not fair."'

The need was clear: Tesco Clubcard had to broaden its offer to give fresh appeal and greater benefit to high-value loyal customers. With Clubcard, Tesco says 'Thank you' to every customer... but a bigger 'Thank you' to some.

Clubcard Deals was launched in August 1999, with a campaign that effectively re-launched the entire Clubcard programme. Tesco didn't hide the significance of Deals to Clubcard's future and to Tesco's overall customer strategy. *The Financial Times* announced on 6 April 1999:

> Tesco... is planning to relaunch its Clubcard loyalty scheme this summer to provide bigger rewards to its highest spending customers. The company intends to create three classes of loyalty points... Analysts said a gold, silver and bronze point system could help Tesco retain more of its highest spenders. However, there could be a danger that other shoppers would be alienated, said one expert.

The Financial Times summed up why Tesco was prepared to take that risk: 'Industry studies show that 80 per cent of food sales at any given food chain are derived from just 20 per cent of customers.'

The business case for Clubcard Deals was even more thoroughly modelled and developed than the original Clubcard concept itself. Some would argue, too thoroughly.

One million free tickets

'It's a new Clubcard Deal' said the promotional fliers that customers were introduced to in 1999. The basic customer proposition of Clubcard Deals was, and is, very straightforward: instead of spending your Clubcard vouchers to put towards your grocery shopping at Tesco, you could save them up for a special treat or trip for the family. By picking up the seasonal Clubcard Deals brochure, customers could choose from a range of Clubcards Deals from airlines, attractions, holiday companies, hotel chains, restaurants, sports venues and cinemas.

The launch publicity boasted 'a million cheap tickets', with partnerships in place with KLM, Euro Disney, Eurostar and Virgin Trains. For the first time, Tesco Clubcard members could redeem their vouchers outside the Tesco stores, indeed outside Tesco's business. Furthermore, with Clubcard Deals the highest-spending customers could quadruple the value of their vouchers when they used them to buy Deals. This meant you could 'Look your beautiful best for only £2.50 in Clubcard vouchers' (an appointment with Color Me Beautiful), or 'All aboard with three-quarters off ferry crossings' (P&O Ferries).

There was no question that Tesco was encouraging some of its top spenders to switch to spending their Clubcard vouchers away from their Tesco store, to create more value for them outside the Tesco shopping trip – but which customers?

The target audience was mainly families with children, households that spent well above the average basket value and visited their store regularly. There were many customers who spent a lot when they came to the store, but they didn't shop with Tesco on a regular basis. Tesco's priority with these 'opportunity' customers was to persuade them to come into the shops more often, so it wouldn't be smart to encourage them to spend their Clubcard reward outside the store. Nor could Tesco justify spending a lot more on rewarding the loyalty of customers who shopped regularly but who spent only a small amount. The priority there was to keep the prices of these customers' favourite products as low as possible so that they got value for money out every visit.

A balance had to be struck between showing the value of the new Clubcard offer to the big spenders, without alienating the other customers who could not qualify for the benefits. It was for this reason that the Clubcard team decided to introduce the concept of a 'Keyholder', based on a target threshold of regular spend. When Keyholders had earned enough 'Keys' they could get access to the Clubcard Deals.

Keys and Keyholders

The idea was similar to the frequent flyer schemes offered by airlines like British Airways, where privileges and special offers are available according to the number of high-value flights taken in any one year. And just as it does for the airline, this mechanism was chosen to give Tesco the maximum control. It allowed the company to target its new loyalty investment at the minority of most valuable customers, without flattening the sales peak enjoyed by the stores when Tesco vouchers are sent to the majority.

Every customer who spent £25 in Tesco in one visit earned a Key, and on the statement a new box showed a little picture of this Key. To qualify for double the value for the deals on offer, customers had to earn 50 Keys in their little box. If they earned 100 Keys in the previous four quarters, they became a 'Premium Keyholder'. That entitled them to a 75 per cent discount. Keys expired one year after they were earned, so each time the customer's statement might show that he or she had gained Keys or lost some. Meanwhile, he or she was unable to earn a Key by buying petrol or ordering from Tesco on the internet. When he or she had the right amount of Keys, and the right value of Clubcard vouchers saved up, that customer could exchange them for double or quadruple their face value from the Clubcard Deals brochure.

Still with us?

Too clever by half

The statement mailing sent the full brochure to the million customers most likely to qualify for Deals. Clubcard Deals was successful enough between 1999 and 2001, steadily growing the base of top-spending Clubcard members who saved up their vouchers rather than spend them in-store.

However, too many customers were turned off by the complexity of the scheme. 'Keys,' as McArdle now admits, 'were a step too far.' The concept of Keyholder status, he adds, is one of the few innovations from Clubcard about which no one fights for a share of the credit.

The creators of Deals concentrated on making the programme work for Tesco, and forgot to make it work for the customer. Because the proposition was too hard to explain pithily, it wasn't promoted widely beyond the launch. 'We couldn't continue to market it above the line, because Keys meant different levels of benefit and that's too hard to get across. So we just produced a brochure twice a year,' McArdle ruefully admits.

Keys may have failed, but the failure shows that customers will not engage with a complex idea: and without engagement, loyalty marketing is useless. 'Keys was textbook loyalty marketing,' says Mason. 'The trouble is, it was rational, not emotional. Customers couldn't be bothered.'

Getting the right Deal right

For those who made the effort, Clubcard Deals offered extraordinary value for money compared to the run-of-the-mill rewards on offer with other loyalty schemes. So much so that 500,000 Clubcard users repeatedly use their vouchers this way, and 27 of the original 30 partner companies who took part in the Deals programme when it was first launched are still part of the scheme, enjoying a good source of business.

Today, McArdle himself buys his summer family holiday at a huge discount thanks to Tesco. 'We went to Thailand,' he says, 'and I took just under £1,000 off the cost of my holiday.'

McArdle is a classic points chaser, just one who happens to have made his shopping habit into a job. He understands the motivations of those loyal Tesco customers who are attracted to Deals. He uses his Tesco credit card to buy his Tesco shopping, doubling the points benefit, and uses the same card for all other purchases. He shops for electrical goods, wine and CDs with Tesco.com. In a typical year he will receive £250 worth of vouchers, and when he converts them to what's on offer from Clubcard Deals, it becomes £1,000 to spend on the family holiday.

Two years after the launch of Clubcard Deals, the Clubcard team simplified the scheme. In the summer of 2001, the invitation to 'double the value of your Clubcard vouchers with Deals' was opened up to every Clubcard holder, not just those awarded the mystical Keyholder status. Clubcard members who spent an average of £60 a week were able to quadruple the value of their vouchers with 'Premium Deals'. This means that a very large proportion of Tesco shoppers qualified. When the Office of Fair Trading investigated supermarket shopping in the UK in 2000, its survey of shopping habits showed that half the adults interviewed spent £51 or more per week on groceries. Of those between 30 and 44 years of age, 70 per cent spend more than £50. C2DE shoppers are as likely to spend between £50 and £100 as ABC1s.

The Clubcard Deals scheme became easier to explain, easier to understand and easier to take advantage of. Tesco marketers slapped their foreheads, and said, 'Why didn't we do that two years ago?'

BROADENING THE OFFER

Air Miles returns

With Clubcard Deals, Tesco broadened the opportunity for its customers to spend their rewards. The precedent for spending vouchers outside the store had been accepted, and the problem of spend substitution was being addressed. In 2002 the opportunity to expand the Deals proposition grew dramatically, thanks to Clubcard's first suitor, Air Miles. Today, Tesco customers can exchange their Clubcard points for Air Miles – for example, £2.50 in Clubcard vouchers gets you 60 Air Miles.

By Christmas 2001, Air Miles had been a partner of Sainsbury's for five years. The 6 million Reward cardholders had been able to exchange points for miles from the beginning, and many tens of thousands had taken up the offer. Of the 1 billion Air Miles issued in 2001, between 200 million and 250 million went to Sainsbury's shoppers. Yet despite its popularity with customers, Sainsbury's decision to outsource its loyalty programme by joining the Nectar scheme created a problem. Air Miles discontinued its contract with Sainsbury's, and by February 2002 had announced the link with Tesco. McArdle says:

> It wasn't important for us to join with Air Miles until the opportunity arose, but there are times when you don't look a gift horse in the mouth. If you have an opportunity to take as much as £100 million in trade off your nearest competitor, you do it.

When Tesco joined forces with Air Miles in March 2002, Tesco predicted its shoppers would swap points for 400 million Air Miles in the first year – in effect, between £12.5 million and £25 million of the £200 million Clubcard points that Tesco issues per year would be converted.

The week that Tesco launched its Air Miles partnership, searches online for the nearest Tesco store jumped 450 per cent. One million new Clubcards were distributed to stores. Enquiries about home shopping jumped 300 per cent.

While Clubcard, Reward (and now Nectar) had long outstripped Air Miles by the numbers of collectors, Air Miles still has an intensely loyal base of fans: affluent, mature and valuable supermarket shoppers. They are self-confident enough to organize their own travel and will change their shopping habits to earn their Air Miles. Sainsbury's found that out. It credited the divorce from Air Miles with a loss of 1 per cent of sales volume – equal to losing 60,000 of its most valuable customers to Tesco.

Air Miles excite emotion in a limited, but sizeable number of customers, as Sainsbury's discovered. Sometimes, customers' commitment to chasing miles in every shopping trip can border on the irrational. But for those customers committed to earning one particular loyalty currency, it's better for Tesco to offer it than not.

Five years after the aborted partnership discussions between Clubcard and Air Miles, the two schemes now sit side by side. Now that

Tesco has realized the need for its own Deals concept, allowing customers to spend their rewards outside the store, Air Miles can be seen not as a threat, but as another way to 'burn' points that appeals to a small but valuable minority. And the fit between the programmes is complementary. According to McArdle:

> It doesn't do things in the same way as us, and that helps. In the early days we would have seen it as a competitor. We have discovered that Air Miles are seen as a different sort of loyalty currency by customers – it works perfectly.

The launch of Freetime

Simultaneously to doing the deal with Air Miles, Tesco decided for the first time in 2002 to bring together all of its Clubcard partnership interests under a new company, named Tesco Freetime. As well as expanding the range of offers to Clubcard members to spend their vouchers, the Freetime team was also responsible for increasing the number of partner brands that issue Clubcard points as part of their own promotional activity. McArdle explained:

> Clubcard is a huge and expensive machine developed by Tesco. But because it's so well established it's also the cheapest way for someone else to run a loyalty scheme. We essentially do it for them. Therefore they can spend on their customers all the money they have saved on building their own system and use Clubcard as their promotional tool.

This sounds like Nectar – but it is different:

- Clubcard is the Tesco loyalty programme, principally aimed at providing benefits to Tesco shoppers. Tesco issues the Clubcard points. Partners like Powergen buy those points, at a rate negotiated with Tesco, and they pass them on to their customers. But they are Tesco Clubcard points redeemable through Tesco or Clubcard Deals.
- Individual customer data are not disclosed, only aggregate data are shared with the other brands. 'We will tell them how many customers shopped at their store using Clubcard, and what sort of customers they were, but we won't tell them that it was you, or where you live,' says McArdle.
- Marketing to Clubcard members is the responsibility of Tesco. McArdle again: 'We might agree to jointly write to customers with one of the partner brands to tell them about a great offer. But the

partner will never know who the customer is unless that customer chooses to tell them. It is critical that they trust us not to misuse data.'

- Unlike Sainsbury's, Tesco has no intention of outsourcing its loyalty marketing activity. Quite the contrary, through its Freetime strategy it was taking on the loyalty marketing operations of other brands under the Clubcard umbrella.

The benefit to the partner brands was that for a fraction of the cost of going it alone, they could benefit from a powerful promotional currency that will be recognized by, on average, about 4 in 10 of their customers. And they got rich customer segment insights into the needs, preferences and behaviours of their clientele that only a broad-based scheme like Clubcard could provide.

Simpler, faster, broader

While Tesco is still conservative about recruiting partners, it is now sufficiently confident of the 'gold standard' status of Clubcard that it sees more opportunity than threat from the strategy. Indeed at the end of the 1990s, Tesco experimented with selling cheque books of Clubcard points vouchers to the businesses often considered to be most under threat from the supermarket's success: corner shops. McArdle recalls:

> It went very well, not so much from a financial point of view, but it helped centre us in the local business community. We moved from being a big ogre on the edge of town to being a key partner for some local smaller retailers.

Deals now offers a much greater breadth of rewards, targeted at every sort of Tesco Clubcard member, not just at points chasers or the big earners. Today Clubcard Deals offer vouchers that Clubcard members can use to buy tickets in 8 out of the top 10 tourist attractions in the UK.

They can even invest their Clubcard points towards planning their funeral. When Steve McArdle met Dignity Funerals, the second-largest chain of its type in the UK, he discovered that the typical customers for Dignity's pre-paid funeral plans were senior citizens, possibly recently bereaved themselves, who were prudent and didn't want to impose a burden on their families. Allowing Tesco customers like these to contribute their Clubcard rewards to a Dignity plan was perceived as genuinely valuable. It also demonstrated that Clubcard Deals were useful to a segment of supermarket customers who were less interested in family activities or holidays. 'We wanted to bring rewards to the widest group of people possible,' says McArdle, 'We actively looked to increase our range and look for niche products, and we asked our customers what they wanted. And a lot of them said that helping to pay for their funeral was a good idea.'

In 2003 Tesco took steps to simplify the Deals offer so that more and more customers could benefit. First it abandoned the £60 spend threshold which had qualified big spending customers for Premium Deals, and allowed them to convert their points at four times the value. Instead all customers could now earn four times the value of their points through Deals. With no Keys and no qualifying spend, the process, in McArdle's words, was the equivalent of 'removing the asterisks' from a Deals offer, no more annoying small print. As long as you have the vouchers, you qualify. In Tesco's opinion it has led to a boom in the number of people taking up offers. Tesco also renamed the company, shedding the Freetime brand and adopting Clubcard Deals as the trading title.

The next step in simplifying the Deals offer will be to make it easier for customers to convert their points into the Deal they want. At the end of 2005, the process was still being fulfilled manually. Customers fill in a form, mail it to the Deals office, and receive the relevant voucher through the post in return. In the near future that process will be automated and fulfilled online. This, McArdle explains, will eventually allow Tesco the chance to offer 'last minute' deals – for example, enhanced offers with partners who are carrying too much stock and are prepared to offer Clubcard members exceptional value for money.

Managing the risk

By the end of 2005, 10 per cent of Clubcard points were being issued by companies other than Tesco stores. Clubcard vouchers may still be very much the loyalty denomination of Tesco, but now the anonymous Clubcard Deals office, with its low-tech processes, is the clearinghouse for a thriving alternative and widely traded currency. Its staff numbers – just over 100 – are supplemented by up to 150 temporary staff after each mailing, as customers send in their Clubcard vouchers to convert them into the Deals of their choice.

Before the four-times value offer was made available to everyone, some partners were legitimately worried that only a hard-core of points-chasing customers would participate, and would accumulate deep discounts on partner products or services by concentrating their spending at Tesco. That would mean that Tesco had most of the benefit of the Deal, because the customers had boosted their commitment to Tesco products, and boosted Tesco turnover as a result. This could potentially have become a crisis when four-times value was made available to everyone – if that change turned a large proportion of Clubcard holders into fanatical points-chasers who would then redeem their vouchers for discounts outside Tesco.

Based on their research into customer spending habits, Tesco and EHS didn't believe that would occur – and they were proved correct. When four-times value was extended to everyone, the average value of a Deal didn't go up. It declined by about one quarter.

There's a side-effect to being able to track which customers are sitting on which vouchers: Deals can now also target its offers better. It doesn't need to mail holiday offers to customers with few vouchers, or magazine subscription offers to customers who save up for one big discount if it doesn't think they would value the mailing.

By over-complicating Deals, Tesco nearly lost the power of its simple promise. It learnt that if its offer to customers was simple, it would succeed, and the more it has simplified Deals, the more attractive it has become. Also, despite not trying to micro-manage the programme, it has still been able to control demand, satisfy partners – but most of all, attract a wide range of Clubcard holders. It realized in time that it was possible to be too clever for its own good. In focus groups, Tesco finds that its Clubcard users who have done a Deal often spend their time selling the benefits of the scheme to the others there, because it's now simple to explain and easy to understand. 'It's one of those mums-outside-the-school type of conversations,' says McArdle. 'How did you get to Legoland by using your Clubcard vouchers?'

13

From mouse to house

▶ 'It's our job to make home shopping work'

▶ Tesco on the internet

▶ Real shoppers, real stores, real advantage

▶ The bubble that didn't burst

▶ How it's different online

▶ Becoming a non-food e-tailer

▶ How Clubcard helped Tesco.com

'IT'S OUR JOB TO MAKE HOME SHOPPING WORK'

Sir Terry Leahy remembers:

> The success of Tesco in the 1990s was based around being prepared to do things that other people, or conventional wisdom, said wouldn't work. We did these things because customers liked them. I remember going to a presentation on home shopping, when it was a sort of laboratory thing,

and all the retailers who were there were saying that it would never work, it couldn't work. I walked out and thought, hang on a minute, it's our job to make it work.

Today Tesco.com fulfils over 200,000 home delivery orders every week. In November 2002, its turnover topped £10 million in a week for the first time. Around 4 million UK households have bought products from it since its launch in 1999. There are 5.5 million visitors to the Tesco.com site every month, and one out of every four customers that come to Tesco via the internet are not regular shoppers of Tesco supermarkets.

Apart from over 25,000 grocery lines and a range of wines, online travel and finance services, Tesco.com offers customers a choice from 380,000 book titles and 250,000 CDs, delivered by 800 Tesco.com branded delivery vans. A full range of electrical goods is also available.

Like Leahy, who learnt his retail science on the shopfloor of a Tesco store, Tesco.com (or Tesco Direct at it was known until April 2000) used a completely different recipe for commercial online success than was the norm for a dot-com start-up. In doing so, Tesco.com outpaced not only every other British e-tailer, but has become easily the largest internet grocery retailer in the world. At the time that the dot-com bubble was popping for other internet grocers like Peapod and Webvan in the United States, and when rival supermarkets in the UK were scaling back their early ambitions, Tesco.com was launching in new districts and announcing its first operating profit.

Leahy's peers, attending that home shopping lab with him in the mid-1990s, were right after all: they couldn't make home shopping work. Tesco, however, did make it work. It made an important strategic choice to launch using a pragmatic low-cost route – and backed its pragmatism with Clubcard.

It is no surprise to see that many of the original Clubcard team have worked at Tesco.com at some time. Tesco marketing director Tim Mason was chairman, Carolyn Bradley was at one time chief operating officer, working with Dave Clements as marketing director. The team is backed with targeting and creative work from EHS and data analysis from dunnhumby. The story of Tesco.com's success is how the combination of Tesco values and Clubcard insight could work on the internet just as well as they worked for the parent brand.

First steps

Leahy recalls:

> It would have been much more difficult without Clubcard. On the
> internet, you need more than anywhere else to understand your customer,
> to create a relationship with the individual customer. So while it would
> have been possible to build up Tesco.com without Clubcard, it would
> have been much harder; the mindset of the company would not have been
> right. If you couldn't be bothered to know about your customer in your
> main business, why would you suddenly want to know about your
> customer in this new business called the internet?

The internet has been the channel for Tesco.com since 2003, but the
origins of home delivery from Tesco pre-date the internet boom, and are
closely related to Clubcard.

When Clubcard got the go-ahead from the chairman's conference in
November 1994, having as Lord MacLaurin said, demonstrated more
knowledge about customers in three months than he had learnt in 30
years, it was not the only idea discussed that day. Home delivery was
also on the agenda. When Grant Harrison, Dave Clements and the rest
of the Clubcard development team were dispatched to 'The bunker' to
plan in secret the launch of Clubcard, they had a ready-made cover
story. Tesco had also decided to launch a home shopping trial, and the
team disguised its work by claiming to be devising a profitable way for
Tesco to deliver groceries to customers' homes.

Both were brave decisions from a board committed to modernization.
Reintroducing a loyalty scheme must have seemed like going back 20
years in time, but at least the Clubcard trials showed promising results.
Reintroducing home shopping was an echo from another era. Home
delivery was hardly new, it had simply been forgotten as neighbourhood grocers became self-service supermarkets. As Leahy pointed
out in a presentation to the 'Digital Britain 2000 Summit', the Army &
Navy store in London ran a 24-hour telephone ordering system before
World War II, with five deliveries a day.

Other retailers were thinking about reintroducing home delivery at
the same time, though with little success. In 1992, Asda was the first to
run a trial programme, offering the service to housebound elderly
customers who needed a shopping service similar to meals on wheels. It
cooperated with Help the Aged in a six-month trial to deliver groceries
to pensioners, although it was not extended. 'Our customers missed

choosing the items themselves,' an Asda spokesman said. In 1993 Somerfield piloted its home delivery scheme from its store in Crieff, Scotland, and Marks & Spencer followed the next year, trialling with five stores. Both experiments were discontinued. In the autumn of 1995 Tesco followed Asda and trialled the service with Ealing Social Services as a partner to offer 400 pensioners in West London the opportunity to shop from home.

Who used the internet?

While Mason had seen the strategic importance of the internet long term, in 1995, it barely existed in the minds of most Tesco shoppers. Market analyst Jupiter calculated that only 3 per cent of users of the public internet lived in the UK in 1995. Dataquest, the independent market consultancy, calculated that by mid-1996 there were around 5 million European internet users, and the UK had 2 million of them, mostly logging on at work. Romtec added that one in four UK homes had a PC, even if only one in 40 homes had a modem to go with it.

Shopping by catalogue too

In September 1996, the Tesco Osterley store in West London, which had been the base for the home delivery service trial, made the first small step towards the nationwide service that would become Tesco.com. While the growth of the internet was the most important factor in winning approval for home shopping from the board, there were not enough internet users to make an immediate internet-only launch practical – so initially, customers could shop either by catalogue or on the internet using either a CD-ROM catalogue or a primitive internet site to place the order.

A small fleet of Tesco-liveried Bedford vans was provided to deliver orders. Catalogues were posted in the catchment area, listing 2,500 out of the 45,000 items carried by the store; customers could order the CD-ROMs, which listed 18,000 products. The households invited to use the service were selected on proximity, ease of delivery and shopping profile. A couple of telephone operators stood by to take orders, and for a fee of £5 the van would deliver to the door at a pre-arranged time.

Tesco Direct in this incarnation was arguably a step sideways in enhancing customer service, rather than a leap forwards. As anyone who has ordered from a catalogue will appreciate, the prospect of browsing through thousands of items of grocery could only be tedious, whatever the medium. Frequently changing store prices made the challenge of updating the catalogues time-consuming and expensive. The inability to present all the products visually (too costly) was restrictive: often customers had little idea whether what they were ordering was the same as the product they bought in-store. It was difficult to describe the choices in customer-speak – how to give a price for 'a bunch of bananas', for example – so there was uncertainty and inefficiency in the order process.

Nick Lansley, now the IT new technologies manager, but at that time an analyst programmer in the Tesco IT department and the sole 'techie' on the Tesco Direct team, recalls:

> To start using Tesco Direct took a lot of effort. With a grocery order being 40 or 50 products, it wasn't like buying a book from Amazon. Customers were put off by the first order. In the time it took them to place it, they could have gone to the local Tesco, bought the stuff and driven back again.

TESCO ON THE INTERNET

One small step

Tesco Direct's project director Ken Towle admitted in October 1996 that he felt like the 'Neil Armstrong of internet supermarketing'. It might have been because he was taking the first step. It might also have been because Tesco strapped him to the top of a rocket and lit the blue touch-paper.

On 5 November 1996, Tesco formally launched the ability to order on the internet, using the CD-ROM as the catalogue of products (connection speeds at that time were too slow to access thousands of products online on a web page) and Microsoft to add the internet connection. Tim Mason shared the stage in the Queen Elizabeth Conference Centre in London with Bill Gates, whose other meetings that day were with Prime Minister John Major and leader of the opposition Tony Blair.

Meeting Microsoft

Although Microsoft's leader was already important enough to pop into 10 Downing Street for a chat, Tesco Direct was massively important for the commercial future of Microsoft. It was the first high-profile commercial customer in the UK for Microsoft's secure Merchant Server Internet software. Despite its success with Windows and Microsoft Office, Microsoft had been slow to recognize the full market potential of the internet, preferring to back its non-internet rival service to AOL and CompuServe, called the Microsoft Network, or MSN. But now the company was looking to be involved in driving the internet's phenomenal worldwide growth, and a partner like Tesco shared many of its own corporate characteristics. Both companies were ambitious, dedicated to being first to market, willing to experiment, to try something and if it wasn't exactly right first time, to fix it and come back for more. Microsoft, like Tesco, had overtaken several larger software companies, such as Lotus Development (now part of IBM), with a combination of aggressive marketing and relentless innovation. It jumped at the chance to be the partner of a major brand offering potentially high volumes of transactions that would prove that its internet software really could do the job.

Microsoft's Internet Server product manager was David Bridger. 'Tesco wrote its application in a few weeks,' he said at the time. 'It's the first full-service internet supermarket in the world.' But even Bridger had his concerns about the usability and long-term viability of Tesco Direct: 'Tesco has to make filling an internet shopping basket with 80 items interesting. That's quite a challenge.'

While Tesco Direct was becoming a pioneer of internet grocery shopping, behind the scenes it was far from a well-oiled logistical machine. As a new channel, it was still at its most experimental, backed up by improvised processes, not integrated with the rest of Tesco's supply and delivery chains. The priority was to maximize customer acquisition. If there proved to be insufficient demand, then it would be a waste of investment funds to build a bespoke infrastructure. While the jury was out, ad hoc arrangements would have to do.

The ad hoc approach

Tesco's ad hoc approach to fulfilling internet orders contrasted with the grander concepts of the dot-com boom, but it was a massively important strategic decision. Instead of building a network of warehouses, Tesco was determined to use its existing store base to manage customer demands (the trial was to expand gradually to 22 stores, mostly in London, by May 1999, when Tesco promised to add five stores a month until Christmas – a promise later extended to 10 a month). This dependency on stores meant finding an efficient way to have staff to shop using the customer's shopping list.

Today, the Tesco 'personal shoppers' as they are known, are a familiar sight in Tesco supermarkets, especially in off-peak hours. They use picking instruction sheets produced by a custom-designed software system, enabling them to fulfil six orders at a time, taking the shortest route round the store. But in the early days of Tesco Direct there was none of this process sophistication. The picking operation had minimal route planning, and used existing staff downtime rather than dedicated staff. The order process was equally unstructured. Internet orders were placed by the customer and transmitted down the line to the Tesco call centre in Dundee. They were then printed out and faxed to the local store.

It worked – sort of – but as an ongoing way to manage the process it was far from ideal. Too often the desired products would be out of stock and so shoppers found that their delivery was short of several items, and would have to visit the supermarket anyway.

Yet despite the teething problems, a significant minority of, usually high-spending, Tesco customers – and non-Tesco store customers – greatly valued the convenience of internet grocery shopping. The first challenge to the Tesco.com pioneers was how to find more of these customers cheaply.

REAL SHOPPERS, REAL STORES, REAL ADVANTAGE

Together again – the Clubcard team

In 1996, Carolyn Bradley had been responsible for the Tesco brand, working with Tim Mason and the original Clubcard team on the TV launch campaign. By 2003 she was the chief operating officer of Tesco.com. She made the switch to become Tesco's e-commerce director in 1999, when the steady growth of the home shopping service promised explosive success.

From the outset she was determined to make the most use of the Clubcard experience and apply it to this new growth opportunity. She remembers:

> One of the things we found, subsequent to launching Clubcard, was the whole impetus we got from understanding customer data, managing it to

improve how we do business. When it came to home shopping Clubcard gave us a huge head start. Our data management skills as a company were way ahead, but more than that the Clubcard database gave us a fantastic list of people to go after, and a sophisticated understanding of those customers. We could be very specific in terms of whom we targeted. That was a huge built-in advantage when starting up a business.

Dave Clements, another graduate from Mason's team of 'bright young things' who launched Clubcard in 1995, later followed Bradley to the internet shopping project. There he was responsible for recruiting more of those profitable customers prepared to pay a service premium for home delivery of their groceries. In 2003, while working as marketing director for Tesco.com, he described the 'classic' home shopper:

> We are not trying to force home shopping on anyone. The profile of the customers who get most benefit from home delivery obviously starts with internet access, then they are most likely to have young families with a need for a lot of shopping but they don't have the time to shop. Or they are young professionals, who buy premium products but don't want to visit the supermarket. Thanks to our Clubcard experience we know where and how to find them, then invite them to try the service.

Tesco's plan to target online shoppers via Clubcard, rather than just fishing in the pool of internet users, has paid off. By April 2001, Tesco.com was looking for a very non-typical internet user to become a typical internet Tesco shopper. Among Tesco.com shoppers, 79 per cent were women, 80 per cent were ABC1 – much higher proportions than the average profile of e-commerce customers.

Young families made up 47 per cent of Tesco's online customer base, and three out of four were buying online for the first time – shoppers that it would have been tough, if not impossible, to find by searching the online population and trying to sell the benefits of internet grocery shopping.

Mass customization

The contribution of Clubcard wasn't just about finding new users: it also made it easier for Tesco to keep its online customers. By 1998, it became clear to Lansley and the others on the team that if Tesco was to create a home shopping service that matched the quality of experience in-store, it needed to be able to mass customize what it did in the same way that Clubcard helped to customize Tesco's communication to its non-internet customers. Because there was always going to be an overlap between the two – few customers shop direct but don't visit a store – Tesco also needed to integrate the customer service offered by the two channels.

The idea was simple: show shoppers what they had already bought in their local Tesco store, so they would have to spend less time looking for it online. 'The Tesco mainframe stored every scan from every checkout, from every store for the previous two weeks. If you use your Clubcard in the transaction, then that is recorded too,' says Lansley.

He begged a small slice of mainframe time for Tesco Direct, and with it, he created 'My favourites'. When shoppers registered online, they could tick a box that would allow Tesco to produce a 'My favourites' list. That list was compiled by asking the mainframe to look for the Clubcard number and find the products that had been scanned that were connected to that number. Next time the customer logged on to Tesco Direct, there would be the list.

'It was a roaring success,' Lansley explains, not least because in the early days of Tesco Direct there were no product pictures, just text descriptions, so customers would often make a mistake when ordering.

There was, and continues to be, a small problem with 'My favourites'. Some customers feel uncomfortable when presented with the fact that Tesco knows what they bought – it is too personal. Lansley says:

> A lot didn't have any problem, but we offered the box to give them a choice – if they didn't want us to, we would not compile the list. But a bigger problem was when it revealed information that some customers might not have wanted to be revealed.

An early example was when Lansley was contacted by a Tesco Direct shopper. She had just received her 'My favourites' list of products bought in the previous two weeks, and she was certain there was an error: the list contained condoms, which her husband can't have bought because he didn't use them. Knowing the list to be accurate, Lansley made a diplomatic decision that became an informal policy afterwards: 'I'm sorry,' he told her. 'There has been a corruption in the data. We will remove it.'

'Whenever something comes up like this, we say we are very sorry and change it,' he says. 'I don't want to cause a marital rift when I can tell a white lie. Customers regard groceries as personal. They reveal a lot about you.'

THE BUBBLE THAT DIDN'T BURST

Internet economics

From the earliest days, the home shopping team used Clubcard data to the full, combined with other data sources, to identify which Tesco stores offered the greatest potential for the service.

The planners at EHS were charged with identifying and quantifying how many customers on the Clubcard database best fitted the ideal profiles: where they lived in relation to the store, the products they bought and the value of their shopping baskets. Additional data gathered from the Tesco.com website and individual response profiles were used to develop an internet-only customer segmentation model to predict customer profitability. Based on a classic 'recency, frequency and value' (RFV) model, the Tesco.com segmentation measured customer commitment on six-levels: 'Dedicated', 'Established', 'Developing', 'Cautionary', 'Logged-on' and 'Logged-off'.

Beyond the Clubcard and online audiences, standard geodemographic data was used to identify 'birds of a feather' households who shared similar characteristics to the Clubcard members, but who were not currently using the Tesco store. The team was able to calculate accurately the number of potential customers living in the area served by Tesco Direct. With this targeting knowledge and the power to communicate with minimum waste, Tesco was able to recruit customers for a fraction of the cost endured by most e-tailers.

For other internet entrepreneurs trying to establish themselves at the time, those costs reached quite frightening proportions in 1999. Reporting in March 2000, management consultant McKinsey found that internet retailers were paying US $250 for every customer they acquired, and that two out of three of these expensively courted individuals never returned for a second purchase. On average less than 5 per cent of visitors to retail websites ever made a purchase. McKinsey calculated that a new customer contributed US $24.50 in the first quarter to the retailer's gross margin, and US $52.50 in every quarter after that – but that for each customer that remained, retailers would have to invest US $1,931 just to keep a website available and up to date. The economics were starting to look grim for the new economy businesses.

Nonetheless, in the late-1990's world of venture capital extravagance, CEOs under 30 and marketing budgets of millions, Tesco Direct looked a little staid and dowdy. One analyst told *The Grocer* magazine that it was 'constructed from balsa wood'. Carolyn Bradley remembers: 'We used to get quite fed up. "Why doesn't anyone talk about us when they talk about dot-com companies?" we would ask.' Perhaps Tesco's instinct for thrift and pragmatism wasn't considered very cool.

According to Bradley:

> Amazon, starting out, was spending about 70 per cent of its sales on marketing. That's a ratio you can't live with for long. It's a lot lower now, but ours is still a tiny fraction of that. Tesco's total marketing spend is never more than 1 per cent of sales. Tesco.com's is higher than that, because we're a young growth business. But it is still a lot less than 5 per cent.

By the time that Bradley joined Tesco Direct in 1999, some commentators were waking up to the inherent problems faced by most of the dot-com start-ups, speculating that the bubble was about to burst. Sentiment shifted to 'clicks and bricks' businesses – part traditional retail, part internet business. Tesco Direct was stronger as a business model as it also had the back-up of its Clubcard loyalty programme, enabling Tesco to identify, segment and incentivize the best potential customers for a lot less than US $250 a head.

Tesco Direct becomes Tesco.com

By the beginning of the new millennium, Tesco's internet grocery service was taking 10,000 orders a week, even though it was still available only in Greater London and Kent. By April 2000 Tesco Direct accounted for 70 per cent of grocery home shopping sales in the UK, and compared to the same month a year before, its turnover had grown 600 per cent. Most exciting for the board was the fact that three out of 10 customers using the home shopping service regularly – almost 100,000 – were new to Tesco.

An impossible flotation

At the time speculation grew that Tesco Direct would be floated as a separate company, taking advantage of the buoyant valuations still accorded to new economy businesses. In April 2000, several newspapers carried rumours that a valuation of up to £4 billion was expected – extraordinarily a quarter of the value of the parent company, such was the economic insanity of the time. A leading HSBC analyst poured cold water on the excitement. 'It would be completely illogical to float Tesco Direct,' she explained. 'In fact it would be physically impossible to do so.'

One week later, as Tesco announced its annual results, Tesco Direct was reorganized to become a fully fledged subsidiary of Tesco and renamed Tesco.com in keeping with the brand fashion at that time. This followed Tesco policy, rather than dot-com convention: for example, its small-format supermarkets are also run as a separate business unit. On the one hand, it gave Tesco.com staff their own identity and motivation, on the other it meant that Tesco.com could still profit from its association with Tesco – and the common link of Clubcard.

With sales of £125 million in the year, Tesco.com had made its planned operating loss of £11.2 million, and was predicted to break even in two years. Tesco marketing director Tim Mason, the original sponsor of Clubcard and home shopping also took on the job of chairman of Tesco.com, while Tesco strategy director John Browett became chief executive, and Carolyn Bradley became chief operating officer. Tesco chief executive Terry Leahy promised £35 million investment to accelerate expansion of the service in the 2000 financial year.

Following its successful trials, Tesco.com's goal was to become the UK's number one internet shopping destination. Its breakthrough year was going to be 2001, and one of the key differentiators was going to be Clubcard.

Measuring the Clubcard advantage

Because it is a remote channel, rather than face to face, online retailing offers few opportunities to provide personal service. The instances where the service 'touches' the customer are often out of the brand's control, as the only face-to-face interaction is outsourced to delivery companies. Tesco deliberately avoided this by quality controlling the deliveries, insisting on branded delivery vans, uniformed drivers and careful staff training. Since launch, Tesco drivers have been asked to unblock sinks, choose wallpaper, baby-sit, drop kids at school, witness a will, and even give a lift to a wedding.

It's a similar approach to Tesco's refusal to outsource the Clubcard scheme. Because Tesco.com had access to Clubcard data, it could track whether Tesco.com was getting it right. As Carolyn Bradley explains:

Clubcard gave us the means to understand how to target customers, which ones would be most likely to try home shopping. Most of all it gave us the ability to validate that what we had done was right. We can analyse our online customer activity by relating it back to the core business. We can analyse based on the existing customer segments, identifying how people are using the Tesco brand. Are they using Tesco.com only, or a mix of dot-com plus in-store shopping? Questions like that. We can look at total customer behaviour, not just what they are doing online, and respond appropriately.

For example, Tesco discovered that some of its assumptions about how customers would use the service were wrong. The belief that they wouldn't want to buy fresh produce without 'squeezing it' proved to be unfounded. Marketing director Dave Clements says:

> To start with, our shoppers may start by buying bulky baskets: bottled water, pet food, washing power. That's the chore of going to the supermarket. Quite quickly, a loyal home shopping user develops to become a normal supermarket shopper. Seven of our top 10 lines are fresh, so it is certainly not true that people will not buy fresh food on the internet.

HOW IT'S DIFFERENT ONLINE

The customer journey

Shopping online offers a different 'customer journey' – the jargon that describes the process by which a shopper trying the service becomes a loyal customer.

By definition internet grocery shopping is not as familiar to customers as store shopping. The customer is left to create his or her own habit. The challenge to the team was not only to maximize visitors to the Tesco.com site, but to persuade as many of them as possible to trial the service for the first time, then win the second order. Experience showed that only after several orders would customers become committed online shoppers.

Working with EHS planners, the Tesco.com team mapped out this customer journey. They had identified that convenience was what online shoppers wanted most. So they looked at the 'journey' and tried to make everything as convenient as possible along the way.

This meant a consistent message whenever Tesco communicated with the customer, from the awareness communications in the store or from outdoor posters and TV advertising; through recruitment direct mail and digital communications; through the customer's first website visit, registration and first shop; all the way to the delivery of the goods to the home and the subsequent use of the service. Tesco.com needed to communicate consistently to reassure customers of the solidity of the virtual alternative to the stores that customers could touch. More importantly, it demanded a consistent quality of service. Customers are attracted to online retailers with the promise of convenience, but one bad experience can destroy that faith in an instant.

As well as 'My favourites', this led to other innovations to make the site quick and easy: customers could preview delivery slots, as convenience of delivery time was the first thing customers looked at before shopping, reassuring themselves they could get what they want, when they want. More evening and weekend delivery slots were allocated to cope with the 'out-of-hours' lifestyle of the typical dot-com shopper. Pages were designed to download faster, with performance targets. 'E-vouchers' – offers and incentives to shop – are now delivered and redeemed electronically.

Improvements to the usability of the Tesco.com site were important but so were improvements to customer management. Conscious that this was a start-up business, the project team devised a programme of online and offline communications to convert as many enquiries as possible to repeat usage. That meant relying on old-fashioned direct marketing, with the goal that they would maximize the volume of new customers to the business. Regular e-mails and mailshots were sent to existing customers to increase frequency and basket value, encouraging as many as possible through the various stages of customer development from 'Cautious' to 'Dedicated' customers.

By planning exactly what messages needed to be communicated at each stage of the relationship, the aim was to talk to the right customers at the right time, with the right offer, encouraging trial, repeat purchase, cross-sell, up-sell and retention. For example, an e-mail follow-up might offer a discount off a customer's next shop in the form of £5 or £10 e-coupons, tested against date-specific three-part offers giving up to £50 off over three shopping trips within a certain period.

The price of a customer

The cost of recruiting through the direct marketing campaign handled by EHS reduced to £20 per customer. Customer referrals increased 92 per cent that year. Average 'cost per click' fell from 29p to 21p.

Tesco also improved its success rate in encouraging customers of competitive e-tailers to switch to Tesco.com. Through data profiling it identified customers whose primary online grocery shop was with a competitor, but who occasionally 'topped-up' with Tesco. It refined the targeting by matching this list against the Clubcard profiles, to identify the highest-spending potential customers. It segmented the wish list of customers, splitting those who lived close to Sainsbury's, and those who did not. The prospects closest to Sainsbury's – the key competitor at the time – were incentivized with a voucher promising '£10 off your first shop'; those further away got a voucher worth £5. Tesco considered its campaign a major victory: each new customer cost £19.

Word of mouth (or in the dot-com lingo of the time, 'viral marketing') contributed approximately one-third of new customer registrations. Another third came through from in-store promotion with advertising, internet and direct marketing activity accounting for the rest.

Only Amazon currently has more online customers in the UK than Tesco.com. Tesco's turnover in 2000 was a little over £200 million – by 2005 it was £719 million. For Christmas 2004, 750,000 customers – one in 25 of the households in the country – had their Christmas grocery shopping delivered by Tesco.com.

In Ireland, there are 145,000 online customers, and online shopping via Tesco.com is just beginning to take off in South Korea.

One-third of Tesco.com customers are substituting online shopping for their existing trips to a supermarket – but one-third are new to Tesco, and one-third are existing customers who are spending more with Tesco thanks to Tesco.com.

Thrift vindicated

Clements says:

> When competitors are trying to catch up with us, they don't always make such pragmatic decisions because they think, 'If Tesco made a success of it, then we should make a success of it.' They look to our experience or to US business models rather than working it out for their customers and their business. We are more single-minded, more confident in designing our own future, I think.

Mason agrees. 'I said at the beginning, let's see if anyone wants to use the internet to shop throughout stores. If they do, and we can't cope, we will build a warehouse – but at least we will know where the first orders are coming from.'

Tesco made the decision very early that its grocery home delivery service would recreate as closely as possible the experience of shopping at your local Tesco store. By comparison, Asda and Sainsbury's decided that to satisfy the needs of their home shoppers they needed to invest in a nationwide network of giant warehouses, purpose built to handle orders, picking and dispatch in an IT-driven environment. In December 1999, Sainsbury's announced its first 120,000 square foot warehouse in Park Royal, West London, dedicated to fulfilling home internet orders. Similarly Asda employed 331 people at two warehouses in Watford and Croydon, and planned 11 more.

For Asda and Sainsbury's, the argument in favour of warehouses dedicated to home shopping was clear:

- They would rarely run out of stock, as they were geared to the needs of internet shoppers. As many orders are placed several days in advance, stock problems were easy to predict.
- They were set up to make it easy to pick orders, so staff could fulfil the orders quickly and accurately, without getting in the way of other shoppers.
- They could be sited close to major transport links, whereas supermarkets were sometimes not set up in the optimal base for a delivery service.
- They could build logistics and customer support systems to accurately track orders and drivers.
- Once the cost of building the warehouse has been offset, they are much cheaper to run, as they are not customer-facing.

Tesco.com has still not built a warehouse. 'You cannot invest £30 million to have an idle warehouse waiting for you to build a business to make use of it,' says Clements. 'We realized at the time that we have 650 really good warehouses already for our internet operation. They are just called Tesco stores.'

The Tesco.com pioneers were convinced from the outset that their store-based model was better:

- The stores were effectively free warehousing.
- They were local to the customers (less than 25 minutes' driving time), cutting delivery times.

- Investment in better logistical systems could be shared between Tesco Direct and the stores.
- The service was easy to scale: you simply added more stores to the system.

Asda has closed all but one of its warehouses, and today fulfils its internet orders from stores, as does Sainsbury's At Home. Neither has access to Clubcard data, which made the in-store model more effective. It helped Tesco identify which stores offered the best potential to expand the service – where the greatest concentration of prospective Tesco.com shoppers could be found, what take-up would be and what sales value could be predicted.

It showed what those shoppers would most likely buy when they shopped in person, and how the basket size and composition changed online, meaning that out-of-stock problems could be minimized, and it demonstrated how to incentivize a segment of shoppers to use the service fully, and quantify what the response rates were likely to be. Through its quarterly statement mailing Clubcard also provided the cheapest possible recruitment medium – outside the store – for new Tesco.com customers. In 2005, Tesco.com profits rose 51.8 per cent, to £36 million.

Webvan crashes

The online grocers that had caught the eye of the press when no one was taking any notice of Tesco Direct didn't fare so well. The deflation of the dot-com bubble for Webvan, the US pioneer of grocery home shopping, and the only home delivery service worldwide to rival Tesco for scale, was dramatic and sudden. Webvan, launched in San Francisco in April 1999, burned through more investment – about $1.2 billion in total – than any internet retailer except Amazon.

Webvan was an internet-only supermarket chain that would have no stores, but giant warehouses in urban locations. The Webvan model was the opposite of Tesco Direct in every sense. Whereas Tesco used the results from a few trials, analysing the data through Clubcard to apply to the rest of the business, Webvan set out to acquire customers first, and analyse their shopping habits later. Whereas Tesco concentrated on serving customers, 'Webvan was so intent on meeting its long-term goal of building a behemoth... that it lost sight of a more mundane task:

pleasing grocery customers day after day,' in the words of dot-com industry magazine *The Industry Standard* in August 2001. It added that Borders' concept was that 'delivering groceries was just a way to get Americans to open their front doors. Once they did, he'd sell and deliver everything and anything.'

'It's going to be a US $10 billion business,' Louis Borders, Webvan's founder told Randall Stross, the author of *eBoys*, a story of the celebrities of the dot-com boom, 'or zero.' 'He was right,' *The Industry Standard* magazine commented in August 2001, after Webvan filed for bankruptcy, with its share price down from US $34 to 6 cents. Its US $1.2 billion was spent acquiring 750,000 shoppers: approximately US $1,600 per customer, 80 times greater than Tesco.com's figure. Only one of its operations made an operating profit – an untypical, small-scale, low-cost warehouse in Orange County, California.

Coals to Newcastle

Ultimately, Tesco.com was able to show the US supermarketing business something that it had forgotten in the rush to expand: take care of the customer.

By June 2001 in California, Safeway Inc's Grocery Works internet shopping service was not working for the customer or the business. Enter Tesco. For an upfront fee of £15 million Tesco licensed Safeway to use the intellectual properties developed by Tesco.com – its processes, its bespoke software, its management tools. Tesco.com sent 10 staff to California to help set it up, serving the exact streets that Webvan had tried, and failed, to serve profitably two years beforehand.

Today Safeway.com runs on the same platform built for Tesco.com. It doesn't have the advantage of Clubcard, but it is using many of the measurement and targeting techniques that learnt from Clubcard. It turns out that far from being built of 'balsa wood', Tesco.com is a robust, profitable business model – refined by Tesco's obsession with knowing its customers not only better than other supermarkets, but better than other internet retailers too, and improved by Tesco's culture of listening to customers and acting on their wishes. San Francisco's dot-com grocery shoppers use the descendent of the ordering system built in 'a few weeks' by Tesco and Microsoft in Ealing, West London.

'It's the modern version of taking coals to Newcastle,' says Leahy.

BECOMING A NON-FOOD E-TAILER

A bigger prize

Tesco stuck to the 'power of a simple promise' for internet delivery, and it worked. But the internet offers a bigger prize:

> The proportion of the population for whom getting groceries delivered is attractive is clearly limited. It will never be the majority of the market – it will be a long way short of that. So what we are doing is broadening out beyond Tesco, getting onto other markets.

Tesco's desire to expand into non-food retailing has been well known for several years: it was one of the drivers for growth that Leahy had identified in the early 1990s. Yet the company's opportunity to realize that growth was limited by a physical practicality: its available floor space.

The internet offers a chance for Tesco to increase its non-food activity dramatically:

> We are not just a shopping destination for groceries, but for anything our customers want to buy. In stores we are limited by space, but online, we will sell anything that we feel customers think we should be able to sell.

Tesco.com had a big incentive to push harder into selling non-food online. Research showed that 30 per cent of its customers limited their online shopping to a single retailer – Tesco. It was almost a 'walled garden' opportunity, with Tesco having privileged access to the online purchasing behaviour of thousands of homes.

Again, Clubcard data helps. Clements says:

> Using Clubcard, we can very quickly find similar prospects to our current customers and identify which of our customers are likely to be customers for electrical goods or home entertainment. But it goes further. Some combinations of grocery products suggest strongly that those customers might be direct wine buyers for instance. We found this through evidence and data analysis, although sometimes it's a fairly obvious thing – if you buy a lot of washing powder, you might be interested that we could sell you a new washing machine.

The targeting is never going to be 100 per cent accurate, but it does reduce waste significantly. Tesco.com wants to reduce acquisition and ongoing sales costs through better targeting. For high-value items like a fridge-freezer, which are purchased at most every few years, Tesco has the opportunity to use its brand awareness and the efficiency of its communication channels. It has found that few fridge buyers will naturally return to the last retailer they bought from. Many more customers will choose to deal with a brand they value and trust, based on their regular shopping habits.

Tesco has responded by creating a single destination for non-food Tesco products online, called Tesco Extra Online. Customers now choose from 380,000 books, 250,000 CDs, a digital download store selling 500,000 music tracks for 79p each (which now has 10 per cent of the UK download market) and a DVD rental service supplying 200,000 DVDs a month through the post.

Virtual warehouses

Rather than following the Webvan route, creating real warehouses to hold and dispatch a vast array of product lines, Tesco started to apply its strategy of building virtual warehouses devoted to specific product ranges. Many of these were created in partnership with specialist suppliers. Using Clubcard data, Tesco can target potential customers.

In the first year that Tesco.com pushed its non-food lines, the results were remarkable – in the run-up to Christmas 2001, it sold 230,000 CDs and DVDs. Wine sales topped 1 million bottles. A single mailing for the Mother and Baby warehouse produced directly attributable sales of more than £500,000. Tracking showed the recipients of the mailing were two and half times more likely to make subsequent purchases.

However, while the non-food opportunity is massive for Tesco.com, Leahy is adamant that grocery sales will never become a loss-leader designed to get a foot in the door, as was the declared strategy at Webvan:

> The promise of customer care that was made in store still applies. We develop a customer for whom a visit to Tesco is just part of running the household, and sometimes it's buying a bike once a year, but it is also about buying socks more regularly, buying presents quite a lot, and buying food very regularly. It's hopefully an extension of our relationship with the customer, not simply about grabbing some different customers infrequently.

HOW CLUBCARD HELPED TESCO.COM

A single customer service

Tesco customers are Tesco customers, no matter how they arrive at the store. By insisting that Clubcard was an inherent part of shopping online with Tesco, a strong link was forged between the clicks and the bricks sides of the business. Clubcard allowed customers to shop in the same way online as in-store by posting their 'favourites' as a saved shopping list, based on their store choices as well as their online purchases. And they got the same rewards for loyalty. The reward to the business is, according to AC Neilsen, that 93.9 per cent of purchasers shop loyally with Tesco.com.

A single customer view

Thanks to the wealth of customer information afforded by the Clubcard database, Tesco can quickly see the similarities and differences between online and offline customers: what they buy, what they don't buy, how they respond to the service, how they mix channels. Looking at transactional data over time, Tesco has demolished some internet myths – for example, that shoppers would not buy fresh food online.

Lower customer acquisition costs

When launching its internet shopping trial, Tesco was in a lot stronger position than rivals – it knew the names, addresses and shopping habits of millions of possible customers already. Without Clubcard the company would have had all the risk and the same unsustainable cost of customer acquisition that killed off services like Webvan. Using best practice direct marketing techniques learnt from the marketing of Clubcard over the years, Tesco's dot-com marketers increased their success rates through, for example, testing trial incentive offers, including free delivery and money off first and subsequent shops.

Bringing new customers to Tesco

'We are not just fishing from the same pool of customers,' points out Carolyn Bradley. By analysing its own customer base to identify the types of shopper who have the highest likelihood of actively using the online service, Tesco could target outside sources of data and market more effectively to shoppers who were not yet Tesco customers. The team profiled cold lists against Clubcard data and used both e-mail and direct mail to test a huge array of lists to establish the most cost-effective recruitment strategy. With dramatic results.

Minimizing costs

By basing the expansion of Tesco.com on its network of stores rather than regional warehouses, Tesco could use Clubcard customer data to prioritize those stores offering the best potential – where the greatest concentration of prospective Tesco.com shoppers could be found, what take-up would be and what sales value could be predicted. Customer numbers could be accurately assessed and planned to minimize out-of-stock problems. Using Clubcard information Tesco was able to target its customers within a 25-minute driving range of each store, maximizing the number of deliveries its vans could make each week.

Accelerating into non-food

Tesco found it could use Clubcard data to profile customers who were most likely to respond to non-food offers online, and make the most of this new medium. Tesco.com was the easiest way for the company to expand radically its range of non-grocery products.

14

Back to basics

- ▶ Ask the audience
- ▶ Simplifying Clubcard
- ▶ Simple marketing

On 12 April 2005, Tesco declared pre-tax profits for the previous year of £2.03 billion, a rise of 20.5 per cent over 2004 and a record for a UK retailer. The statistics underlying those headline figures were impressive: £37.1 billion sales worldwide, an extra 10 million customers gained every week, 1,779 stores of all sizes across the UK, 4.9 million customers with Tesco Personal Finance (TPF) accounts, 15 million books sold, and a market capitalization of almost £25 billion. And, of course, 11 million active Clubcard holders.

The next day, the *Independent* newspaper cleared its front page to report the results under the giant headline 'The supermarket that ate Britain'. The *Independent* was not the only newspaper to temper its admiration for Tesco's business achievements with a suspicion that the company had become too powerful.

Having broken through the 30 per cent market share barrier, Tesco had long since become the most successful supermarket in the UK. Now, with £1 in every £8 spent in retail spent at Tesco, it had become the UK's most significant retailer by far; its sales accounted for 2.6 per cent of the GDP of the UK. That, some commentators had decided, meant that Tesco's dominance was too great (one lobby group even going as far as starting an anti-Tesco campaign based around a website called 'Tescopoly').

'Tesco is generating its own particular brand of loathing,' an article in the *Guardian* had claimed during January 2005, quoting the National Federation of Women's Institutes, who had called for an investigation into its power by the Office of Fair Trading. Another 13 organizations had joined the WI in a campaign called 'Breaking the Armlock' to try to rein in the power of supermarkets in general, and Tesco in particular, and to encourage the UK government to appoint a supermarket regulator. A WI spokeswoman said about Tesco:

> They have steamrollered the competition. They are becoming too powerful. Our members don't like to see local shops closing. So many live in small communities and they are losing the focal points of those communities. We also want members to question the whole concept of convenience. We are asking them to think about what they are doing, and think about the impact of their actions.

It wasn't just Tesco's diversification and its growing share of supermarket spend in the UK that was alarming its critics. Tesco had made two major strategic purchases: first, in 2003 it had paid £377 million to buy approximately 1,000 small shops and kiosks operated by T&S, the largest chain of high street convenience stores in the UK. A few months later, in January 2004, it spent £53 million more to buy 45 central London supermarkets which traded under the brand names Cullens, Europa and Harts. The stores had prestige locations in London's busiest shopping streets: Notting Hill Gate, Bayswater, Trafalgar Square, Holland Park and Marylebone High Street. Tesco now owned more traditional British 'corner shops' than anyone else, and central London's poshest supermarkets. Strange to recall that only 20 years earlier, Tesco had such a reputation for poor quality that some advisers seriously suggested it should change its name.

With out-of-town planning permission hard to get and an ever-widening range of product categories available in its large-format stores, Tesco had decided that there was an opportunity to grow by expanding its small-format Tesco Metro shops, many of which would occupy the locations it had just acquired. The UK Government's competition regulator decided that these store purchases did not need to trigger an official enquiry, as the two retail markets – convenience shopping and large-scale supermarketing – were distinct and therefore subject to different competitive dynamics. From now on Tesco would be capturing more of the share of high street spending from more of the population on more days of the week than ever before.

While Tesco's critics were becoming increasingly vociferous, sales results suggested that the shopping public took a different view. At least for the time being. Tesco was determined to protect the positive relationship it had enjoyed with the British public. The management was aware that if they ever lost that fund of goodwill they would have a bigger problem than a few critical headlines.

ASK THE AUDIENCE

Signs of decline

Unknown to the journalists, Tesco had already been engaged for more than a year in a ferocious bout of self-analysis. This led to a root-and-branch review of every aspect of the brand's communications and service to customers. One of the key outcomes was the relaunch of Tesco Clubcard in 2004.

When UK marketing director Simon Uwins started his job in 2001, he inherited a powerful brand but he quickly identified a subtle problem. While the brand promise of 'Every little helps' was popular and well known both inside and outside the company it was in danger of being something that Tesco said – rather than what Tesco did. Uwins was determined that 'Every little helps' should permeate the whole business guiding all its contact with customers. He calls it the 'body language of the business'. He says:

> When you think about what customers actually want from their shopping – they want us to help them make their shopping trip a little bit easier, and if we can do that year in year out, that's all that 'Every little helps' is. We're not trying to pretend that it changes the world – but actually you can count on Tesco that, every year you shop with us, every year it gets a little bit better.

Uwins saw his job to be the conscience of Tesco's brand, standing up for the values that Tesco promises to its customers. And the evidence was that Tesco had some work to do in this area. An example that Uwins uses as a lesson for his staff was the experience of Christmas 2002, where Tesco did not enjoy the lift in sales it was expecting – despite a large number of promotions and seasonal offers. When it asked customers what the problem was, they pointed out that in its desire to make its best promotions easy to spot, Tesco had placed many of them in the centre of the aisles. This, in turn, made the aisles difficult to navigate when the shop was busy. The desire to sell had overwhelmed the mission to make shopping easier.

Uwins thought Clubcard was a useful barometer of the changes in customer engagement with Tesco as a brand. Every year since the peak of participation in 1997, when more than 80 per cent of Tesco sales were linked to Clubcard membership, Clubcard usage had shown a slight but steady decline. In the late 1990s, this could be explained as a natural trend: a settling down to a sustainable level of participation. After the loyalty card frenzy of 1996 and 1997, many users simply didn't want to carry a loyalty card all the time, or only carried one or two. But as the trend continued into 2001 and 2002, it became obvious that there was a danger of more serious customer apathy. In 2001, 74 per cent of Tesco's sales were trackable by Clubcard. In 2002, it was down to 72 per cent. Unless checked it meant that by the end of 2003, the participation rate would hit 70 per cent, and that set alarm bells ringing.

There was a very clear reason why the higher reaches of Clubcard penetration were tougher to achieve. Tesco's growing expansion into small-format stores, where credit cards are used less frequently to pay for impulse purchases and small shopping trips, and therefore customers' loyalty card usage is less habitual, necessarily depressed the overall Clubcard results.

There was nothing statistically important about the 70 per cent threshold. It had never been set as an internal target below which participation must not go. It would still deliver a phenomenonally accurate indicator of the dynamics underlying Tesco sales and the trends in customer behaviour. So looked at from the point of view of data analysis, it wasn't important at all (remember, Tesco had started by analysing only 10 per cent of its Clubcard data). But as the figures coasted gently downwards, the Clubcard team knew that 70 per cent Clubcard penetration was a figure that several years previously they would have never accepted. It was a signal that some customers were becoming disengaged from Clubcard. Tesco staff had a mantra on retaining customers taken from Frederick Reichheld's 'Loyalty Effect' drummed into them: 'Grow by fixing the leak in your bucket'. Clubcard's leak was becoming worrying.

Relaunching Clubcard

Uwins called a meeting of the Clubcard team in March 2003. 'Simon said, look at the scheme. Simplify it. Do what we have to do to make it responsive to the needs of all our customers again,' says Helen Godley, head of Clubcard operations and development, 'Sales penetration was our key measure, and over the last few years that had been in steady decline.' But for a programme that had, on the surface, strong customer engagement the question was: why was this happening?

'The whole premise of Tesco's business is to understand customers better and give them what they want. You find that out by listening to them,' says Uwins. 'We asked customers, and discovered that there were still some very appealing things about Clubcard, but some things needed changing.'

To keep listening closely to customers Tesco runs a continuous programme of Customer Question Time sessions – in 2004, more than 9,000 participants from up and down the UK had their say in one of these face-to-face sessions. When they dedicated one of these sessions to Clubcard, Tesco found out exactly why usage was declining.

'What they told us was, "We know what it is about, but it's getting old-fashioned, staid and a bit boring. It seems less rewarding than it used to be",' Godley recalls.

Clubcard's deteriorating image was the result of four commonly voiced complaints:

- It's too confusing. Uwins says:

    Customers said Clubcard had become complicated. Which was understandable. Since we had launched Clubcard Deals we had in effect been running three different currencies. As well as the Clubcard points you earned at the checkout, there were keys that you converted for Deals, and all the vouchers we sent to you were in pounds and pence. So the customer was seeing these three currencies in one Clubcard statement. People didn't understand what was going on any longer.

    The result was that a growing number of customers who were not enthusiastic points-chasers, or who were simply too busy to work out what was being offered, no longer felt it worth their while using their Clubcard.

- It's too anonymous. From the time when Clubcard was proudly launched in every Tesco store in the land the programme had progressively dropped down the store managers' list of priorities. It was becoming part of the background noise of the store rather than front of house. 'Clubcard's presence in stores was a lot less than it used to be. Customers thought, maybe Tesco isn't as committed to Clubcard any longer. It didn't seem to be as important,' says Uwins. 'They were saying, "Why would I bother using it if you are not proud of it?"' adds Godley.

- It's too hard-sell. Uwins says:

  This was really worrying. Customers were saying that some of the Clubcard stuff felt like a second-hand car salesman, very promotional. What with all the trade-driving mailings and bonus coupons we were sending out, imperceptibly over time we had made the reward to customers more and more like a sales promotion and less a simple thank you.

  Tesco had embraced its new marketing mantra: 'Reward the behaviour you seek', but it seemed it had been applying it too crudely. Any loyalty strategy is pulled in two directions. One is to develop long-term customer relationships through a customer-focused approach, responding to their needs and priorities. The other is the imperative to drive short-term sales. By making 'lifetime loyalty' its core corporate purpose and creating Clubcard as its 'Thank you' strategy, Tesco had committed itself to prioritizing the longer term value of building customer relationships. Now Clubcard members were saying that this commitment was no longer so clear.

- It's too old fashioned. Clubcard's members said that they saw new things in their Tesco store all the time, but they couldn't recall seeing anything new from Clubcard. 'We were stuck in the 1990s,' Godley admits.

It was clear that Clubcard had four problems that had been allowed to take root. Now Uwins, the Tesco Clubcard team and their agency partners at EHS Brann were in a race to solve these fundamental issues before customer participation hit 70 per cent.

SIMPLIFYING CLUBCARD

A single currency, a simpler Deal

From the outset Tesco always intended that Clubcard shouldn't be hard work for customers. Increasingly customers were telling them that good intentions were not matched by reality.

Two things were making Clubcard more mentally taxing than it should have been. First, there was the mixture of currencies on the statement – points, keys and pounds and pence.

Then there were the Deals that invited cardholders to spend their Clubcard vouchers outside the store on travel and family treats. These were causing some confusion. To qualify for the best offers customers had to maintain a minimum spend threshold of £60 a quarter, in order to gain what was called 'Premium Deal' status. This was an alien concept for customers to grasp: they were accustomed to a simple pound-a-point swap. It was also the reason why a secondary currency – keys – was quoted on each statement. When people browsed the Deals catalogue looking for ways to spend their vouchers they were confronted with two levels of pricing; this made it difficult to work out exactly what they could get. Special status for Premium Deals was the only example of tiering in the Clubcard programme, something that sat uncomfortably with Tesco's 'democratic' brand values.

The symptoms of the problem were clear. The next thing to do was tackle them.

When Tesco is running a project, it creates what it calls a 'Natural work team', where everyone who is personally responsible for delivering part of the solution to the problem, from whatever part of the business regardless of job title, has representation. Every week, the team meets to report what it has achieved over the last seven days and agree next steps. Tesco runs its meetings in the same way it runs its business: strict timekeeping, a succinct agenda and clear actions coming out of the meeting. The person given those tasks has the power to complete them, and the responsibility to report back that they have been completed. Anna Dobson, the Tesco account director at EHS Brann, was asked to participate as a team member for the Simplifying Clubcard project, representing the communications task, which meant attending the meetings at Cheshunt every Tuesday for six months. 'Everyone attends, and everyone listens to what everyone else has to say. No one is an outsider or an observer. No one is out of the loop, and it forces you to do exactly what you promise,' she says.

It also creates a culture of consensus between managers, and between Tesco and partner agencies, because decisions are made in full view. Not everyone has to agree with them, but no one can say they didn't know what was going on.

Simplifying Clubcard meant two things: sort out the currency confusion and strip out the complexity from Deals.

To solve the first challenge the team came to the conclusion that Clubcard had to return to basics and be unequivocally proud of its own currency: Clubcard Points. Customers would be reminded that they earned a point for every pound they spent (with multiples for using a Tesco credit card, for example), and their bonus offers would also be expressed in terms of Clubcard points too rather than money-off or percentage discounts. The thinking was clear: encourage customers to concentrate on and value the earning of more Clubcard points and don't distract them from that pursuit. But there was an equally clear risk: would fewer shoppers take part in the tactical promotions that Clubcard offered them if they were collecting their value in points rather than an instant discount?

Mike Emery, head of the Clubcard direct mail programme recalls that the plan to move to a single currency wasn't overwhelmingly popular with a very important constituent: the suppliers who funded the promotional coupons. By offering shoppers points rather than a direct cash discount, the supplier funding was being recycled into the Clubcard currency. Suppliers worried that this would have a reduced effect on a shopper's responsiveness to their offers, even if they valued the points reward. 'Suppliers said it was good for Tesco, not good for them,' Emery recalls. Nevertheless, for Tesco the change was not negotiable. Earning Clubcard Points had to be the centre of attention for the whole programme.

In stripping out complexity from Clubcard Deals, Tesco was to consider taking an even bigger gamble. The project team looked at all the options but in the end the most radical was the one they backed; get rid of Premium Deal status for the minority of most valuable customers and elevate all Clubcard members to the most generous offer. That meant that instead of offering four times the value of Clubcard points via Deals to Premium customers only, they would offer it without restriction. There was to be no threshold of spend, no keys, no unnecessary small print. Deals, which had proved enormously motivational for the minority who had qualified thus far, would from now be open to all. It was an idea that Uwins remembers was like a 'light bulb going on':

> The thing that motivates customers is not trying to get to an imposed £60 a week spend level, that's looking at the offer from the wrong perspective, the business not the customer... What motivates customers is earning enough points to do a Deal they can enjoy with their friends and family. We had built in a false step in the original scheme that made it look difficult to take part. Even so we had demonstrated that once a customer did a Clubcard Deal, they would really get enthusiastic about getting another one and they would increase their participation much more with

us, in what we call the extended brand. People start to chase points, just because the value for money you get with Deals is so good, nothing else, no kind of manipulation is needed.

Steve McArdle, head of Tesco Deals, admits it was a 'leap of faith'. The risk was that hundreds of thousands of Tesco customers would convert their Clubcard rewards and swap them for Deals vouchers at four times the value. If they expressed their loyalty outside the store, it might lead to less engagement with Tesco as a brand, not more.

So both Simplifying Clubcard strategies carried significant risk for the business. At worst the moves could combine to damage Clubcard's return on investment for Tesco by making it much more expensive to run, and much more rewarding for a minority of promotions-hungry customers – that would accelerate Clubcard's decline rather than arresting it.

In November 2003, the changes were put to the Tesco board in a brief discussion paper. They discussed the risk – but approved the changes.

Throughout 2004, the Clubcard statement mailing, which drives so much of Clubcard's sales effect, switched over to points-only offers. Says Emery, 'Offering points rather than money-off discounts has allowed us to be less conditional in our offers.' Offering a coupon giving money off always implied that customers had to buy something first to get the benefit. Too many of these coupons were helping to create the idea that Clubcard was all about promotions. Offering points meant that sometimes points could simply be given as gifts: for example, offering double the points on the same shopping trip for a limited time for customers who were in danger of lapsing.

Mixed in with the coupons offering bonus points were 'gifts': a coupon that a customer hands in at the till to claim 100 extra points, for example. Customers have to visit the store to claim the gift, but they don't have to buy anything more to benefit.

Customer response was immediate and very positive. Redemption rates almost doubled, and in some cases the results were even more spectacular. Says Emery:

> In our November 2004 mailing we targeted people who shopped with us regularly, but who we knew also shopped elsewhere and we gave them a gift coupon for a free Christmas pudding or a box of mince pies. We were getting redemption rates of 50 per cent. That meant a few simple unconditional offers were able to generate massive increases in in-store traffic. And when we analysed the sales effect of doing that we learnt that when people use these coupons, they start using our stores a lot more.

So what about the effect of simplifying Clubcard Deals? The number of Clubcard members who took advantage of the four-times value offer from the Deals scheme shot up by 260 per cent after the Premium status condition was removed in May 2004. More customers of all segments were getting involved in the Deals programme. It also changed their shopping behaviour.

> We believed that the majority of new Deals customers would be more loyal and increase their shopping behaviour if they switched to using their Clubcard points for Deals, but we didn't know just how massive the effect would be until we tried it, remembers Dobson at EHS Brann, after the agency had lobbied for the radical option for Deals rewards. The sales impact exceeded all expectations. Shoppers who took advantage of a Clubcard Deal became significantly more likely to visit a store more frequently afterwards, and they were much more likely to concentrate more of their spending at a Tesco store.

After Simplifying Clubcard, there was less need for a hard sell to get customers to remember to use their Clubcard in-store, because the pull of a simplified Clubcard did the work.

A consistent message

Sometimes, Uwins notes, you don't see what the customer sees until they remind you. 'As we reviewed Clubcard, we saw some internal stuff we were doing that made things more complicated for them. Every statement mailing had a new creative on it. It never looked the same. It was needlessly complicated,' he says.

For nearly a decade 'Every little helps' had been as useful as a rallying call for staff as it was for customers, reminding Tesco people to concentrate on making the customers' shopping trip a little better every time. It also reminded the business as a whole to avoid any 'we know best' arrogance. Whatever you do for customers, the brand promise said, it has to about being helpful to them.

Yet when the Tesco Clubcard team sat down and reviewed the wide range of communications in mail and e-mail that it was sending to customers, too often it fell short of this standard. The team looked at everything that was being sent out to Clubcard members and everything in-store that invited customers to join – but this time, exclusively from the customer's perspective. Was it clear? Was it simple? Was it motivational? Was it relevant? Was it helpful? Most importantly, was it 'Tesco'?

From that review they created a 'communications journey'. First, they saw how poorly new members were welcomed into the programme. When someone signed up in-store, they took their card, used it, and waited for something to be sent to them. That wait could be two months, or sometimes longer. Tesco had never acknowledged a new Clubcard member soon after they joined, or explained fully what they could expect from their new Clubcard membership. Often customers would take the card but not supply a name and address. As they used the card they would earn points, but Tesco could never identify them to send them their reward. These anonymous points collectors, referred to as 'skeletons' by the Clubcard team, often assumed that their points were accumulating automatically on their card – and when they failed to get their benefit, they lost interest in the scheme. Skeletons worried Tesco, because they were literally unreachable – and there were more than a million of them on the Clubcard database.

It was a lost opportunity on all sides, and the team decided to use this overhaul of the programme to regain it. Dobson explains:

> We changed the way people got their Clubcard. The application forms were redesigned to make it easier for new joiners or home movers, who were too often lost. Instead of picking up a permanent Clubcard in store you got a temporary card to get you started, then a welcome pack in two weeks with your permanent, personalized card enclosed. We made it clearer than ever that unless you provided your name and address you hadn't activated your account. The result was an immediate reduction in the number of 'skeletons' among new members. What is more, the message got through to many of the existing anonymous cardholders, who were reminded that they weren't getting a reward. They took a new temporary card and transferred their skeleton points balance to their new, named Clubcard account.

In the first six months of the change the number of skeleton Clubcards declined from 1.3 million to 1.1 million. The Clubcard Welcome Pack was a measurable success. But there was a more fundamental rethink needed of the Clubcard mailing programme. 'Simon likes things to be clear and simple,' Dobson says of Uwins, 'So when it came to the Clubcard statement and all the other mailings that went out, we decided to scrap the lot and start again'.

Instead of completely different creative themes for every mailing, EHS Brann set out to bring order to the creative chaos with a Clubcard style manual and a single set of guidelines. The colour palettes available to designers would be different for different parts of the business – but the overall look would be consistent, clearly denoting that this was a communication from Tesco Clubcard

Most of the attention was given to the statement mailing. The time had come to replace Clubcard magazine. All the research showed that customers were ceasing to value it, and a dwindling minority were even reading it. In the spirit of Simplifying Clubcard the decision was made to swap it for something that would communicate more straightforward value for money to customers. EHS Brann designed what it called 'The Postcards': five connected cards offering a different combination of offers or invitations targeted by nine customer segments. Any of the cards can be simply torn off, filled in and mailed. Instead of having a magazine that sat on the table or was immediately binned, the postcard format was engaging, giving customers five reasons to respond. For those who wanted a magazine from Tesco, a new format Tesco magazine was free in-store.

From the envelope inwards, the redesigned statement mailing aimed to have, in the direct marketer's jargon, 'matability' – that is, the opposite status to junk. It should not look like the sort of direct mail people file in the bin. It had to be as familiar and valuable as a statement for their savings account. The plan was that a customer could tell from the top of your stairs that it was from Tesco – and that it was worth opening.

Tesco's Godley says:

> When we reviewed the old work we were aware that the mailings had become holdalls for all the offers the business wanted to put out. How many messages were we putting into the statement? Too many. No wonder customers thought we weren't proud of Clubcard anymore. Now when we lay out all our design work, and it is all in the same style, clean and simple, it almost sends a shiver down my spine, it's work we are all proud of.

The most important audience, the Clubcard members, responded favourably to the changes too. In the first year of the redesigned mailing programme, the percentage of customers who judged that Clubcard was 'modern and up to date' rose by 11 per cent.

One day during the redesign, the Clubcard team was looking at all the printed materials and realized something was missing. 'The reward vouchers never had the words "Every little helps" on them. Never. Only after we noticed that, did we realize that Clubcard itself didn't carry the message either,' recalls Uwins. 'Amazing'.

Immediately the new Clubcard design and reward vouchers were changed to incorporate the essential message that Tesco was trying to convey – but which for 10 years it hadn't noticed was missing.

Living the promise

Uwins' concept of 'body language' describes how a retailer backs up its promises with actions. Without realizing it, he says, customers pick up the signals that the business – often accidentally – is putting out. They will see through any insincere claims or a lack of conviction in what the brand stands for. Customers might not be able to articulate exactly why they are not convinced. What matters is that if they aren't, it's because they sense the retailer lacks self-belief. Then they turn off from what the store has to offer.

Which is why, when customers started to tell Tesco that it didn't seem committed to Clubcard any longer, Tesco's marketers took the hint very seriously. If Tesco's commitment to Clubcard wasn't being communicated in the brand's 'body language', something needed to be done.

Alongside the relaunch of Clubcard, Tesco created a concerted 'hearts and minds' campaign among Tesco staff. In the larger format stores many staff had been there for years. In the recently acquired and rebranded Tesco Express stores, few staff came from a Tesco background. At the checkouts, customers were much less likely to be asked for their Clubcard, for example. The Clubcard team found that fewer of the staff in these stores had been fully briefed on what Clubcard was offering, and so they were not aware of the importance of communicating the benefits to shoppers. Enthusiasm among Tesco staff had been the catalyst for Clubcard's popularity at launch: the same strategy was used to make sure that checkout operators remembered to ask for the card and could explain why it was useful.

This has helped solve the problem that customers thought Tesco didn't care about its loyalty programme. Today, nine out of 10 Tesco customers say that they feel Tesco is proud of Clubcard.

A special interest in food

Since the first sub-club was launched in 1997 the sub-club strategy had been successful in demonstrating Tesco's commitment to particular groups, rewarding their decision to sign up with gifts, discounts and helpful information. Baby Club remained the most popular of all – attracting hundreds of thousands of new members every year. As part of its review of Clubcard's role, the team took another look at the current choice of clubs, and decided that the time was right for potentially the biggest club of all: 'Of all the clubs we had offered, we had never had a food club,' Uwins says.

Launched in January 2005, the Tesco Food Club attracted 370,000 customers in its first eight weeks. By signing up, members received recipes, nutritional advice and a generous helping of money-off coupons. As with the other sub-clubs there was no joining fee or quali-fying conditions: it was used as a way for Tesco to say 'Thank you' to customers who were particularly interested in good food.

There was, however, a problem in the depth of the commitment that club members demonstrate. Emery recalls:

> The special interest clubs were ticking along, and we knew that members are more loyal both in the depth of their commitment and the breadth. When we did an audit of the performance of the club mailings, we found that those customers who joined were more loyal to Tesco, spent more with us and were often our most valuable customers. But when we looked at the redemption on the coupons we sent out to them, the rate had dropped to 5 per cent.

This flummoxed the team. Here was another worrying sign of declining interest. From research groups there was no obvious customer discontent, just a failure to engage. When they looked in detail at the choice of offers being made, they realized why. Because the sub-clubs were part-funded by suppliers, the coupons were based on what the brands wanted to sell rather than on what Tesco customers wanted to buy. The Clubcard team judged that members of the special interest clubs were not getting the reward they deserved for their decision to join. To address the problem Emery lobbied for a substantial slice of marketing support – around £1 million of promotional budget – to pay for better targeted offers for sub-club members. It was another leap of faith to back Emery's case that this diversion of investment would pay off. It did: one year later, the redemption rate for the sub-club coupons was between 25 and 30 per cent. The customers were re-engaged.

The Clubs refocused on a 'What can we do for them?' approach. 'We started to use the phrase: "Unconditional love". No one does it in retail. No one loves customers without expecting a quick return. With Clubcard we thought we could be more radical. Let's just try just giving people things,' says Emery.

There was sound business logic in making this work. Emery could justify the concentrated effort of the business to re-engage the 2.4 million sub-club members because of the enormous potential they could have on Tesco's profitability. 'If you are a member of the World of Wine, and you redeem one or more your coupons, Tesco research shows that on average you spend £1.14 more a week at Tesco than if you don't,' Emery says. Multiply by the number of Club members, and the effect is significant: today the average sales uplift of club mailings is £5 million.

A disloyalty programme

Getting Clubcard back on track was not just about changing what the scheme offered and how it did it. It was also about who it made those offers to.

A growing amount of attention had been focused not on the most loyal customers of Tesco, but on many of the least loyal customers. This is common to many 'loyalty' programmes.

First, there is more potential growth among customers who only use Tesco on an occasional basis, and clearly do a lot more spending elsewhere, compared to customers who already spend a big proportion or even the majority of their household budget at Tesco. There are a limited number of reasons you can give to a regular customer to visit the store more frequently. The 'opportunity customers', as they are dubbed in Clubcard jargon, offer the headroom to create greater return on investment from a programme like Clubcard.

Second, it was easier to attract supplier funding for promotions that promised to win over a large number of new customers than it was to reinforce current shopping behaviour.

This explains why there had been a drift towards targeting promotional spending to these customers. Simon Uwins admits:

> The best value for money coupons in our statement mailing were for people who were less loyal, rather than the loyal customers, because we were trying to change behaviour and entice them to spend more with us more frequently. It was the result of a logical business case, but we were getting a bit too hung up with short-term measurement of the incremental uplift from Clubcard. We were doing it for us, not for the customer. The outcome from a broader customer point of view was that Clubcard simply felt too promotional.

Another bold decision: Uwins massively cut the money that Tesco invested in driving trade from 'opportunity customers' and the money was shifted into saying 'Thank you' to customers who were genuinely loyal to the brand.

In 2003, Tesco invested £150 million to drive more trade from less-loyal customers on the Clubcard database. At that point you got a better deal from Clubcard if you weren't loyal. It made short-term trade sense and delivered a sales spike, but it was the antithesis of the reason Clubcard had been introduced. During 2004, the majority of Clubcard's trade-driving budget was used to provide better offers for loyal customers.

Tesco also spread the rewards for loyalty more consistently across the customer segments, instead of concentrating investment on high-spending groups only. So for those families struggling on a tight budget they resurrected an old retail favourite, the Christmas Club. The idea of a scheme which lets customers save steadily over the year to pay for Christmas groceries dates from the early 19th century. In 2005 Tesco sent a targeted mailing inviting loyal price-conscious shoppers to save up their Clubcard points all year round to put towards their big Christmas shop – with a bonus of up to 4 per cent. They could also pay cash into their Christmas Club account at the checkout. Around 100,000 took up the offer.

'We could look at ourselves in the mirror and say that we genuinely rewarded loyalty. One year previously, I'm not sure we could have said that,' Emery says.

Modernizing Clubcard

'It's a plastic card,' says Dobson, 'How can you make that more modern?' Answer: you make it into a key fob.

If evidence was needed that Clubcard was ready for an update, Tesco's top management needed to look no further than their own wallets. As loyal Tesco customers most of them had received their Clubcards back in 1995. Their cards had a dated design and, more important, they weren't working as well as they should when presented at the checkout.

At the tills, the old cards were causing a problem because the magnetic stripe that identified the card's unique number were wearing out. Millions of Clubcards had to be swiped several times before they registered, many others had to have the user number entered by hand. Swiping a magnetic stripe was an old-fashioned, laborious process at the best of times. One that did not work first time added hassle for the customer and an alarming cost to the business, particularly when you consider that Tesco is processing 20 million transactions a week. Says Helen Godley, who headed the re-carding project:

Re-swiping was costing us £4 million in lost time a year, and using a barcode instead of a mag stripe would save another £4 million. Swiping a card takes six seconds, scanning a barcode takes three seconds. Add up the time across the business and it was costing us a fortune. And because barcodes don't fail like magnetic stripes sometimes do, it's a lot less embarrassing for our customers when there's a queue.

The hassle for customers was becoming more expensive too. Focus group evidence suggested that when Clubcard holders popped out to a small local Tesco store, they would often grab their keys and some cash – and leave the troublesome card at home. This, customers told Tesco, was especially the case for men.

The Clubcard team had seen the technology they wanted in replacement. Advances in plastic barcoding meant that there was now a fool-proof way to get one-swipe scanning from a mass-produced card that would not wear out. 'Until then we also hadn't the capability to handle the number of bar codes through the tills. That capability came on line in 2004,' says Uwins, 'So then we took the opportunity to re-card with a new technology.' When you have a barcode instead of a magnetic stripe, the Clubcard doesn't even have to be a card any more. It can be printed on any format. Like a key fob, for example.

That idea was checked with customers. 'Key fobs were especially popular among men,' Clubcard's Godley notes, 'because they could attach them to their car keys and so only have one thing to remember... apart from their money.'

The re-carding campaign in autumn 2004 was a logistical challenge as daunting as the original launch of Clubcard in 1995. It meant manufacturing and mailing almost 10 million key fobs, in a pack with two new personalized Clubcards. It meant training all checkout personnel staff in how to process the new Clubcard formats. The cost of production and mail would be huge, but thanks to the bean counters at Tesco who calculated the time cost saving, there was a clear business case that meant the budget was soon made available.

Dobson points out another reason why the new-format Clubfob will save cash over time. 'The main reason that people called the Tesco call centre in Dundee was for misplaced and lost Clubcards.' The observation was that while many people misplace their cards, sometimes they even lose their wallets, they rarely misplace their keys. Since the advent of the key fobs the call volume at Dundee, Dobson says, has reduced by 10,000 a week.

The positive effect was just as marked. Clubcard penetration increased by 4 per cent in the sales period after the fobs were mailed. At Tesco Express stores, where Clubcard use remained doggedly low, it climbed by 50 per cent in one year. At the end of 2005, sales penetration was still on its way up, for the first time since 1997. 'A lot of that is on the back of the re-carding exercise, particularly the popularity of the fob,' Uwins says.

SIMPLE MARKETING

Keep it simple

Clubcard's relaunch didn't happen in isolation. Uwins' broader project was to make 'Every little helps' a governing thought for all Tesco marketing, and that included Clubcard. He demanded that the Clubcard team embraced his drive for 'simple marketing' – a discipline based on the insight that too many companies over-complicate their communications to customers

The 'Simple Marketing model' that Uwins espouses starts from a suitably simple premise: 'Understand customers better than anyone'. From that, it has four objectives:

- making Tesco available;
- delivering the 'Every little helps' shopping trip;
- using 'Every little helps' to drive trade;
- saying 'Thank you' to customers.

In working towards these combined objectives the business aims to achieve long-term customer loyalty. Everyone in the Tesco marketing department has a flowchart that explains the model. At the end of the flowchart is the question: 'Is our activity consistent with this model?'

If it isn't, Tesco cannot achieve long-term customer loyalty. As an example of how clear the Simple Marketing model is, trade driving is now defined as a 'secondary activity' of Clubcard. Being unconditionally rewarding and focusing on retaining loyal customers are the primary activities.

Another graphic now familiar to everyone on the Clubcard team is The 'Virtuous Circle' of Clubcard. It describes a cycle of communication that reinforces the right message to customers. Tesco sends customers offers that they want, customers value it as a 'Thank you', they spend the vouchers at Tesco, which means they collect more Clubcard points, so Tesco can send them more coupons to say 'Thank you'. Rethinking Clubcard has brought every aspect of its activity into the Virtuous Circle – including Clubcard Deals.

Dobson says:

> When we changed Clubcard Deals so that we were offering four-times value to everyone it was a perfect proof of the Virtuous Circle. All we were asking of customers was that they continued to shop at Tesco in the normal way and then they could get this fantastically generous offer. The customers took it up enthusiastically, and in focus groups became almost evangelical.

This not only reinforced the circle, but potentially brought more people into it.

Keep it controlled

Clubcard's most loyal 40 per cent of customers are responsible for generating 88 per cent of Tesco's UK retail sales. The most loyal 20 per cent creates two-thirds of its turnover. What are referred to as 'Premium Loyals' are also most likely to buy into more than one of the extended Tesco branded businesses, like TPF. They are most likely, in fact, to be responsive to almost anything Tesco offers them. Which is very good news. But also part of Clubcard's problem. Because there is a constant danger that these super loyalists will be over-sold and over-mailed.

Today, the principle of 'air traffic control' governs how much direct mail lands on any customer's doormat. No matter how much suppliers would contribute to a mailing, Tesco will often prefer to say 'no' rather than abuse the relationship they have built up with loyal customers. The rough limit is that customers should receive no more than one piece of mail a month. 'This is not a mailing free-for-all,' says Steve Grey, at dunnhumby, 'we have to be the guardian of the customer's interests, and if necessary, to educate the marketers who pay to contact the Clubcard database.'

'We built guidelines around what an "Every little helps" mailing is,' says Uwins, 'it's all laid out on one page, with simple guidelines, and every mailing gets submitted to the mailing group. We simply say: does it conform to our guidelines? If it doesn't it won't get mailed.'

The controlling committee is led by Andrew Mann, Director of Clubcard, who has to review and approve every mailing before it goes out. This direct mail air traffic control system is tricky to manage – not least because it has to track all mailed communications to every Clubcard household, wherever they come from. But it is vital if the Simple Marketing model is to work in practice.

Permission-based marketing

On the one hand Tesco is determined not to over-mail customers and alienate them from Clubcard. On the other, there is plenty of evidence that many customers want to hear more. Indeed, one of the most surprising aspects of Tesco's Clubcard experience is the degree to which customers actively demand more communication. Every time the Clubcard statement is mailed the call centre at Dundee has to handle calls from impatient customers asking when they will be getting their pack. To manage this demand Uwins has steered as much of Clubcard communications as possible towards an 'opt in' – that is, offers that customers actively request – on the premise that it is better to be a chosen than a given. Experience shows that customers value offers that they have requested more than those that arrive unannounced. This is why the Clubcard team have put so much emphasis on developing special interest clubs.

The key to success in permission-based marketing is to make the opting in as painless as possible for the customer. Clubcard coupons make the process easy; for example, customers who buy a lot of health and beauty products in-store are likely to want more information and offers in this category. If they receive a barcoded coupon in their statement mailing inviting them to join the Health and Beauty Club, all they have to do is present it at the checkout and they're automatically in. 'It has been fascinating to see how people respond: you can join a club just by swiping a coupon through the checkout,' says Uwins, 'You get a welcome mailing, see if you like it, and if you do – off you go.'

Unconditional love

Another key lesson from the Simplifying Clubcard project has been the importance of returning to basics. 'We'd gone a bit too far, with all the right intentions, but we'd got too clever. Refocus and lo and behold we revitalized the whole scheme,' says Uwins.

By making Clubcard's rewards too conditional and rewarding 'opportunity' customers at the expense of the loyal ones, Tesco had unwittingly begun to undermine the reasons why Clubcard was so successful. Tesco's 'body language' had sent a message to customers that Clubcard had changed. Clubcard was meant to be a 'Thank you' to customers, a tangible demonstration of Tesco's brand promise 'Every little helps'.

By listening to customers, and having the confidence to reward customers in a less conditional way, Tesco was able to refocus both the business and the membership on the benefits of Clubcard. 'If you really listen to customers, what you end up saying is, "Oh no, that's obvious, how could we have misunderstood!"' says Uwins. Simply saying 'Thank you' and giving less conditionally, changed the 'body language' of Tesco's rewards to customers: 'The net effect is that after the relaunch we signed up more than 1 million more customers to Clubcard in one year. It was the highest recruitment into Clubcard since 1997.'

15

Clubcard overseas

- ▶ Is customer loyalty the same everywhere?
- ▶ Crossing the Atlantic
- ▶ Slaughtering sacred cows
- ▶ dunnhumby USA
- ▶ A journey with Kroger

On 4 March 2002, 'the Fantastic Four' touched down at Cincinnati-Northern Kentucky International Airport. Their mission: tell Dave Dillon, then the chief operating officer of Kroger Inc., and today the company's chief executive, what he didn't know.

'The Fantastic Four' is the ironic name that dunnhumby US chief executive Simon Hay gave to a team comprising his three colleagues – Sarah Myatt, Mark Hinds and Adrian Coy – and himself. They certainly weren't superheroes, instead four rather tired British data analysts with an unspecific remit, big expectations and no US office space. But arguably, they did have superpowers – the knowledge and experience gained from running the data strategy of the world's most successful retail loyalty programme.

They had been transported from their headquarters in West London to the US Midwest for one reason. Kroger, a US retailing giant with sales of more than US $50 billion and 2,500 supermarkets across the United States (making the company approximately the same size in sales as Tesco), was looking to analyse the mass of data it had accumulated from running its long-established loyalty card. Kroger had challenged every relevant available data specialist in the United States to help, and so far everyone had come up short.

As with many loyalty cards in the United States, the KrogerPlus Card was used primarily as a way to offer instant discounts to regular shoppers at the point of purchase. The Kroger Card produced large amounts of data, but the management team had little experience in turning that data into insights that would help them make their business work better. Surprisingly it didn't seem that the local data community had much experience either. 'Every time [Kroger] spoke to a company that looked likely to be able to help, that company admitted that they hadn't done this before,' Hay recalls. 'That's like saying "I can't drive a car, but let's learn in the Indy 500. It's only driving round in a circle, how hard can it be?"'

When Dillon saw what had been achieved by Tesco and its Clubcard, he believed he might have found a team who knew how to drive his data strategy. What's more this was a data company directly linked to Tesco itself. Realizing the value of the insight that dunnhumby's methods were generating, Tesco had taken a 53 per cent stake in the company in 2001. The investment aimed to develop two new revenue-generating opportunities. First, to share the insights from Clubcard data with Tesco supplier brands in order to gain greater share of their in-store promotional budgets; second to partner with other retailers in markets to exploit commercially the data-driven techniques that dunnhumby had developed for Clubcard.

For Hay – dunnhumby's first employee other than the founders, and one of the original data analysts on the Clubcard trials in 1994 – the opportunity to work with Kroger was energizing.

Just like the original Clubcard project, the team would have to build from the ground up. There was no established data analysis platform underpinning Kroger's loyalty strategy, and just as with Clubcard, they didn't have a large staff or a huge office to start the building work. 'We had gone from working with the data ourselves in the UK with Tesco, to building a big team who did it for us. It was enormously refreshing to do it again, just like we did at the beginning with Clubcard,' Hay says. And just as with Clubcard, the team knew that if they could crack the data challenge, it would have huge financial benefit for their client.

Kroger's first test for the Fantastic Four was deceptively simple: 'Prove you can discover something that could add value to our business from the data we've got now'. That meant taking a sample of its customer data, tracking almost 100 million transactions a month, and working on it to find something valuable for the business. To do this the four-strong team had a local IT infrastructure of four laptops.

Vitally, it also had wireless internet access to dunnhumby headquarters and the much deeper IT resources in London. Hay says:

> We would work out of Starbucks. That was our office. We had three-bedroom apartments, and the third bedroom was office space. For US $30 a month as a broadband connection, we could work on dunnhumby's virtual private network, use the e-mail system and run the data on our existing servers. One year previously, none of that would have been possible.

The big question was: could they export the principles of Clubcard into the US market? If so, which principles would travel best? Equally fundamental: would it be possible to apply a new loyalty marketing approach to a mature business which had worked for half a century in a significantly different way to Tesco?

This was not the first to attempt to recreate a nationally proven programme in the United States. Keith Mills, the Air Miles and Nectar founder, had successfully exported his loyalty model to Canada and Holland, but success in the massive US market had proved elusive. As some of the most successful practitioners of loyalty marketing, indeed marketing in general, have learnt, what looks familiar on the surface can be very different underneath.

IS CUSTOMER LOYALTY THE SAME EVERYWHERE?

The Billion Dollar Club

Mills is a member of a select club, he says. It's the 'Billion Dollar Club' of loyalty entrepreneurs who looked to the US market with high hopes of launching a successful loyalty marketing brand, and failed. His fellow members are companies like Citibank, AT&T – large organizations that care about their customers, want to serve them better, and have wanted to use an ambitious loyalty programme concept to secure greater customer commitment. 'The idea is the easy bit,' Mills says. 'The hard bit is executing it. Very few companies in the world can do that.'

One lesson he has learnt over the years is that loyalty programmes don't always travel well. Superficially, there are common shopping traits around the developed world, but customer attitudes and behaviour in different markets often vary in subtle but important ways. For example, shoppers in some markets may be moved more by immediate discounts and have no patience with accumulating rewards, even if the ultimate payback is better. Other countries might have underdeveloped retail brands and more fragmented markets, so customers are far more likely to graze for bargains across a number of shops in their area. Even the legal environments can be significantly different. For example, Germany has a number of uniquely restrictive laws such as the Free Gift Ordinance and the Discount Act, which make loyalty marketing more difficult.

In its own global development, Tesco has an unusually flexible approach to retail expansion. Rather than insisting on a uniform, centrally governed model, respect is paid to local tastes, with distinct product ranges and locally produced goods. 'Retailing is extremely local,' says Mason. 'You should go into one of our stores overseas and feel like a foreigner, and if you are a local, Tesco should always feel just like home.' Instead, to reinforce what we could call the 'Tesco-ness' of all its stores, Tesco has created a core set of shared values based on delivering a broadly similar quality of customer experience. In all its overseas markets Tesco employees are given cards as a reminder of the familiar Tesco core purpose – 'to create value for customers to earn their lifetime loyalty', and the company values: 'no one tries harder for customers' and 'treat people how we like to be treated'.

What their customers do not all get, however, is another card: Clubcard. Although the stores in Hungary were purchased in 1994, those in Poland in 1995, and the Czech and Slovak stores in 1996, Clubcard is not yet part of the offer. This isn't due to a lack of confidence in Clubcard, says Mason. Tesco may introduce Clubcard in all its markets, but only when the necessary conditions exist for what is quite a sophisticated marketing tool. 'I think Clubcard will follow us round the world, but it's a question of timing,' he says. For now, he adds, the fundamental challenge is giving customers better quality and, most of all, lower prices.

Dave Clements, one of the original Clubcard team and today Tesco's international marketing director, says:

> We don't rush into every country we can and try to launch Clubcard. We are very conscious that customers must have a good shopping trip as a priority. Loyalty programmes work as the icing on a good cake. They can't

fix a problem, for example if your layout is a nightmare or your prices are too high. Customers see through that very quickly.'

There's one other principle governing Clubcard's glacial progress internationally: it has to be able to create long-term benefit to customers, rather than just being a deferred discount programme. That means being able to create useful insight from customer data. 'We want to avoid being one of those businesses that has the data, but does nothing with it,' Mason says.

Clubcard in Ireland

Tesco purchased the stores in Ireland owned by Associated British Foods plc (many trading under the name Quinnsworth) in May 1997, paying £643 million. The Irish retail environment was advanced, with strong competition in a crowded market, and with a rival loyalty scheme called Super Club already in place in the largest rival chain, Superquinn. As soon as was practical, Clubcard Ireland was launched, using the expertise gained in the UK.

Fear of competitor attacks meant that the Clubcard Ireland project was a secret until the last minute, with the staff briefing packs delivered personally on a plane to Ireland and collated in the departure lounge of the airport on the morning of the announcement to the company. Irish shopping habits are not identical to those Tesco had found in the UK (there is a significant segment of consumers that visits the store every day, a rarity in the UK), but the tools developed by the Clubcard team to identify those habits, and to incentivize customers to maintain and grow their custom with Tesco, have proved just as relevant and effective.

There was no doubt that Tesco Ireland staff took to Clubcard with enthusiasm. Tesco launched a competition to find the store that could convert the largest proportion of sales from Clubcard holders. Store staff took the Clubcard applications and took to handing them out in the street, as well as on buses and trains to the surprise of fellow passengers.

Sir Terry Leahy explains that the early introduction of Clubcard was a vital tool to win over customers who might have been wary of a British supermarket brand like Tesco. The scheme was used, for example, to let customers know that Tesco Ireland sourced as much of its fresh produce locally as its competitors. 'One of the most important things for us in Ireland has been to change and improve our relationship with customers,' he says.

Clubcard in South Korea

The other exception to the 'not quite yet' strategy (if we ignore a one-store trial in Thailand) is South Korea, another well-developed retail market. The bright red 'Familycard' – red being associated throughout much of Asia with luck and prosperity – was launched in 2001, and boasts over 2.5 million active users, and 5 million registered cardholders.

In South Korea, the Tesco Homeplus chain is a joint venture with Samsung Corporation, offering electrical goods and jewellery and hosting in-store concessions as well as selling groceries. It is more akin to what we would know as a department store. But it's not just the choice of products in-store that makes the Familycard different to its Clubcard parent.

Familycard offers a smaller 'Thank you' than Clubcard: 0.5 per cent instead of 1 per cent, but that's enough to ensure that 80 per cent of sales are made to cardholders – meaning card use is slightly above that in the UK. The fundamentals, Clements says, are the same: for example the quarterly statement mailing is just as powerful in driving incremental sales in-store. There's also a Baby Club, and targeted mailings are sent to customers who have defected to competitive retailers. But there are important successes that are unusual to the market. The stores are usually part of giant shopping malls, and Tesco has negotiated partnerships with other stores in the malls, so they too can offer Familycard points which can be redeemed at Tesco. There are also differences in the shopping culture that Tesco's loyalty marketing has embraced. 'In Korea Tesco Homeplus runs a lot of what are known as "Culture Centres",' says Clements, 'It's like hundreds of activity classes, and they are extremely popular with customers, who take 12-week courses in cookery or a foreign language.' In the spirit of 'Every little helps', some of Tesco's most redeemed coupons are those which give a discount on this popular form of adult education. One of the biggest drivers for Baby Club membership is the offer of a free course in caring for toddlers.

The Culture Centres are an example of how different cultures can respond to loyalty marketing: Tesco staff report that on the opening days of new Homeplus stores, the longest queues are always for the Culture Centres as customers sign up for courses.

In Korea, it's also culturally more acceptable to use SMS to send marketing messages targeted to customer segments using the proven Clubcard data analysis techniques. It might be an invitation to come to the store to pick up a free gift, or a one-day-only sales promotion offer.

'But fundamentally we don't change the core principle,' Clements says, 'we support the local CEO and share best practice, but it's still a thank you, a simple reward, and of course, it helps us to understand our customers.'

CROSSING THE ATLANTIC

What Kroger knew

Meanwhile, in the United States, Kroger's Dave Dillon and his key lieutenants – Don McGeorge, now President and COO, and Rodney McMullen, Vice Chairperson – didn't need Clubcard or dunnhumby to point out the obvious fact that supermarket loyalty retailing in the United States was very different in character from retailing in the UK. Unlike Tesco, which had successfully managed to maintain or improve its market share against Asda, they had one challenge bigger than anything else: Wal-Mart. And a big task: how could Kroger tune its business to compete more effectively with the world's largest retailer?

In 1995, when Tesco launched Clubcard in the UK, it wanted a final push to take it to the number one position in the UK; Clubcard helped achieve that within months. US supermarket chains have a more pressing ambition: how to resist Wal-Mart's seemingly unstoppable growth. The world's largest retailer has been taking customers from its rivals for years. Figures from US analyst Retail Forward show that the percentage of US shoppers who visit the three largest non-Wal-Mart supermarkets – Kroger, Albertson's and Safeway – was 56 per cent in 1999. Five years later, it was down to 46 per cent.

Two-thirds of Kroger stores are within 20 miles of a Wal-Mart supercenter, with its enticing 'Every Day Low Prices' (EDLP) promise for customers. In common with most other US retailers, Kroger urgently needed to find an answer to EDLP that was effective and sustainable.

Dillon knew that he had a potential advantage that Wal-Mart couldn't match: the Kroger card, a loyalty card that had been offered to customers across all of Kroger's variously branded stores and attracted customers with the benefit of instant discounts in-store. For years Kroger had been collecting data for most of the transactions from its 42 million customers. It had become the sort of business that Mason talked about: one that captured torrents of customer data, but was doing little with it to make the business more competitive.

Now the priority was to see if that vast reservoir of data could be harnessed by Kroger to fight back against Wal-Mart's EDLP promise.

Every Day Low Prices

Wal-Mart's much-imitated EDLP strategy offers low prices on everything, even if it is at the expense of consistent brand choice. It's a price-cutting juggernaut, spreading discounts evenly across throughout the store and across the range. The advantages for customers are obvious – whatever they can find to buy, they can be confident they are getting a keen price. The more they buy, the more they save. Customers like EDLP because they don't have to pick and choose or hunt for bargains and, most critical to Kroger, they don't need to shop at other stores. And EDLP is a simple promise to customers because it's so easy to communicate.

It has disadvantages, however, particularly for the retailer. In the United States, where most supermarkets work on margins of 2 per cent or less, there is little cash available for deep discounting. EDLP can be an efficient mechanism for eliminating profitability for a small gain in customer numbers. In a 1994 study published in the *Journal of Marketing*, the authors Hoch, Drèze and Purk found that in a typical US example, although a 10 per cent EDLP price decrease in one category led to a 3 per cent sales volume increase, it also resulted in a profit reduction of 18 per cent. Not many businesses can cope with that for long on their own.

This is why the only sustainable EDLP strategy is to cut overheads and spread risk, first by squeezing out costs ruthlessly in the business and its processes. Then the successful EDLP retailer must push some of the burden of the EDLP discounts back on to suppliers. Cutting overheads may well result in best business practice – for example the improvements made by retailers around the world in stripping out unnecessary cost from their supply chain – but it can also result in 'efficiencies' which might seem attractive on paper, but might not be as attractive to customers in the store. One example might be offering a much-reduced choice of products and brands. EDLP also cuts out the freedom of retailers to offer compelling short-term promotions, restricting their ability to encourage customers to try new categories.

A pure EDLP strategy works exceptionally well for Wal-Mart though, chiefly because it is so ubiquitous. Controlling roughly half the US grocery market, Wal-Mart has both the economies of scale to drive out cost and the buying power to convince suppliers to sell at the lowest price.

Because of Wal-Mart's success a pure EDLP price platform is not a sensible option for competitors – even ones the size of Kroger. It had to look at other ways to demonstrate value to win and retain customers.

Hi-Lo pricing

Without Wal-Mart's buying muscle and its ability to achieve such economies of scale, a retailer like Kroger can never hope to compete on EDLP. In mass-market retailing no amount of difference in service quality can realistically make up the competitive deficit. This is why for many years Kroger, like most of Wal-Mart's rivals in the United States, has favoured Hi-Lo pricing as the alternative to EDLP.

Hi-Lo is simple: retailers do not attempt to maintain lowest prices on everything all the time, but attract shoppers to the store in search of unbeatable bargains for some essentials. Stores add excitement to the shopping trip by offering dramatic price cuts on popular items. These heavy discounts are always short-term, and may even be loss-leaders, but the results show that customers value the chance to get a bargain and will then go on to buy from the range of products that are not discounted that week. With Hi-Lo the customer trade-off is between the desire for a bargain and the convenience of getting everything they need in one place. The risk for the Hi-Lo retailer is that customers may become organized and determined enough to buy only 'Lo' at the Hi-Lo store and then pop over to a rival EDLP store for the rest of their shopping. In that scenario the Hi-Lo strategy is simply a way to attract unprofitable customers.

Also, Hi-Lo has the disadvantage that it is comparatively expensive and risky to communicate. The retailer has frequently to communicate a completely new set of offers – for example Carrefour in France distributes price bulletins door-to-door to many millions of potential shoppers. Each promotion has to be a winner. An offer that doesn't pull the right sort of profitable customers will dramatically effect that period's sales. It is also a blunt instrument: every customer and potential customer gets the same sales message at the same time. Without detailed information on customer behaviour, it's almost impossible to predict which promotions will be profitable, and which will destroy value by attracting promotional 'cherry pickers'.

Despite these problems Hi-Lo continues to be a successful strategy for supermarkets worldwide because it does not have such a long-term depressive effect on margins. Unless EDLP price cuts are wholly funded by suppliers or increased efficiency, they can be devastating to margins in a way that Hi-Lo promotions are not. Promotional discounts are generally funded or joint funded by suppliers, and because they are short term the margin sacrifice is less onerous for both sides of the deal. In the 1994 *Journal of Marketing* study previously referred to, diverting the investment required to fund 10 per cent EDLP cuts into a Hi-Lo promotional pricing strategy led to an overall 3 per cent decrease in top line sales – but a 15 per cent increase in bottom line profits.

The intriguing questions for Kroger were: could it combine the customer attractiveness of EDLP with the excitement of Hi-Lo, and could it reconcile the customer loyalty that EDLP generated with the financial advantages of Hi-Lo? The key would be the ability to use customer information.

What Kroger wanted to know

On 17 October 2002, dunnhumby's expat team was ready to present what they had found out from analysing Kroger's customer data to Dillon, McGeorge and McMullen. Kroger had been very open and cooperative, giving dunnhumby access to all the data they needed. Kroger's reward was to learn some harsh realities. As dunnhumby's Hinds recalls, they had to tell Kroger's senior management that after testing their findings from the data: 'The challenges you have today won't go away. Hi-lo won't deliver loyalty. Customer acquisition strategies won't deliver growth unless you do a better job of serving the customers that you have.'

With such a stark prognosis Kroger's management might have been forgiven if they had decided to end the experiment at that point. Dillon, like Terry Leahy at Tesco, was a lifelong retailer – his great grandfather had founded Dillon's stores, one of the many chains that Kroger had acquired during its growth in the previous 30 years. He had built his career at Fry's, another Kroger acquisition. Kroger already had a sort of hybrid model in place to defend against Wal-Mart, adapting EDLP to offer competitive pricing in everyday products: 'Save on the items you buy most'.

Now Simon Hay and his team were questioning the fundamentals of Kroger's strategy and suggesting there was a completely new way to fight Wal-Mart. This went even further than what Clubcard had done for Tesco. At Tesco, Clubcard was an enhancement of a successful business strategy. For Kroger, the data team was proposing that data-fuelled loyalty marketing would change the way Kroger did business.

'We needed to make the difficult decisions tangible,' Hinds recalls. 'Do you want sales data on frozen peas, or do you want customer data on who buys frozen peas?'

Dillon, McGeorge and McMullen were convinced. Today Dillon describes customer data as Kroger's 'secret weapon' against Wal-Mart – and with its policy that EDLP is its loyalty strategy, it's the one weapon that Wal-Mart, so far at least, has no answer to. But as Kroger has discovered, customer data is only a weapon if it is used as an agent of change – which meant ignoring some of the received wisdom of US retailing.

SLAUGHTERING SACRED COWS

Sales promotion doesn't create loyalty

While Kroger was open to new thinking, not all of the data team's assertions were easy for Kroger executives to accept. 'First we had to slaughter one of the sacred cows of [US] retailing,' says Mark Hinds, 'the one that said that marketing was all about bringing more new customers to the store'. 'At the beginning, Kroger's people would say to us, "If you bring in the customers, our store will do the rest",' agrees Hay. 'We've been hearing this since 1995, repeated by retailers all over the world, and yet it is fundamentally wrong.' A simple example: 99 per cent of US customers buy laundry products. But if you look at the penetration of laundry products bought by Kroger shoppers, it is way below that. This means that customers were coming to the store, but the store was not 'doing the rest' for a large proportion of them. 'Using the penetration figures for all the departments in store, we showed Kroger that they didn't need any more customers to step change their business, they just needed to sell more to the customers they already had.'

Hi-Lo and EDLP can coexist

Hi-Lo pricing strategies often create some spectacular promotions in US supermarkets – but at some point the loss-leader can serve to attract too large a proportion of bargain hunters, and become a loss-maker. 'In the US, the price difference on a single product can be 60 or 70 per cent between retailers at any time. But choose any product and offer it at a ridiculously low price, and who do you attract? Cherry pickers.' Hinds points out.

Hi-Lo stores often carry larger ranges than EDLP stores, because a fundamental part of the EDLP discount is gained by supermarkets buying in bulk. So although most Kroger stores are smaller than the massive Wal-Mart Supercenters, Wal-Mart often carries fewer products than a Kroger supermarket. Offering choice makes it almost impossible to match EDLP on every product that overlaps with Wal-Mart's range, because that would mean embedding a mini Wal-Mart in your store, among more expensive choices. 'When Kroger carries 40,000 products it's going to be impossible to be cheaper than Wal-Mart,' Hinds says.

Kroger needed to deploy customer insight. Instead of blanketing EDLP discounts across the store (including all the most-bought products) or just at the products where the supplier would contribute promotional funding (a Hi-Lo approach), a customer-insight led approach allowed Kroger to get the best of both worlds. 'Saying that when we reduce those prices we sell more of those items isn't exactly genius, but what's cleverer is that we can produce a halo effect,' says Hinds.

For Kroger, this process is in its early stages – but for Tesco it had already been applied consistently and deepened over several years as the core of its discounting strategy, as we will see in the next chapter.

Conventional sales promotion doesn't work

Kroger's marketing was driving sales, but not profit. A heavy focus on sales promotion was creating customer behaviour that destroyed value. 'All the radio advertising, for example, had a product focus and was promotionally driven. What did that drive? Promotional behaviour,' says Hinds.

The focus of Kroger's Hi-Lo strategy, as for many supermarkets in the United States and Europe, is a mass-produced colour booklet of special offer products delivered door-to-door in every neighbourhood in the store's catchment area. For many retailers, compiling this sort of discount bulletin every week is an all-consuming, ongoing effort that is almost institutionalized into how the business operates. For internal reasons, as well as for external expectation, it can seem impossible to stop. Many supermarkets live with an over-riding fear that customers would be upset if their weekly discount fix was taken away – especially if nothing else could fill the gap.

This approach to communication doesn't stand up to too much logical analysis. We know there are many different types of customer. Tesco had found that their differences often outweighed their similarities – even customers who lived in adjacent streets. Mailbombing booklets every week rests on the assumption that one size can ever fit all. There is no attempt – or indeed opportunity – to target the promotions. The choice of offers is conventionally driven by the supplier brands and their promotional funding rather than what customers actually need, partly because the detailed information on what customers need isn't available. At Kroger, as with many similar food retailers around the world, gut feel was driving the most important communications strategy.

When Kroger invited dunnhumby's team into the decision-making process, this customer-blindness could at last be cured. By analysing transactional data in fine detail, they were able to show which customers bought which promoted products – and could confidently predict what their transactional behaviour would be during their shopping visit, and afterwards. 'Historically, everyone sat around and argued about who got to be on the front page. But we could tell them, definitively, that one offer would only affect 1 per cent of customers. The other 99 per cent would not care, while another offer would have far wider appeal. Argument over,' says Hinds.

Deferred rewards can work

Most US retail loyalty programmes, including the Kroger programme, have focused on immediate gratification, usually offered as preferential pricing (that is, if you have the loyalty card, the price is cheaper) or discounts at point of sale. The reasoning is that US consumers are used to clipping coupons for that week's shopping and expect the same immediacy from their membership of a loyalty programme. The logic continues that customers will not respond well to a Tesco Clubcard-style offer which rewards them by accumulating a loyalty dividend over a three-month period, then receiving their benefit in a statement mailing.

Kroger's management team was convinced enough that it could adapt the Tesco model to test the idea of a mass-customized mailing to its base. With 42 million households holding a Kroger card, a mailing could be a powerful sales generator if the experiment worked. The Kroger 'Loyal Customer Mailing' is a way of targeting discounts to regular shoppers as a reward. The first results have been encouraging: the redemption rate to the first coupons was 20 times the industry average. It will probably be a long time before the Clubcard mailing model replaces the instant rewards offered across the Kroger estate – if it ever does. Yet by targeting the rewards at what customer segments demonstrably want, rather than continuing only with a one-size-fits-all approach, the Kroger card has proved that a quarterly mailing can create new business and target rewards more relevantly to the US super-market customer.

Merchandizing creates marketing

Whether a statement, catalogue or advertising is used, customers are traditionally targeted with overt messages. To change customer behaviour, you tell those customers what you are doing, for example, that week's discounts, and wait for the customer to respond. Kroger has been able to experiment with a different approach – using customer data to analyse what happens in-store, and improve that experience, without necessarily communicating directly to customers the changes it is making. It's the ultimate test of what Uwins called 'body language'.

An example: how did customers respond when they were forced to seek alternatives? Looking at the customer data showed that it was often possible to offer a smaller range without damaging customer loyalty. This was a new insight for dunnhumby, because the problem is much more apparent in the US market. In the UK, retailers might carry two pack sizes for a laundry product, whereas in the US the same product might come in five pack sizes. This creates logistical problems and increases the possibility that a product will be out of stock. It also reduces the amount of shelf space available for other ranges that might be more exciting for customers and more profitable for the retailer.

By looking at the choices that shoppers would make when they were forced to look for an alternative, dunnhumby could provide a simple insight: that often, customers would still find what they wanted if the supermarket carried a smaller stock, with no damage to the size of their shop, or the likelihood that they would return to the store. Sometimes, the customer benefits of stocking a reduced range outweighed the disadvantages. So stocking two pack sizes instead of five would help a smaller format store – of which Kroger had many and Wal-Mart few – to compete against large out-of-town outlets.

This is just one way in which customer data could be used to directly affect ranging and store layout to create and preserve loyalty.

DUNNHUMBY USA

At the beginning of 2003, Tesco's majority-owned data company dunnhumby and US retailing giant Kroger formed a 50–50 joint venture, dunnhumby USA.

McGeorge explained why Kroger wanted to increase its commitment to this new way of marketing by creating a joint venture:

> Our merchandisers will learn which products and categories are important to each customer. We will learn more about how to fulfil our customers' needs in a more relevant way. In short, dunnhumby's insight will enable Kroger to make more informed merchandising and marketing decisions while improving our customers' shopping experience.

Hay now has one floor of an office building in downtown Cincinnati and is expanding on to a second floor, and so doesn't have to work in a coffee shop any more. On 14 October 2003, the company had 14 staff. Today it is recruiting, aiming to reach 200 staff by the end of 2006.

The joint venture company continues its work on the merchandising side of Kroger's activity, fast building a close and trusted relationship at the highest level. Hay says:

> It is genius on their part. We can be internal when we want to be internal, and speak to who we want and have access where we need it. We can pick up the phone to executives, walk into Kroger offices. There's no feeling of "I'm the President, no one walks into my office" here. And when we have to be external, to think differently and communicate new ideas, we can be that too.

It also allows dunnhumby USA to create an intimate relationship which allows the management to communicate its ideas across the 2500-store Kroger network – a much bigger challenge than communicating across Tesco's tightly-knit UK stores. 'We can't be everywhere, because in Kroger there are 4,000 miles between the most easterly and the most westerly store. We had to find a way to encourage the organization to think in a data-focused way when we were not there,' Hay says.

Hay admits that without Kroger's desire to change, the project wouldn't have had a chance.

> We came here from Planet Zog, we spoke a different language and believed different things. And to Kroger's credit, they greeted us with

open minds. It's hard for managers to accept that everything you have practised for 30 years is wrong. It's a big ask of any senior executive in any industry. Kroger's executives have been brave and open-minded.

Hinds adds:

> We encouraged collaborative learning, so when the regional managers get together, instead of saying "We had a great sales week", they could say "We tried this idea, and it worked for us". The refreshing thing is that with some retailers in the UK, you could discuss radical ideas, and you know they would work, but you also know there isn't a hope they would be adopted. In the US they embrace change because people only judge you by your results.

What Hay calls 'a lack of cynicism and a willingness to accept new ideas' does not mean that Kroger has relinquished control of its marketing strategy to the joint venture, nor is it about to become a Tesco clone. Instead it has allowed its thinking to be challenged by the success of the Tesco loyalty model in the UK. Some of the arguments over how to implement new customer insights last for a long time. 'Often the results from the data that we have given have been hard for Kroger to accept,' adds Hinds, 'their people may ask us to go away and slice the data differently, to make sure the result was really the result. Invariably we would come back with the same result.'

Echoing Lord Maclaurin's observations about Clubcard's effect on Tesco nearly a decade before, Hay quotes one of Kroger's senior employees on the impact of customer data on the business: 'There has been more change here in the last two years than in my previous 23'.

Employees are a segment too

In most US retail loyalty programmes, as in many such programmes worldwide, the company's staff are not embraced by the programme. Often they are simply unaware of the benefits. Yet as Tesco discovered, staff are potentially the most powerful generator of a loyalty programme's success. With this experience in mind dunnhumby incorporated staff communications into the plan. They sent some of the first communications to employees to thank them for shopping at Kroger, and to let them know the potential of the Kroger card. By increasing the effort taken to explain the coupons and the benefits available to shoppers, Kroger staff are being encouraged to educate customers about the benefits they could earn.

A JOURNEY WITH KROGER

Kroger's journey with its joint venture with dunnhumby is in its early stages, but the data have already given up some important information – and created an agenda for the future.

Kroger is at the beginning of a bold new direction in US retailing: using data to transform a massive business from the inside out. Like Clubcard, this approach is working by creating a common language, and a common set of priorities for marketing and operations based on customer knowledge. However, it is an evolution, not a revolution:

Hay admits:

> We have to help Kroger make choices where it spends its money – because budgets are finite. If we recommend spending it on something new, we have to say where the money should be taken from to fund it. We believe some of the old ingredients of the Kroger strategy don't contribute to its overall success, but it is hard to say what all of those ingredients are immediately. So we're still on our journey.

Despite this evolutionary approach, Kroger has already been able to break out of a business model by ceasing to worry too much about the customers they haven't got, and serving better the ones they have got. When he looks at the increasingly desperate Hi-Lo discounting offered by some supermarkets in the United States, Hay likes to quote Albert Einstein: 'Insanity is doing the same thing over and over again, and expecting different results.'

And as we shall see, back in the UK, Tesco has discovered that 10 years into that particular journey, Clubcard has become one of the most important engines of growth for Tesco's UK business.

16

'Tesco's most potent weapon'

▶ A critical function

▶ Smart weapons in the price war

▶ The Shop

▶ Making promotions work harder

▶ Three little words

Investment Bank JP Morgan Cazenove Limited issued a surprising research report on 31 August 2005 – at least, surprising to most people outside Tesco headquarters. The authors asserted:

> Contrary to popular belief, Tesco's most significant competitive advantage in the UK is not its scale. We believe Clubcard, which conveys an array of material benefits across virtually every discipline of its business, is Tesco's most potent weapon in the ongoing battle for market share. Very simply; Tesco is big because it is good, not vice versa.

The analysts chided investors who, they suggested, had undervalued Tesco stock by as much as 20 per cent compared to its peers. Their report said:

Despite its centrality to Tesco's success over the past decade, and ignoring the scope it offers as an ongoing engine of growth, we believe the importance of Clubcard to Tesco is a material area of investor misunderstanding that contributes to a widespread misperception of the UK business as a quasi-mature operation. Clubcard is the principal reason that we expect Tesco to continue to outperform all its UK peers into the medium term and, indeed, it could also become an important force in Tesco's global expansion.

A CRITICAL FUNCTION

JP Morgan Cazenove picked 10 areas in which Clubcard gave Tesco competitive advantage:

- identifying customer trends;
- targeting communication;
- better promotions;
- basket building;
- defence against competitors;
- ranging;
- negotiating power;
- cross-selling;
- site selection;
- driving footfall to the store.

The most striking thing about the list is how many of those categories – supplier negotiation and site selection, for example – are strategic areas that Clubcard would not influence if it was solely a promotional marketing tool.

What Tesco insiders know is that Clubcard has been influencing these decisions almost from the beginning. The two main movers behind Clubcard are now the group's worldwide CEO and the CEO of its new venture in the United States; but the commitment to Clubcard extends throughout the business.

Tim Mason, Tesco board marketing director and now boss of Tesco's new store chain in California says:

To us, it's self-evident. You could argue that we've done a poor job of explaining it to the wider world – or conversely, that we have put all our energies into doing it rather than explaining it. I think that you do need to go back to 1997 when we set about describing our mission for the business after Lord Maclaurin and David Malpas had gone and there was a change of leadership and direction. We said that this business would 'create value for customers to earn their lifetime loyalty'. Probably with the benefit of hindsight, that is a more remarkable thing for practising retailers to express rather than marketing theoreticians. Not a word about the prices we were going to charge, not a word about the sorts of stores we would run – but a notion of understanding customers, value and loyalty.

Instead of assessing the full implications of Clubcard, many analysts have continued to dismiss Clubcard as a short-term gimmick and have criticized the company for holding and using customer data. There's an argument – which Tesco certainly believes – that the 'Big Brother' argument is created by a small minority. After all, most Tesco shoppers use their Clubcards most of the time. 'It does irritate me, of course,' Mason adds, 'in much of the commentary there is an implicit accusation of a conspiracy theory, which is nonsense. Most customers let it pass them by, they don't feel conspired against at all.'

As Clubcard became an integral part of the business landscape at Tesco, there have been more and more opportunities to use the insight produced by the transactional data to reshape the business. Today Clubcard's values and Tesco's 'Every little helps' values are aligned more closely than ever. Internally, Clubcard has become an agent of change and a symbol of what Tesco does well. Better, as JP Morgan Cazenove's analysts noted, than its competitors, and perhaps better than investors still give it credit for.

Mason says that suggestions that Clubcard is effectively a 'business within a business' rather than a critical function of Tesco itself are 'fatuous nonsense'. As Tesco's ability to innovate improves, and as the Tesco brand evolves, Clubcard's contribution to that evolution has never been greater.

SMART WEAPONS IN THE PRICE WAR

Start with the customer

Some of the clearest evidence that Clubcard had the power to change fundamentally how Tesco does business came from exploiting the Lifestyles data to guide the store's discounting strategy.

Among the broad range of customers Tesco's rival Asda has always had, and continues to have, a reputation for being the low-price benchmark. The reputation is bolstered by the long-term success of the 'Asda price promise' advertising campaign, the brand's version of the 'Every Day Low Prices' (EDLP) strategy of its Wal-Mart parent. As we have seen, Asda has also consistently rubbished loyalty cards as a needless expense when, it claims, customers would prefer the cost of loyalty schemes to be redirected into price cuts.

In 1998, Tesco was faced with the imminent takeover of Asda by the US giant of low-price shopping, Wal-Mart. Tesco was aware that this could mean an even more focused discounting strategy from Asda – but also that during the takeover, when Asda management might be distracted, there was an opportunity to take some of its customers. There was no argument where the battleground would be – price. Tesco had to be in a position to beat the Sainsbury's price, the Safeway price and the Boots price. Most important was that it had to be seen to match the Asda price as well.

The traditional way to approach this would have been to track every Asda price for every product line, do a like-for-like comparison to all the prices that Tesco offered, and calculate the cost of reducing all Tesco prices to the Asda level. This 'nuclear option' would mean an a no-holds-barred price war. It might buy some business, but the negative effect on margin, and later shareholder value, might erase any advantage gained.

Using Clubcard data, there was an alternative. That alternative was to identify and assess the effect of discounts on certain products for the most price-conscious customers.

Tesco wanted to make sure its price cuts had the biggest impact possible in the first year. This would attract customers away from rivals, and the increase in sales would help to fund more price cuts in years two and three. To do this it analysed the Clubcard data – especially the Lifestyles segmentation – and decided to target price-sensitive staple products.

How did this targeted discounting work? Take bananas. Millions of people regularly buy bananas. That's why when you walk into any supermarket, there they are, hundreds of them. Surely bananas would be ripe for price cutting. Actually no, because the Clubcard Lifestyles data had given Tesco a more intelligent way to use its discounting investment.

As Mason points out:

> Customers who are really strapped for cash don't buy as much fresh fruit and vegetables, and really poor people don't buy bananas, they're too

unreliable, they're too perishable. [Those customers] can't afford to risk their limited food budget on them. So discounting bananas would not impact on the people who are most price-sensitive. When you look at what those customers do buy, for the cost of cutting the price of bananas to everyone by a few pence, we could cut the price of ten products by ten times as much, and those ten products appear in the majority of baskets of people strapped for cash.

In 1998 this targeted discounting strategy was led by former management consultant Laura Wade-Gery, who joined Tesco as targeted marketing director. Her first task was to review how the business used Clubcard data to look more analytically at its pricing.

She recalls:

Like every other supermarket, what the business had traditionally done was look at the prospect of sweeping price cuts across all categories and come up with a huge cost of becoming cheaper. And then everyone would throw up their hands in horror and say, 'Oh no that's too much, where do we start?' Then we would start working our way down the biggest-selling items, slashing prices purely on the basis of quantity sold. We changed that approach completely. Instead, we looked at the most price-sensitive customers, people without a great deal of money, and looked to see how their shopping choices were different from everyone else.

The logic is simple: we all want low prices, but only a section of us shop exclusively on that basis. And the low-price reputation of a supermarket is driven by the choices of the most price-sensitive customers. So cutting the cost of a bunch of bananas was emphatically not the place to start, because Tesco would have been aiming the discount dollars in completely the wrong direction. Thanks to Clubcard and the insights it gave into customers' shopping behaviour it was now clear to Tesco management how to minimize the cost of price cutting while maximizing the competitive impact.

Wade-Gery's analysis found a product that fulfilled the new criterion perfectly: Tesco Value brand margarine, purchased by price-conscious shoppers and very few others. The customers who Tesco was most likely to lose to Asda because of lower prices bought lots of this product, and relatively few others did. There was an equally well-defined shortlist of similarly relevant products. Invest the cash for price cuts in those products, Tesco reasoned, and the payback would be greater.

Changing perception

In the financial year 1998, Tesco invested around £130 million in targeted price cuts. Releasing the results from the year in September 1999, Terry Leahy promised to double the investment, and was also able to show that Tesco prices overall had reduced by 6 per cent in the previous three years.

In effect, Tesco got to make its price cuts for a lower net cost. By targeting the investment at the customers it would most likely have lost, this increased business volumes, which allowed Tesco to buy greater volumes from suppliers at lower cost prices, which in turn meant that the subsequent price cuts could cover a wider range of products.

Subsequent research conducted by Warwick Business School on Tesco shopper behaviour revealed that not only had the company targeted its price cuts more effectively (in rough terms, Tesco estimates 50 per cent more impact compared to an across-the-board strategy), but it also successfully changed its price-competitive perception with those shoppers. The study also confirmed that targeted discounting had a disproportionate effect on Tesco's image with those price-conscious shoppers. Their perception of how cheap Tesco is, is directly proportional to the number of discounts they notice during a shopping trip.

'Bloody obvious when you think about it,' says Mason: not that any supermarket had thought to do it – or had the capability to do it – before.

THE SHOP

Harnessing the power of Clubcard

One of the most revolutionary ways that Clubcard has given Tesco competitive advantage was almost named after a toilet cleaner. Luckily, someone checked to see whether 'Indigo' was a brand name before announcing the creation of the new research tool based on Clubcard data. Instead, the tool was renamed more prosaically, 'The Shop'.

For years many major brands who supplied Tesco had wanted to find out more from Clubcard about which customers were buying their products. Until the launch of The Shop, that was not possible. The Clubcard charter forbids any sharing of information about the shopping preferences of individual customers. The advent of The Shop gave suppliers another way to use Clubcard data, From now on they could gain access to anonymized sales data detailed by customer segment, by brands selected, by region or even store, and analyse it using nothing more complex than an internet browser.

The Shop is a set of analytical tools that brands can buy into to help them build reports on how their products are performing in Tesco stores in the UK. With the insight gained by analysing transactions by every Clubcard member they can balance their ranges, track trends, optimize prices and evaluate the true performance of promotions. They can even measure availability store by store, and improve it by looking closely at the effect of promotions or advertising on demand in target areas.

The Shop doesn't claim to be the answer to every brand manager's problem: it can flag when things are going wrong, and when they go right. It's up to the brand owners to work out why. 'It begs as many questions as answers, ' says dunnhumby chief operating officer Steve Grey, 'but marketers can learn things they would never have been able to learn any other way.'

At present around 40 brand owners have committed to accessing The Shop. It's not cheap – though no one is saying exactly how much they pay for access, the cost is measured in tens of thousands of pounds. However, for companies prepared to act on the information it provides, it can pay for itself many times over.

The sources of data held on The Shop are as young as 10 days, which is itself a breakthrough in the recency of data available to suppliers. Subscribers can interrogate the information stretching back 104 weeks allowing them to see seasonal ebbs and flows in their sales performance. The users ask for a data set, supply the times, dates, products and views that they are interested in, and wait for a few hours while the servers that hold The Shop data pull out customized information. It's a massive data set, but not everyone wants to see everything: for example, businesses using The Shop usually buy into it at a category level, as the manufacturers of detergent are unlikely to be obsessed with information on wine sales.

In each selected category, marketers can view the performance of their brand against direct competitors. For example, they can see which types of customers have been trialling and repeat purchasing their new product, and which brands of products in the sector they were buying beforehand. They can see regional differences, and monitor the impact of TV advertising. They can see whether the new product cannibalizes sales from their own range or draws sales from competitors.

What is also invaluable to the brands shopping at The Shop is the accuracy of customer profiling that it gives. You don't need to know customer names and addresses to discover the characteristics of the customers most likely to buy particular product versions; the data can help show whether promotions really work – are you selling exclusively to 'cherry pickers' who will abandon you when you are not discounting? Does a brand appeal to a segment of customers you never noted before? Is there a customer group you want to attract but that is generally avoiding your product?

In the past these trends could be masked by healthy overall sales figures. Just as Tesco discovered through Clubcard, averages are dangerous in retail, as they may disguise fundamental weaknesses in a brand's performance or profitable opportunities.

Acting on the knowledge

The Shop is only useful if the subscribers, like Tesco, are prepared to act on the insight it gives. This could be as simple as setting up focus groups made up of target customers the data shows are not loyal to the product. It could mean a seasonal price reduction to address fluctuating customer behaviour.

Some brands using The Shop have taken more drastic action based on what they have learnt from The Shop. It has led suppliers to change or even cancel nationwide promotions costing hundreds of thousands of pounds. It has led to them introducing different pack sizes or formats. It might even mean discontinuing a product entirely. The key to deriving value from The Shop is to make decisions as a result. 'We sometimes have the problem that the marketers don't have the knowledge to derive the benefit they could get from a report,' says Dave Worden, who helps run The Shop in the United States, where it is used by around 20 suppliers to the supermarket chain Kroger in a similar way. 'We also see that they don't have the time to do anything about what they have learned.'

Nevertheless, The Shop is becoming recognized as a powerful new way for brands to use transactional data to drive their strategies. And if a brand's direct competitor is using the insights The Shop gives, few marketers will not wish to catch up. After all, if your competition has knowledge from The Shop, they not only know more about the habits of their own customers than you do about yours, they know more about the habits of your customers as well.

MAKING PROMOTIONS WORK HARDER

Every year billions of dollars worldwide are spent by brands promoting their products. It's a phenomenal, if largely hidden, cost of trading. Extraordinarily, the true return on this massive investment is very unclear. Among professional marketers, few can answer the question in detail: do promotions really work?

We know that promotions drive sales, which is not the same thing at all as knowing that they work. Since supermarkets rose to dominance in food retailing in the 1960s eye-catching, time-specific promotions on products have been an essential in the sales armoury and a conspicuous way to stimulate interest in a store's offer. Retail promotions can be characterized in six main categories:

1 Same for less. Here's a favourite at a lower price ('£1 off').
2. Same plus. Here's a favourite with an added extra ('25 per cent extra free').
3. More of the same. You normally buy one packet. Now buy two at a bundle price ('Three for the price of two').
4. Switch brands. You normally buy the market leader brand. Here's a cheaper alternative ('Taste the difference for less').
5. Trade up. You bought the secondary brand – but now you can try the market leader, without having to pay more ('New low price').
6. Try something different. You've never bought anything like this from us before, now you can ('Introductory offer').

Both the suppliers and the supermarkets constantly play variations from this repertoire. With around 8,000 new products launched every year in the UK, and many more in the United States, promotions are not just a way of brightening the store experience for customers – they have become a commercial necessity.

At a superficial level, it seems simple for a supermarket and the brands they sell to decide whether specific promotions have worked or not. If compared to the previous month, say, twice as many units of an item were sold in the month it was promoted, then surely that's a successful promotion? Not so. The 'positive' effects of promotions can be unpredictable and often counter-productive over time. Indeed, it is perfectly possible to double sales in the short term, yet unless you change customer behaviour among your target customers after the promotion has ended, you might have a disastrous effect on profitability in the longer term.

So without knowing who has bought the promoted product, why that might be, and what happened afterwards, no one can be certain whether the doubling of short-term sales is a successful promotion. Measuring a promotion only by its 'sales rate' is as one-dimensional as measuring customer loyalty only by last week's basket value. It's just that in the past it's really been the only measure that supermarkets had.

If a promotion does succeed in attracting a sizeable number of new or occasional customers, the other hidden danger is that they are habitually promiscuous 'cherry pickers'. In the UK, a significant minority of shoppers come into this category. In the United States the coupon-clipping bargain predator is far more common. Cherry pickers have minimal loyalty to any particular supermarket or supplier brand. Instead, they buy a disproportionate number of products on a promotional discount, and disappear elsewhere until the next bout of discounting. You could even argue that by definition, price promotions reward cherry-picking behaviour and punish loyalty.

Data bridges the knowledge gap

The transactional history of millions of customers bridges the knowledge gap between what customers say they do, reported through a research sample, and what they really do when they are shopping, tracked through billions of product purchases.

Since Clubcard's earliest Lifestyles segmentation, Tesco has been able to identify accurately which customers react positively to promotions, and in which ways their brand preferences are affected in the future. These are powerful insights. For example, analysis of Clubcard data allows Tesco's marketers and their brand partners to see which promotions create a lasting change in shopping habits, and which are one-offs. This has helped Tesco reduce the quantity of promotions in the store by around half, and improve the quality of the promotions that it runs, by concentrating on those that have the greatest potential to be successful with the target shoppers. It means that Tesco attracts a greater share of promotional budget support from the brands, focuses more marketing support on the winners, and gets more active engagement from store management to back up promotions.

The evidence is that customers respond better to Tesco's 'less is more' strategy. Instead of being bombarded with too many so-what offers in the store, they are presented with promotions that are designed to provide maximum value to the maximum number of shoppers. The result is a series of bigger, more impactful promotional 'events' in the crowded retail calendar.

The influence of Clubcard has also been felt by customers who historically have been neglected by Tesco promotions. Most promotional money goes on building new brands. So conservative shoppers, like those who still do most of their own cooking and purchase a large number of ingredients, have rarely benefited from promotional investment in recent years even though they are some of the most loyal and committed customers in the shop. Tesco is focusing more promotional effort directly at these segments. This has created a different category of in-store promotion, based on enduring brands and commodities. The ultimate goal: to share promotional investment more equally across the customer base, and cut out the 'noise' that does not generate enough return for customers – or indeed for the business.

THREE LITTLE WORDS

'Every little helps' is not just the strapline on the Tesco advertising. As the relaunch of Clubcard in 2003 demonstrated, the brand promise is the fundamental driver of Tesco's business. Mason says:

> Go back to 1992 and the creation of 'Every little helps', then look at the vision and values we wrote down in 1997, and you will see it is a three word summation of all our values. At its heart, our Clubcard scheme is personal proof to the customer that the Every little helps promise is real. It's run by marketing people whose primary object is to improve the shopping trip for customers.

'Every little helps' has created a framework on which Tesco develops its business. 'The difference between Tesco and many other brands is that Tesco brings 'Every little helps' to life with what it does in the store. They give it meaning. It's not about a company just speaking well of itself,' says Paul Weinberger, the advertising executive who created the 'Every little helps' line, and who as a partner in Tesco's advertising agency The Red Brick Road is still responsible for Tesco advertising in the UK. He adds:

> No matter how good an advertising campaign is, it won't last unless people who see it go into a store and find that it is true. Normally advertisements use a third party to talk to the consumer on behalf of the

company, because the consumer and the company can't talk to each other directly. But if you're a retailer like Tesco, you meet your customers every day, and we wanted to push the glitz out of the way and talk directly to them in the same way.

As JP Morgan Cazenove discovered, customer data is powerful – but only if Tesco continues to use it to create value for customers to earn their lifetime loyalty. At the end of 2005, Sir Terry Leahy wrote about the power of the customer for the *Economist*: 'The bigger a brand becomes, the more sensitive it has to be to what its customers want,' he said. He pointed out that 25 years ago, when he joined Tesco, it had just one computer.

> Today, our capacity to store information is limitless, and our ability to use it to understand our customers is limited only by our imagination. There is a great opportunity here not just to build closer relationships with customers, knowing what they like just as well as the high street shop does, but also to see the provision of information as a marketing tool in its own right… companies that keep close to their customers will grow – but make no mistake, the power is in the hands of the consumer.

Acknowledgements

THANK YOU

A project as big and ambitious as Tesco Clubcard consumes the energy, imagination and sheer hard work of many people. Over the last 12 years there have been many individuals and companies who have significantly contributed to Clubcard's success. Time takes its toll on memories, so to those we omit our apologies and thanks. To those we remember please accept your place on the following roll of honour:

from the Tesco team: Alison Hobson, Helen Milne, Mikaela Morgan, Kate Anderson, Kate Walton, Elizabeth Bartlett, Catherine Harman, Clare Chambers, Jordan Womack, Ann Sinnett, Dylan Harrington, Nick Mccormack, Debbie Read, Ian Crook, Catherine Conroy, Claire Smith, Crawford Davidson, Dave Clements, Donna Orman, Helen Godley, Paul Cable, John Browett, John Mcintyre, Joyce Kelly, Jan Ross, Karen Burbridge, Laura Wade Gery, Andrew Mann, Mike Emery, Neil Southworth, Richard Brasher, Richard Levin, Simon Uwins, Steve McArdle, Terry Leahy, Tim Mason, Wendy Jordan, Alison Gamble, Zoe Rogers Lewis, Rob Mason, Steve Roberts, Sylvie Gourdon, Sarah Dolan, Michelle Morre, Sue Higham, Bob Green, Paul Sumner, Rachael Flint;

from dunnhumby: Andrew Hill, Doug Jeffery, Ed Blake, Edwina Dunn, Euan White, Giles Pavey, Hannah Marshallsay, Rachel Eccles, Mark Hinds, Matt Kerswill, Matthew Keylock, Matthew Lovett, Nicola Doidge, Peter Miles-Prouten, Rosie Poultney, Sandra Townley, Simon Hay, Stephanie Robin, Stuart Appleby, Sheena Ewing, Sam Winterson, Jemma Bristow, Anna Davis, Shane Silberry, Mark Evans, Adrian Hado, Hugo Minoprio, Julian Baxter;

from Evans Hunt Scott (EHS Brann): Matt Atkinson, Guy Culshaw, Anna Dobson, Nigel Clifton, David Macmillan, Emma Hicks, Claire Hutchinson, Natalie Hutton, James Casey, Alyssa Aldersley, Roxanna Fournier des Corats, Libby Clay, Rachel Heathfield, Chris Okesola;

from Forward Publishing: Hilary Ivory, Sarah Morris, Sarah Wyse, William Sieghart;

from Polestar: Craig Hall, Emma Rogers, Tina Johnson, Chris Rawthorne, Lisa Mastin, Ann Keime, Ash Keime, Andy Pheasant;

from Cap Gemini: Julia Wood, Steve Cawkwell.

We would also like to thank the team at Kogan Page for all the hard work they have put into making this book successful; and Professor Merlin Stone, for his help and guidance.

Index

NB: page numbers in *italic* indicate figures and tables